D0849946

# Telling Histories

# Telling Histories

BLACK WOMEN HISTORIANS IN THE IVORY TOWER

*edited by* Deborah Gray White

THE UNIVERSITY OF NORTH CAROLINA PRESS Chapel Hill

*This book was*

*published with the*

*assistance of the*

*Z. Smith Reynolds Fund*

*of the University of*

*North Carolina Press.*

Library of Congress Cataloging-in-Publication Data
Telling histories : Black women historians in the ivory tower /
edited by Deborah Gray White.
p. cm. — (Gender and American culture)
Includes bibliographical references.
ISBN 978-0-8078-3201-1 (cloth: alk. paper)
ISBN 978-0-8078-5881-3 (pbk.: alk. paper)
1. African American women—Historiography.
2. African American historians—Biography.
3. Women historians—United States—Biography.
4. African American women—Biography.
5. African American women—Social conditions.
6. Historiography—Social aspects—United States.
I. White, Deborah G. (Deborah Gray), 1949–
E185.86.T379   2008
398.2089'96073—dc22   2007045654

cloth   12 11 10 09 08   5 4 3 2 1
paper   12 11 10 09 08   5 4 3 2 1

*In tribute to*

ANNA JULIA COOPER

*and*

MARION THOMPSON WRIGHT

# CONTENTS

A section of illustrations appears after page 122.

## ACKNOWLEDGMENTS

Many people made this book possible. It would not have happened
had I not had to respond to papers given on my book *Ar'n't I a Woman?:
Female Slaves in the Plantation South* at the 2003 Southern Historical
Association meeting. I thank the members of that panel and the Program
Committee co-chairs, Steven Lawson and Nancy Hewitt. Many thanks also go
to Kate Torrey for supporting this project from the beginning. Of course, the
contributors made the book, and I am very, very grateful for their
participation. I thank them for trusting me with their stories. Words of
encouragement, especially from Darlene Clark Hine, Jacquelyn Dowd Hall,
and Anne Firor Scott, made me realize that a book like this was necessary.
Vanessa Holden, Felicia Thomas, and Rebecca Tuuri, the graduate students
who helped compile and gather all the biographical information, provided
invaluable assistance. So too did Laura Fuerstein, who over the years taught
me the value of personal testimony.

# Telling Histories

# Deborah Gray White

## INTRODUCTION

### A TELLING HISTORY

*I know of more than a score of girls who are holding positions of high responsibility, which were at first denied to them as beyond their reach. These positions so won and held were never intended for them; to seek them was considered an impertinence, and to hope for them was an absurdity. Nothing daunted these young women[.] Conscious of their own deserving [they] would not admit or act upon the presumption that they were not as good and capable as other girls who were not really superior to them.*
*—Fannie Barrier Williams, 1905*

Some might think Fannie Barrier Williams's 1905 commentary on "the colored girl" a peculiar place to begin this examination of late-twentieth-century African American women in the historical profession. But Williams's words, as well as her experiences, resonate in the autobiographies compiled in this volume and in the history of black women in the historical profession. Williams was, after all, an educator and a tenacious trailblazer for professional African American women. She was, like the Chicago "girls" she refers to, audacious. One need look no further than her refusal in 1894 to withdraw her nomination for membership in the all-white, very prestigious Chicago Woman's Club. White friends had put her name forward, and despite the fact that there were no other African American members, Williams had not expected to have to fight publicly for over a year to gain membership. She certainly did not count on being the only black member for more than thirty years. Despite her impeccable credentials, she met opposition at every turn, opposition fueled by prejudice.[1] But she, like the "score of girls . . . holding positions of high responsibility," held fast to her sense of herself as deserving and capable and did not retreat. So did the African American women historians whose stories unfold here.

They are the spiritual descendants of women like Williams. This is not hyperbole because Williams and her cohort of intelligent, educated, articulate women were revisionist historians before the history of black women was recorded. Their very bodies stood in opposition to a national script that held black women to be immoral and reproachable. Williams made this point when she rose to speak before the World's Congress of Representative Women in Chicago in 1893. She took her very presence at the speaker's podium as evidence that black women themselves were beginning to rewrite the conventional wisdom. Still she found it lamentable that there existed "no special literature reciting the incidents, the events, and all things interesting and instructive concerning them."[2] Clubwoman and activist Addie Hunton was likewise concerned. In a 1904 article entitled "Negro Womanhood Defended," she spoke of an "unwritten and an almost unmentionable history" that had been generated, not by black women and "not by those who have made a systematic and careful study of the question from every point of view." When it came to black women, Hunton called for "real study, friendly fairness, and appreciation of her progress."[3]

All of the historians in this volume have answered Hunton's call. Although not all have chosen to study and write African American women's history, like Williams their very presence as historians is a testimony of revisionism and change—change in the national history that was previously written by men and whites, and change in the subject matter that all too often was written either without consideration of race and/or gender or for the political purpose of suppression. By querying the late entry of black women to the professional world of historians, this introduction will set the stage upon which the first of them set foot in the early 1970s. It will attempt to speak for those who did not leave the kind of record produced by those whose telling histories appear in this volume. Like the essays that follow, this introduction will put a face and a soul on women historians who might have, like the Chicago women Williams refers to, appeared on the surface to be undaunted by their assigned inferiority but who struggled mightily against the devastating effects of racism and sexism.

Anna Julia Cooper was the first black American woman to receive the Ph.D. in history in 1925, but she received it not from an American university but from the Sorbonne in Paris. Fifteen years later, Marion Thompson Wright received the Ph.D. in history from Columbia University. The lateness of their entry has been a source of inquiry because the first American woman to receive the doctorate in history, Kate Ernest Levi, did so in 1893, and the first black American man to receive the degree, W. E. B. Du Bois, did so in 1895. Besides the all-important question of why black women did not enter the historical profession in significant numbers until the post–civil rights era, there is the question of why both credentialed and noncredentialed black women students and practitioners of history eschewed black women's history despite their intimate understanding of how their history had been misrepresented and used against them.

If for no other reason than to set the record straight, it would seem that credentialed black women historians would have rushed to study and write the history of their group.[4]

There were many reasons why they did not. If we take our cues from those who could have been historians, prominent educated black women, we might conclude that they freely chose not to pursue academic careers in any discipline, much less history. Fannie Williams, a graduate of the State Normal School at Brockport, New York, understood that black women, even the college educated, not only had to make a living but also had to serve the race. "The ideal of scholarly leisure and the life of the student recluse is very attractive," Williams wrote in 1904, quoting a statement she had heard at a conference entitled "Women in Modern Industrialism," "but in the days to come, the true education will not be that which is devoted to pure academic work, but rather that which prepares for service." Knowing too all the obstacles black women faced in the world of work, Williams quoted further: "Parents of a girl in college know, that even if they are not compelled to, their children should be able to take care of themselves."[5]

That black parents knew that their daughters, in particular, had limited employment opportunities is reflected in their socialization practices. The few who could afford to give their daughters the chance to escape field or domestic work, says historian Stephanie Shaw, expected them "to make some difference in the lives of the many people in their communities who did not enjoy the advantages that they did." They were socialized from infancy to use their education to uplift themselves and their communities at the same time.[6] It should come as no surprise that Gertrude Mossell's 1908 *The Work of the Afro-American Woman*, which Mossell described as "historical in character," detailed the contributions of black women who were able to make a living doing race work. Many were teachers, but Mossell was careful to point out that Frances Watkins Harper, a writer, lecturer, and woman's rights advocate, not only advanced the race but also "sustained herself and her family by her pen" and that Edmonia Lewis, the sculptor whose work often depicted African Americans, was able to sell her work to titled persons of Europe.[7] Marion Cuthbert's 1942 dissertation confirmed Mossell's and Shaw's observations. The 181 women in her sample were motivated to go to college by "their interpretation of what should be helpful in meeting the grave economic situation which confronts the Negro." She added, "They perceive the need . . . to become self-supporting."[8]

As important as the need to be self-sufficient race women was the need to project a proper image. Mossell herself wrote under her husband's initials—as Mrs. N. F. Mossell—in part to project the image of a moral woman under the authority and protection of a man.[9] Mossell did not hold up only professional women as examples of women who did important race work. She also complimented "the most humble of our women." Quoting a southern journalist, Mossell heralded industrious black women who "hoe, rake, cook, wash, chop, patch and mend, from morning to night," women who worked hard in the field all day and then did domestic chores at night, women who in addition to everything else raised chickens and turkeys, geese and ducks. In other words, for Mossell, it was important for educated women to do race work, but it was even more important for *all* black women to uphold an image of industriousness. This too constituted uplift race work.[10]

This is important to this discussion of black women in the historical profession because it is easy to conclude, and in fact it has been argued, that black women did not pursue careers in history because history did not lend itself as easily as other professions to racial uplift. It has also been argued that when black women did write history, they did so as part of the project of racial uplift and thus avoided the particular history of African American women.[11] These arguments may help us understand why black women arrived late to the historical profession, but there is more that we need to look at, something suggested by Mossell.

An education enabled black women to practice a profession that provided sustenance to both the individual and the race, but any woman could help uplift the race by projecting an unimpeachable image. Image, therefore, was a central concern for black women because conventional historical wisdom defined them as promiscuous and explained them to the nation as ignorant and uneducable. To say that black women were disadvantaged by this history is to understate the obvious. More important for the project at hand is that these historical interpretations so circumscribed the black woman's existence that it was impossible for even the college educated to escape the consequent discrimination that prevented her entry into the professional ranks of those who wrote history. In other words, it was nearly impossible for black women to become historians because they were caught in the hopeless dialectic that went something like this: in order to enter the historical profession, black women had to escape a race *and gendered* history that perpetuated discrimination, but the only way to escape that history was to become historians.

This dilemma was not lost on some could-be historians. They felt the burden of discrimination, and in what amounted to some rather classist statements, they unhesitatingly complained. Said clubwoman Sylvanie Francoz Williams of Louisiana, "For the educated Negro woman has been reserved the hardest blow, the darkest shadow and the deepest wound."[12] In a similar vein, Addie Hunton, the first black graduate of Philadelphia's Spencerian College of Commerce in 1889, regretted that "those who write most about the moral degradation of the Negro woman know little or nothing of the best element of our women."[13]

These women understood how history functioned not only to oppress them but also to keep them from becoming historians, professional or otherwise. Their particular history, the black woman's history, was especially oppressive.[14] Hunton alluded to its prohibitive nature when she delicately noted the "almost *unmentionable* history of the burdens of those soul-trying times when, to bring profit to the slave trade and to satisfy the base desires of the stronger hand, the Negro woman was the subject of compulsory immorality."[15] Sylvanie Francoz Williams was more direct. So painful was the wound of the black woman's history, she argued, that "her detractors rely upon her not voluntarily reopening it, even to probe it for its cure." Perceptively, Williams maintained that the black woman's "sensitiveness on this point has been the greatest shield to the originators of the scandal." Using the slanderous remark of a reporter who wrote, "I cannot conceive of such a creation as a virtuous black woman,"[16] Williams demonstrated how historical reality could be as much of a hindrance as mythology and why so many chose to leave both alone:

> On reading such an expression, the first impulse is a burst of righteous indignation, but it is soon followed by a wave of pity for one who has "lived all her life" amid such environments, [who] at last, driven to desperation, violently tears aside the curtain to expose the skeleton existing in her own private closet.[17]

Williams's statement becomes all the more salient in light of Shaw's observation that black women of the middle and striving classes were socialized from infancy to avoid any hint of immodesty. According to Shaw, parents understood the economic and sexual exploitation that black women were subject to, and they also understood that if their daughters were to make the most of the opportunities available to them, "they would have to be extremely circumspect and never give the slightest hint of impropriety, otherwise they might be negatively typecast." Childrearing practices, therefore, especially those involving girls, were aimed at instilling "Victorian ideals of restraint regarding matters of female sexuality." Knowing that their daughters did not have to "*do* anything to 'attract' the kind of attention that resulted in sexual abuse," parents "expected their daughters to project a flawlessly upright appearance."[18] To talk about or study the black woman's "enforced immorality," even to expose the wanton power of white men, the evil of systemic raced sexism, the admirable qualities of black men and women, exposed the could-be historian to the boomerang effect outlined so well by Williams. Could-be black women historians were too smart not to know the figurative molesting potential of the "unmentionable history" Hunton alluded to. Surely it was easier and less dangerous to rewrite history through work that uplifted, and thus altered, the community that whites analyzed with disgust than to risk being slandered for revising the historical canon.[19] Just as historian Darlene Clark Hine argues that twentieth-century black women developed a culture of dissemblance and a supermoral persona as a defense against rape, I suggest that this same conscious and unconscious mindset was one of several factors keeping educated black women away from writing anything but celebratory history and away from the historical profession in general.[20]

But there were compounding causes. One was the raw unmitigated discrimination that kept all but a few black people on the economic margins of American society, fighting not for a college degree but for mere survival. If black men and white women had minimal access to degree-granting institutions, it goes without saying that black women had even less. For most of the twentieth century, it took gargantuan effort to obtain even a bachelor's degree. By 1898 only 252 black women had college degrees. Although the number seeking degrees increased significantly after 1900, most black women went to black colleges and most were enrolled in their certificate-granting normal school departments.[21]

Getting the Ph.D. in history was hard, and statistics compiled by historian William B. Hesseltine and librarian Louis Kaplan inadvertently show just how hard it was for black women. In the early 1940s, when they took stock of women and blacks who had obtained the history Ph.D., they found that as of 1936 the fifty Ph.D.-conferring departments in the United States had awarded 2,055 degrees, 334 of which went to women and only 9 to blacks.[22] There were no blacks in the women category and no women in the blacks category.

Nothing illustrates the extent of discrimination against black women better than the scope of invisibility of those who did have the degree. Their exceptional status should have made both Anna Julia Cooper and Marion Thompson Wright visible, but Hesseltine, a socialist and antiracist at the time he published the findings, and Kaplan did not include them when they listed all the blacks who had achieved the degree from 1895 to 1940. Cooper and Wright were similarly absent from their discussion of women Ph.D.'s. Archivist Jacqueline Goggin is, of course, correct in her description of the historical profession as one "dominated by white male practitioners since its inception."[23] But her observation is useless unless we unpack the how and the why of their dominance. We can start with the erasure of Cooper and Wright.

We can continue with a look at the profession itself, which at the turn of the twentieth century was in the process of professionalizing. At the center of that process was the ideal of objectivity—"the rock on which the venture was constituted . . . the key term in defining historical scholarship." As one scholar of the process has noted, in America, professional historians were to be neutral, disinterested judges and not advocates or propagandists. History was not to be written for utilitarian purposes, and the historian's primary allegiance was to "objective historical truth." It was not until well into the second half of the twentieth century that American historians began to ask whether true objectivity was really possible; for most of the century, the profession and history departments took pride in the fact that practitioners studied societies with which they had no organic connection.[24]

These practitioners were mostly men, for part and parcel of the professionalization of history was the gendering of important or "real" history as male. As explained so brilliantly by historian Bonnie Smith, late-nineteenth-century white male scholars believed they needed to separate themselves from the home and the household, from passion and sex, in order to write objective history. Only in the world of disinterested contemplation—a world necessarily separate from emotional, subjective women, whose concerns hovered around the quotidian—could real history—that of wars, politics, and important men—be written. Professionalization was, therefore, a means of exclusion. It was gendered male and, by and large, raced white.[25]

This made the profession inaccessible to black women. Notwithstanding the difficulty that the objectivity principle presented to the race woman who had been socialized to be an advocate for her people, turn-of-the-century historical writing on blacks and women was so dominated by scientific racism and sexism, and by southern apologists, that the race woman who attempted to set the record straight about black women's history, including the subject most dear to her heart—the sexual exploitation of black women by white men—would, by definition, have been judged a sentient partisan, even a propagandist, and thus unfit for historical work. Since for most of the century conventional wisdom followed "scientific" assumptions that blacks were naturally subjective while whites were objective and that women were naturally intuitive while men were analytic,[26] could-be black women historians did not stand much of a chance as professional historians. One can only imagine what it would have been like to try to enter a field dominated by the likes of Ulrich B. Phillips. His *American Negro Slavery*, written with the required air of detachment and neutrality, actually championed an Old South view of slavery that depicted idyllic plantations where planters civilized childlike slaves. Published in 1918, Phillips's book characterized female slaves as women who were protected by their masters and overseers, unusually prolific, and inclined, but for the master's interception, toward infidelity and wonton sexuality.[27] It dominated the field of slavery studies until Kenneth Stampp's 1956 publication of *The Peculiar Institution*. Any could-be black woman professional historian might well have decided to climb Mount Everest before trying to enter a profession so obsessed with objectivity but blind to or accepting of the biases of the white male giants in the field.

According to historian Francille Wilson, they would not have gotten much help from W. E. B. Du Bois either. Although there is no evidence that the first African American recipient of the history Ph.D. stifled the ambitions of the black female students who took his classes at Atlanta University, he was among the mass of male academics who considered the small number of black women who were enrolled in college courses at the turn of the century to be "natural," and he was much more solicitous of his male students, particularly R. R. Wright and George Haynes, who became social scientists, than of the women who studied under him.[28]

Even if American society and the historical profession were not inclined to brand them as propagandists, it is highly unlikely that could-be black women historians could have swallowed the "objectivity principle" in its entirety. The nature of their assigned status in America demanded that they plead the case of their people and offer a view of the past and present that was different from that offered by their white contemporaries. "The value of any published work, especially if historical in character, must be largely inspirational," wrote Mossell. In countradistinction to the "objectivity principle" under which the historical profession was professionalizing, Mossell understood history to be functional. For her it was motivational; race instinct and race pride were behind it, and it always had "for its development a basis of self-respect." The task she set for herself in her historical tract, *The Work of the Afro-American Woman*, was to show both the nation and black women just how far black women had come since being "trammeled by their past condition."[29] According to historian Elsa Barkley Brown, Delilah Beasley was another black woman who defied academic historical conventions in order to offer African Americans a usable history. Beasley, a journalist and amateur historian, researched and then self-published *The Negro Trail Blazers of California* in 1919. Criticized unmercifully by Carter G. Woodson for defying conventional footnote style, mixing documents throughout her story, and failing to present a continuous narrative, uninterrupted by her informants and other sources, Beasley's work was, in Woodson's view, the antithesis of good history. But Barkley Brown suggests otherwise. Beasley, says Barkley Brown, "challenged accepted scholarly conventions regarding historical periodization and historical time, developing a process of historical documentation that used the present to authenticate the past, used the past to remember the future." Beasley's ways of telling history, while unacceptable to the profession, allowed African Americans to reinsert themselves into the history of California on terms established by themselves instead of by the white historians who had eliminated them in the first place.[30]

Women like Mossell and Beasley remind us of the many black women who wrote history as amateurs or, as Pero Dagbovie notes, "without portfolio."[31] They took their insider status not as evidence that they could not be objective but as a license to prove black ability and motivate others. Susie King Taylor, for example, wrote her account of life behind the Union lines "to accomplish some good and [give] instruction for its readers" and to plead for justice for black people because blacks had fought so hard and sacrificed so much for the nation.[32] Elizabeth Lindsay Davis wrote her history of the Illinois Federation of Colored Women's Clubs so that the younger generation of black women would appreciate what had been done for them and "be inspired to 'Carry On.'"[33] Elizabeth Ross Haynes wrote her book of African American biographies for children, *Unsung Heroes*, so that the accomplishments of African Americans would inspire the young to "succeed in spite of all odds."[34]

For these women and the many others who wrote outside of the profession, history proved the black woman's worth. It is not surprising that so many wrote about the organizational life of African American women because they believed, as did Josephine Silone Yates, one of the first presidents of the National Association of Colored Women, that women's organization "was the first step in nation-making," the means by which one measured the progress of black Americans.[35] Their club histories directly challenged the contemporary wisdom that only men made and were the center of history. Anna Julia Cooper raised the alarm as early as 1892 when she began her treatise, *A Voice from the South*, with the admonition that "the busy objectivity of the more turbulent life of our men serves . . . to cloud or color their vision somewhat." Cooper wanted everyone to know that black history began not with the politics of great black men—the Martin Delanys of the world—but with homes, the woman's sphere. "The atmosphere of homes is no rarer and purer and sweeter than are the mothers in those homes. A race is but a total of families. A nation is the aggregate of its homes," she wrote. As the maker of homes, it was the black woman who best represented the race and who was, therefore, at the center of race history. This was the point of Elizabeth Lindsay Davis's history of the club movement, *Lifting As They Climb*, and all the other histories cited in Floris Cash's *African American Women and Social Action* and Cynthia Neverdon-Morton's *Afro-American Women of the South and the Advancement of the Race, 1895–1925*.[36] The women listed in the bibliographies of these books who wrote numerous histories of their clubs and social movements were following the lead of Anna Julia Cooper, who many years earlier had proclaimed that "no man can represent the race." Their histories did more than put women's social-uplift work on a par with men's political work. To their mind, their stories made women's work the center of black history and the motor driving black progress.[37]

Just as important, these histories of women's social-uplift work served a redemptive function. They were not only the means by which black women circuitously refuted contemporary and historic defamation of their character but also a therapeutic way of handling their history of "enforced immorality." Like the works by early-nineteenth-century amateur historians featured in Bonnie Smith's *The Gender of History*, histories of the club movement and black women's many good works "were also detours around the site of the author's own trauma." Their explicit references to their organized creation of mothers' clubs, kindergartens, settlement houses, book clubs, nursing homes, and hospitals were a "better story" than the "unmentionable history" Addie Hunton alluded to. This "better story" helped them challenge the tropes of deficient motherhood and moral depravity without falling into the abyss described by Sylvanie Francoz Williams.[38]

History was, therefore, a means by which black women could help themselves while serving the race. As noted so well by Julie Des Jardins, black women became the force behind the success of the Association for the Study of Negro Life and History (ASNLH), founded by Carter G. Woodson in 1915. Although early on in that organization men set themselves apart from women as interpreters of history while reserving for women the role of collection custodians, by the late 1920s and throughout the 1930s women in their capacity as clubwomen, teachers, reformers, community activists, and professional librarians not only collected documents, raised funds, and wrote community histories but also made the ASNLH's first Negro History Week possible by heading and mobilizing the ASNLH branches that took black history into school districts and libraries. From the District of Columbia to Los Angeles, women did the work of popularizing black history for the masses. By the mid-1930s, Woodson's preference for academically trained historians gave way before lay women's real power to make a usable and positive black history accessible. According to Jardins, "In the beginning his desire to legitimate race history as a scholarly field caused him to disregard women's abilities to advance it. Only after a decade of assessment would he realize that in their social duty to children and community, women could impart historical ideas and shape collective memory in ways male historians could never achieve alone." While Woodson's *Journal of Negro History* began publishing history written by female lay historians and other professional women, the *Negro History Bulletin*, which by 1942 was staffed and written almost entirely by women, often highlighted the work of female African Americans.[39]

Despite the increased stature of lay historians and women doing history work, in the pre–civil rights era, only a few women joined Anna Julia Cooper and Marion Thompson Wright in the ranks of academically trained professional historians. To the minuscule pool came Merze Tate, Lula Johnson, Margaret Nelson Rowley, Elsie Lewis, Susie Owen Lee, Helen Edmonds, and Lorraine Williams.[40] To say the least, their professional lives were not easy; they had all of the problems of black male historians and more. Few had mentors to train them or introduce their work to the profession. They could not attend many conferences because meetings were often held in segregated cities with segregated facilities. To add insult to injury, the few who could take time from their teaching to do research met discrimination in research archives. Moreover, they correctly perceived that academic racism prevented them from presenting their work for publication to mainstream journals. According to Jacqueline Goggin, between 1895 and 1980 the *American Historical Review* published only one article by a black historian and that was W. E. B. Du Bois's 1910 article on Reconstruction. The *Mississippi Valley Historical Review* (which became the *Journal of American History* in 1964), founded in 1914, tripled that number when between 1945 and 1975 it published two articles by Benjamin Quarles and John Hope Franklin's 1975 presidential address to the Organization of American Historians. The *Journal of Southern History* published only nine black-authored articles between 1955 and 1975.[41] This denigration by exclusion is one of the reasons black scholars shied away from black history. Since white scholars believed that black scholars could not be objective about their own history, African American historians feared further exclusion brought on by being typecast as a Negro historian who could write only Negro history. Of the thirteen articles published in the leading mainstream journals mentioned above, one had nothing to do with black history, eight did not concentrate on it, and only five, which appeared in 1955, 1958, 1959, 1960, and 1975, focused on black history.[42]

These were difficult obstacles to surmount, but black women historians endured *both* racism and sexism. White female history Ph.D.'s had a difficult time in the profession as well. Between 1890 and 1940, they composed only 16 percent of the field (334 compared to 1,721 men); could not get fellowships and college jobs; were not allowed to work once they got married; endured what today would be called sexual harassment; were excluded from most of the profession's governing boards, committees, and programs; and had to put up with the devaluation of women's history.[43] According to Goggin, conditions got worse before they got better. Whereas in 1930 16 percent of academic women historians were full professors, in 1970 there were none. Black women historians were subject to these same impediments. Moreover, they could not, like white women historians, find employment at the white women's colleges or a welcome place at the Berkshire Conference of Women Historians. They surely could not penetrate the homosocial world of white women scholars.[44]

For black women historians, the black scholarly world proved almost as difficult to enter as the white. Black male scholars were just as engaged as their white counterparts in the project of masculinizing history by associating themselves with scientific methodology and objectivity. Despite the efforts made by black women writers to place women at the center of black history, black male scholars, like the male historians that Bonnie Smith studied, privileged men over women by "contrasting male truth and female falsehood, male depth and female superficiality, significant male events and trivial female ones, male transcendence and female embodiment."[45] Largely excluded from the white masculine political sphere, black male scholars established intellectual organizations where they could not only distance themselves from women but also perform a masculinity parallel to that established by white male scholars. Thus, the men of the Philadelphia-based American Negro Historical Society designated themselves as historical experts and women as collection custodians. Women were absent from the rolls of the American Negro Academy, the Committee of Twelve, the Negro Society for Historical Research, and the early ASNLH, organizations that at the end of the nineteenth and beginning of the twentieth century spearheaded the New Negro History movement, the goal of which was to counter negative images by resurrecting a positive black history and putting it to work for the benefit of the race.[46] Although, as noted previously, Carter G. Woodson had by the 1930s come to depend on black women to disseminate black history, during the 1920s, only one article written by a black woman, Elizabeth Ross Haynes's article on African American women, was published in the *Journal of Negro History*.[47] For most of that decade, the *Journal* and its editor were invested in retrieving black history from racist scholars who had denigrated black men, especially their role during Reconstruction.[48] The same focus permeated the attitude of historian Earl E. Thorpe. As late as 1958, when he published his revised history dissertation, "Negro Historians in the United States," he wrote, several times, that the central theme of black history "is the quest of Afro-Americans for freedom, equality, and manhood." He then proceeded to write a history of lay and professional black historians that barely recognized the existence, much less the contributions, of black women.[49] Black colleges were notorious for their unfair treatment of black women, from students to faculty to administrators. Until 1925, when the first African American woman, Margaret Nabrit Curry, joined the faculty of Spelman College, white females had a better chance than black women of working at the nation's two black women's colleges (Bennett was the other). The same can be said of all the black schools of higher education, where whites and black men held the majority of positions.[50]

The late entry of African American women into the historical profession is not, therefore, beyond our comprehension. Educated black women were socialized to be race women, to "pay forward" to the race the advantages they had received from a higher education. As lay historians, many put African American and African American women's history to work for that purpose. Had they made it their profession, however, they would have met a world that was closed, if not hostile, to them and blind to the hurdles they had to jump. Just as important, however, was the paradox presented by their own history. Educated African American women believed they had to overcome their history before they could do their history. Yet the nature of the history they sought to overcome was so embarrassing and demeaning that it kept them from engaging that history in all but the most indirect manner. It was not by choice, therefore, but by necessity that we came late to the historical profession.

Although we will perhaps never know all of what the first two black women holders of history Ph.D.'s endured and sacrificed, what we do know should make us pause. Anna Julia Cooper, the child of her enslaved mother and her mother's master, received her B.A. and M.A. (in mathematics) from Oberlin College in 1884 and 1887, respectively. She did not seek the Ph.D. until she was in her mid-fifties, well after she had lost her position as principal of the M Street School in Washington, D.C. Although the cause of her dismissal had more to do with her support of an academic over an industrial curriculum, and not a little bit of envy of her educational credentials on the part of her detractors, Cooper endured charges of inefficiency and, even worse for a black woman, immorality before she was dismissed in 1906. Since Cooper was a widow, her need to support herself took her to Lincoln University in Missouri, where she was hired to teach languages. By the time she began studying for the Ph.D., she had returned to the M Street School (1910) and spent several summers in Paris. She had not planned to seek a degree from the Sorbonne but had intended to study at Columbia University, where she was accepted in 1914 on the basis of her summer studies. By 1917 Columbia had certified her proficiency in French, Latin, and Greek, and she had earned thirty-two credits toward the doctorate. But unexpected life crises interrupted her quest. First, she became the guardian of her nephew's five children, who ranged in age from six months to twelve years old. This meant finding a suitable house and stretching her already-lean income to care for them. Then she assumed the care of her brother's wife when he fell ill. On top of this, she took over her brother's fight with the government to receive pension benefits for his service in the Spanish-American War. By the time she turned her attention to the doctorate, she realized that there was no way she could fulfill Columbia's residency requirement for she could not move to New York City.[51]

The final push for the Ph.D. presented special challenges for Cooper. A bout with influenza forced her to take a year's leave, during which she returned to Paris to complete the requirements for the Ph.D. Only after she transferred her Columbia credits to the Sorbonne did the secretary to the dean of Columbia seemingly relent on the residency requirement, telling her that transferring the credits to the Sorbonne was "impossible, *unnecessary*, undesirable."[52] Cooper went nevertheless but not without hardship and sacrifice. The Washington school system made her pay a substitute a salary greater than her own. Then, after only fifty days, a friend wired her with the news that she would be fired from the M Street School if she did not return within sixty days—well short of the year she thought she had been given. After making arrangements to have her sources copied and sent to the Library of Congress, Cooper returned to her classroom five minutes before the appointed time of her dismissal. The school, now named Dunbar High, raised additional barriers when it came time for her to defend her dissertation, entitled "The Attitude of France on the Question of Slavery between 1789 and 1848." She put in for an emergency leave but was given only the ten-day Easter break to prepare and travel to Paris to take her oral exams—in French—entitled "Legislative Measures concerning Slavery in the United States between 1787 and 1850" and "Equality of the Races and the Democratic Movement."[53] In 1925, at the age of sixty-six, she was awarded the Ph.D. Although this was quite an accomplishment, not a year later, Cooper was subjected to the ignominy of having to plead her case for promotion and a salary increase against school administrators' claims that she had failed their written examination. One reads with sadness Cooper's complaint:

> I believe that I have had many evidences of the sincere esteem and appreciation with which my service is regarded by the humble laity whom I serve, and yet it is to be admitted that official recognition still seems tardily and grudgingly accorded and pecuniary emoluments, so eagerly sought by most persons, are stubbornly withheld while every opportunity is seized in some quarters to excuse this material injury by detraction and misrepresentation.[54]

We can only guess at the combination of racism and sexism that Cooper struggled against, but hers was not a story alien to other black women academics past or present. Jealousy and lack of support from male and female colleagues; overwhelming familial responsibilities that delay the pursuit of degrees; administrators who bend the rules for everyone but women and persons of color; public assaults on personal integrity; and limited opportunities to do research because of excessive teaching loads and the lack of alternative pecuniary support—all have plagued black women academics in every field, seemingly from time immemorial.

Marion Thompson Wright's ordeal underscores black women's difficulties. A little over forty years after Cooper received her B.A., Wright won a scholarship and entered Howard University's undergraduate program. In order to enroll at Howard, she had to keep her marriage and two children secret because Howard, like many other coeducational schools, prohibited attendance by married or divorced women. In 1927, she graduated Phi Beta Kappa and magna cum laude and was awarded a fellowship to continue her studies at Howard. On the one hand, this gave her the opportunity to work with noted educator Charles H. Thompson (no relation), founder of the *Journal of Negro Education*, but on the other, her success meant that she had to continue to live apart from her children, a deception she continued after she received the Ph.D. in history from Columbia University's Teacher's College and returned to Howard as an assistant professor in 1941.[55]

Life at Howard could not have been easy, especially after Mordecai Johnson became the first black president in 1927. Under pressure to prove that a black-run university could succeed and please the all-white male Protestant board of trustees, Johnson ran the school with an autocratic paternalist hand. Disliked by both men and women, he was especially condescending and sexist toward women. He refused, for example, to give Inabel Lindsay the title "dean of the School of Social Work." Although all other deans were called "dean," he called Lindsay "director" and only relented after other women faculty and administrators objected. He still persisted in calling her "daughter," a term he used to refer to all female faculty. His conflicts with Lucy Diggs Slowe, the first dean of women at Howard, are legendary. In direct opposition to Slowe's attempts to transform the job of dean of women from that of matron to that of a specialist in the education of women, Johnson tried to make Slowe live on campus and resisted her efforts to eliminate the constant surveillance of women. When black and white women protested that the dean of men had no such residency requirement, Johnson only dug in his heels and, in what was billed as an economy measure, dismantled the entire women's program that

Slowe had built since her arrival ten years earlier. According to educator Margaret Crocco, in 1937, when Slowe became ill, Johnson publicly accused her of malingering and demanded that she return to work. When she did not, he fired her and changed the locks on her door. Slowe died shortly thereafter, and her family requested that Johnson take no part in the funeral services. Some of her friends attributed her premature death at age fifty-three to her struggles at Howard.[56]

Marion Thompson Wright's struggles were no less difficult. Unlike most black female academics who seldom studied or worked in places where black women had any authority or under anyone who cared deeply about the higher education of young black women, Wright was fortunate to have had Lucy Diggs Slowe as a mentor. She was also fortunate to have had Merle Curti as her Ph.D. adviser. One of a handful of white scholars in the United States who tried to integrate black history into American history and black scholars into the historical profession, Curti guided Wright's meticulously researched dissertation on segregated education in New Jersey.[57] Entitled "The Education of Negroes in New Jersey," it anticipated the U.S. Supreme Court's 1954 *Brown v. Board of Education* decision by emphasizing the damaging psychological effects of separation on black youth. Despite the publication of her work in 1941 and the acclaim and awards that her research garnered—it met the objectivity requirement, and Wright was judged detached from her subject—Wright's life was apparently unhappy. Her marriage to Arthur M. Wright, a postal worker, was short-lived. When she returned to Howard in 1941, she was one of only two female assistant professors on the faculty and the only member of the College of Education with a Ph.D. Her return marked the continued estrangement from her children, whom she never really got to know. When she was found in October 1962 in her closed garage slumped over the steering wheel of her car, it was judged a suicide.[58]

The eulogies suggest that Wright gave much, perhaps too much, to academe. One tribute celebrated the "calm and dispassionate exposition" of her research, which helped both students and educators; the numerous at-large academic and service organizations she served on; the university committees that sought and received her help; and the time she gave to students and friends. It noted that she was willing to give up her leisure time to help prevent student failure, provide remedial experiences, and alleviate difficulties in college adjustment. Along with recognizing the "time, energy, devotion and resources" that she "generously shared," the tribute reflected on her "untimely death" at age sixty.[59]

Of course, the lives of Cooper and Wright do not tell us everything we would like to know about these first professionally trained black women historians, but they are instructive. Since they are the foremothers of the African American women who have contributed to this volume, their lives suggest many of the themes that unfold here and explain why this book is needed. Cooper and Wright might have taught us much more if they had left us their own accounts of their struggles, triumphs, and reasons for choosing the discipline of history. When Anne Firor Scott, one of the founders of the modern women's history movement, wrote about the first historians of southern women, she pondered her initial lack of curiosity about four of the five women whom she had met. They had paved the way for her career, but their histories only later intrigued her. "I failed to learn," she says, "while there was yet time, what I would now give a good deal to know."[60] Although *Telling Histories* only begins to tell the story of African American women in the post–civil rights historical profession, it is my hope that it reveals some answers to questions that will be asked by the next generation of historians.

The civil rights movement and subsequent women's rights movement pried open the doors of the ivory tower and the history profession as well. They were the causal factors behind the entry of blacks and women into higher education in greater numbers than ever before, making it possible for them to establish the all-important foundation for careers in academia. The demand for a more-inclusive American history that accompanied the rights movements began the long process that made black and women's history legitimate areas of inquiry. It did not happen overnight, nor did established academics and historians yield ground without a fight. The rights movements provided the political and ideological justification for the entry of women and minorities, but it was up to individuals, usually isolated on predominately white campuses and in predominantly white male departments, to turn politics into praxis.

And that was lonely and precarious business. As suggested by historian Eugene Genovese's 1969 *Atlantic Monthly* article, "Black Studies: Trouble Ahead," for the black scholar, academia was an intellectual and political minefield. The title of historian John Blassingame's 1971 essay, "Black Studies: An Intellectual Crisis," was similarly foreboding.[61] In short, the ivory tower and the history profession had been forced to change, but neither was particularly welcoming. Old issues mingled with new ones, creating a virtual storm around the 1970s black historian and graduate student. Were black studies departments legitimate? Was black studies itself a worthwhile area of study? What was the role of the historian in black studies? How culpable were white historians in the stereotyping of African Americans, in the discrimination and racism that blacks regularly faced? Could white historians do black history? Could black historians do anything but black history? Could black historians achieve legitimacy as historians writing black history, or did they have to prove their mettle by first researching and writing on some other subject? Would white historians have to lose their jobs in order to make a place for black historians? Could black historians be impartial, could they be as "neutral" as white historians? Would universities wind up lowering their standards by adopting black studies programs, and would these programs become centers of mayhem, disrupting the academy at every turn?

For black historians, the age-old juxtaposition of objectivity and race work took center stage. Some academics still held the presumption that African American historians could not be "objective" or write history "dispassionately." Indeed, we were cautioned by one of our very own, John Blassingame, against writing myth. "Even while recognizing the Negro's need for increased self-respect and the contribution that history can make to this," he warned, "young black scholars must be constantly aware of the relation between means and ends." "Instead of becoming a propagandist," counseled Blassingame, "the young scholar must live up to the historical tradition" created and maintained by the likes of, among others, William Wells Brown, W. E. B. Du Bois, Rayford Logan, and John Hope Franklin. As if we had to be told, Blassingame reminded us of historian Charles Wesley's warning that there could be no unreliability, no mythical or legendary bases for our interpretations.[62]

If Blassingame warned us against advocacy and propaganda, historian and civil rights activist Vincent Harding schooled us on our responsibilities to the black community. What we owed the black community could never be sufficiently repaid, he claimed. Black scholars had to remember that they were made not by the universities that gave them their degrees but by black people, the black community, and in their writing and speaking, they were obliged to "affirm the people, celebrate the people, to clarify all those elements of their life that have been built through the pain of the land, all those elements of their life that have been built on the way to a new life." According to Harding, even as we strove to gain acceptance in academic circles, to gain professional credentials, tenure, and the like, we could not forget our sources—not the cold hard data we collected but our people. Our responsibility as scholars was to "work out new concepts, and try to set afoot a new woman and a new man." Our job, Harding insisted, was to "sing" for the people from which we came.[63]

That the black historian had stepped into a quagmire of sorts was alluded to by the titles of many of the articles that described this generation. "The Dilemma of the American Negro Scholar" was the title of one of John Hope Franklin's influential essays. "On the Dilemmas of Scholarship in Afro-American History" was the title of an essay in August Meier and Elliot Rudwick's *Black History and the Historical Profession, 1915–1980*. Constance Carroll entitled her contribution to *All the Women Are White, All the Blacks Are Men, but Some of Us Are Brave: Black Women's Studies*, "Three's a Crowd: The Dilemma of the Black Woman in Higher Education."[64]

Indeed, the rights movements made access to the university easier for black women historians, but surviving there was just as difficult as ever. As both black and women's studies departments were established, African American female scholars were caught in the political and intellectual cross fire. Would women's studies steal the resources and the "attention" that "rightfully" belonged to black studies? Since women weren't really a minority and didn't have a similar history of oppression, many black scholars protested the creation of women's studies departments and expected all black women scholars to join in that protest. Many demanded that black women scholars choose one or the other. Others questioned the wisdom of further fragmenting history, afraid that the "big picture" of the American nation would be lost. Not facetiously, the question was asked, "What about white men? Shouldn't they have their own departments?" How much fragmentation could the field take, and how marginal did one really want to be? For the black female scholar who chose to research African American women, it was possible to find oneself so far in the outer circle that the center was not even visible.

There was a reason for the title of Gloria Hull, Patricia Scott, and Barbara Smith's book, *All the Women Are White, All the Blacks Are Men, but Some of Us Are Brave*. According to Constance Carroll, who in 1982 was president of Indian Valley College in Novato, California, a 1968 survey of doctoral and professional degrees conferred by black colleges (which in those days still granted most of the degrees that black professionals received) revealed that 91 percent were awarded to black men and 9 percent went to black women. At the university from which Carroll received her degree, the University of Pittsburgh, in 1982 white men constituted 50 percent of professors at the associate and full level, black men were 31 percent, white women were 19 percent, and black women were 3 percent.[65]

For Carroll, many of the experiences of Anna Julia Cooper and Marion Thompson Wright were repeated. She had no one with whom to share experiences, no one with whom to identify, no one on whom she could model herself. It took a great deal of psychological strength for her just to get through the day. Her formula for survival was to tell herself over and over:

You must be *better qualified* than the men.

You must be *more articulate.*

You must be *more aggressive.*

You must have *more stamina* to face inevitable setbacks.

You must have *more patience,* since you will advance *more slowly.*

Above all you must remain *feminine* and *not appear threatening.*[66]

Carroll was not atypical. As joint appointments became popular, it was not uncommon for black female professors to find themselves the only African American in a traditional discipline and the only female in a black studies department. When racism marked the former and sexism raged in the latter, the only thing left for the African American female professor to be, as Hull, Scott, and Smith suggest, was "brave."

Brave is what the contributors to this volume are—brave to be among the first large cohort of black female American historians and brave to share with readers some of their experiences in the profession. I asked the contributors to address two questions: "Why did you choose history as a profession?" and "What have been some of your experiences?" No one reported that they had an easy time addressing my queries. In fact, most told me that they struggled with writing these very personal essays, and quite a few declined to participate because of the personal nature of the project.

In fact, in the course of editing this work, I detected a disquieting phenomenon. Over and over, I encountered refrains such as "I don't want to sound like I'm whining, but . . . " or "I don't want to complain, but. . . ." As noted earlier, Sylvanie Francoz Williams demonstrated the silencing effect of African American women's history of sexual exploitation, how the very people responsible for that exploitation were protected by black women's reluctance to expose their experiences. We have seen too how the history of oppression, and fear of slander, kept them from entering the historical profession. I note the current circumspection to highlight the continued predicament of black women historians, the real bravery involved in illuminating that predicament, and the true accomplishment of these contributors, who overcame their trepidations and successfully avoided the trap that snared earlier twentieth-century educated women.

My comment on the persistence of silence is one of the few personal observations I have chosen to make regarding these essays. I note it because the reluctance to participate and the tentative critique of the historical profession are facts that would not otherwise be known. However, I've left most comparisons and analyses to the reader. For sure, as I received the essays, I noted their differences and similarities, and I marveled at what could be done with them—the ways they could be interpreted, how they either confirmed or disputed different historiographies, what they said about the current and past political climate, what they revealed about race, class, and gender in academia. I resisted, with great difficulty, the temptation to interject an editorial voice, to point things out to the reader, to make comparisons, to underscore change, to interpret and analyze the contributions. I considered inserting a paragraph at the beginning of each essay and including an afterword and an index. But in the end, I feared that my interpretative voice would spoil the book by telling the reader what to think and feel. As primary sources and teaching tools, these essays have unlimited potential, in the present and future, and I feel they deserve to be as unmediated as possible. My editing, therefore, consisted of smoothing out language, clearing up ambiguities, and nudging contributors to be more revealing of their subjective selves. On this last point, I had to remind them that this was their history, their testimony, and that there was value in the telling of it. I also asked the contributors to submit a picture of historical content that they felt revealed a personal side of themselves.

*Telling Histories* focuses on American historians not only because I needed to establish some boundaries but also because other fields of history have different dynamics. Despite the number of historians who declined to participate, I tried to achieve some regional and generational balance, but by necessity, almost all of the contributors are tenured faculty. In order to document a wider variety of experiences, I also tried to include faculty from different kinds of four-year schools and universities. In order to satisfy an important analytic requirement of historical study—change over time—the essays are arranged in chronological order by date of Ph.D.

*Telling Histories* is in no way the definitive history of African American women in the historical profession. As both primary and secondary source, it only begins to enrich our understanding of the way that race and gender come together in history departments in the ivory tower. It is my hope that it does not just chronicle the recent past but that it serves as a sort of "how-to" survival manual for those who are currently struggling against entrenched historical methods, historiographies, and faculties. Insulated from spaces where intellectual activity or knowledge for knowledge sake is frowned upon or even ridiculed, the ivory tower can be an exhilarating, stimulating place. But it can also be isolating, debilitating, and lonely, especially for those who not only buck the status quo but whose very bodies stand in opposition to the conventional wisdom regarding academia. *Telling Histories* is as much for these individuals as it is in tribute to Anna Julia Cooper and Marion Thompson Wright.

NOTES

1. For a brief sketch of Fannie Williams, see "Williams, Fannie Barrier," in *Black Women in America*, 2d ed., edited by Darlene Clark Hine (New York: Oxford University Press, 2005), 352–54.

2. Bert James Loewenberg and Ruth Bogin, eds., *Black Women in Nineteenth-Century American Life: Their Words, Their Thoughts, Their Feelings* (University Park: Pennsylvania State University Press, 1976), 271.

3. Mrs. Addie Hunton, "Negro Womanhood Defended," *Voice of the Negro* 1, no. 7 (1904): 280–82.

4. These questions have been studied and partially answered by a few historians. The most complete studies are Pero Gaglo Dagbovie, "Black Women Historians from the Late 19th Century to the Dawning of the Civil Rights Movement," *Journal of African American History* 89, no. 3 (Summer 2004): 241–61, and "Black Women, Carter G. Woodson, and the Association for the Study of Negro Life and History, 1915–1950," *Journal of African American History* 88, no. 1 (Winter 2003): 21–41; and Julie Des Jardins, *Women and the Historical Enterprise in America: Gender, Race, and the Politics of Memory, 1880–1945* (Chapel Hill: University of North Carolina Press, 2003), 118–76.

5. Mrs. Fannie Barrier Williams, "An Extension of the Conference Spirit," *Voice of the Negro* 1, no. 7 (1904): 302.

6. Stephanie Shaw, *What a Woman Ought to Be and to Do: Black Professional Women Workers during the Jim Crow Era* (Chicago: University of Chicago Press, 1996), 13–40.

7. Mrs. N. F. Mossell, *The Work of the Afro-American Woman* (New York: Oxford University Press, 1988 [1908]), 9, 13, 22, 24.

8. Jeanne Noble, *The Negro Woman's College Education* (New York: Garland, 1987 [1956]), 47.

9. See Joanne Braxton, "Introduction," in Mossell, *Work of the Afro-American Woman*, xxviii.

10. Mossell, *Work of the Afro-American Woman*, 23.

11. See, for example, Des Jardins, *Women and the Historical Enterprise in America*, 120, 131.

12. Sylvanie Francoz Williams, "The Social Status of the Negro Woman," *Voice of the Negro* 1, no. 7 (1904): 298.

13. Hunton, "Negro Womanhood Defended," 280.

14. This argument diverges from the argument by Julie Des Jardins that with the

exception of Anna Julia Cooper, black educated women, including clubwomen, did not understand that their history was distinct from that of black men and white women, despite the fact that the case had been made by black women like Sojourner Truth and Frances Watkins Harper. See Des Jardins, *Women and the Historical Enterprise in America*, 119–20.

15. Hunton, "Negro Womanhood Defended," 281 (emphasis added).

16. Sylvanie Francoz Williams, "Social Status of the Negro Woman," 298–99. Although Ida B. Wells was similarly slandered by Missouri Press Association president James Jacks, Williams does not attribute this remark to him.

17. Ibid.

18. Shaw, *What a Woman Ought to Be and to Do*, 14, 21–26.

19. One need only examine the verbal abuse suffered by Ida B. Wells from both black men and whites to understand why black women steered away from practicing history. See Deborah Gray White, *Too Heavy a Load: Black Women in Defense of Themselves, 1894–1994* (New York: W. W. Norton, 1999), 23, 24, 60–61.

20. Darlene Clark Hine, "Rape and the Inner Lives of Black Women in the Middle West: Preliminary Thoughts on the Culture of Dissemblance," *Signs* 14, no. 4 (Summer 1989): 912–20. Julie Des Jardins notes the practice of dissemblance but argues that black women needed to abandon it in order to use the past for empowerment. She fails to explain how the past was used to silence black women and keep them from probing their history, how it was their very history that kept them from practicing history. See Des Jardins, *Women and the Historical Enterprise in America*, 137–38, 171–72.

21. Francille Rusan Wilson, *The Segregated Scholars: Black Social Scientists and the Creation of Black Labor Studies, 1890–1950* (Charlottesville: University of Virginia Press, 2006), 103, 277 (n. 27). Paula Giddings's statistics are a bit different. According to Giddings, by 1905, 7,488 blacks had earned academic or professional degrees from American universities. Black colleges and universities awarded the bulk of them, and as late as 1900, they had awarded only 22 to women. By 1910, that figure had risen to 227. See Paula Giddings, *In Search of Sisterhood: Delta Sigma Theta and the Challenge of the Black Sorority Movement* (New York: William Morrow, 1988), 18.

22. William B. Hesseltine and Louis Kaplan, "Negro Doctors of Philosophy in History," *Negro History Bulletin* 6, no. 3 (December 1942): 59, and "Women Doctors of Philosophy," *Journal of Higher Education* 14, no. 5 (May 1943): 254. They used the term "Negro." Both of these articles were written long after Cooper and Wright had received the Ph.D.

23. Jacqueline Goggin, "Challenging Sexual Discrimination in the Historical Profession: Women Historians and the American Historical Association, 1890–1940," *American Historical Review* 97, no. 3 (June 1992): 770. Unfortunately, Goggin herself neglected black women. Although she argued that her dates did not extend to the period when black

women historians entered the field, she apparently felt no need to discuss their absence. Regrettably, she focused only on discrimination against white women in the historical profession.

24. Peter Novick, *That Nobel Dream: The "Objectivity Question" and the American Historical Profession* (New York: Cambridge University Press, 1988), 1, 2, 469–70.

25. Bonnie Smith, *The Gender of History: Men, Women, and Historical Practice* (Cambridge, Mass.: Harvard University Press, 1998), 81–82. This is a gross oversimplification of Smith's thesis, which is put forth in several chapters (ibid., 70–156).

26. Novick, *That Nobel Dream*, 471.

27. Ulrich B. Phillips, *American Negro Slavery: A Survey of the Supply, Employment, and Control of Negro Labor as Determined by the Plantation Regime* (Baton Rouge: Louisiana State University Press, 1966 [1918]), 269, 270, 273, 298–99. Interestingly, Phillips seldom comes right out and states his beliefs; he lets others do it for him. He, therefore, quotes extensively from select sources and "objectively" represents the contemporary statements as statements of fact. See also Philip A. Bruce, *The Plantation Negro as a Freeman: Observations on His Character, Condition, and Prospects in Virginia* (Williamstown, Mass.: Corner House, 1970 [1889]). Bruce, a prominent Virginian, was a historian who wrote about black promiscuity: "A plantation negress may have sunk to a low point in the scale of sensual indulgence, and yet her position does not seem to be substantially affected even in the estimation of the women of her own race" (ibid., 20).

28. Wilson, *Segregated Scholars*, 102–4.

29. Mossell, *Work of the Afro-American Woman*, 9.

30. Elsa Barkley Brown, "Introduction," in Delilah Beasley, *The Negro Trail Blazers of California* (New York: G. K. Hall, 1997 [1919]), xxxvii, xxxviii–xxxix.

31. See Dagbovie, "Black Women Historians," 247–51; and Des Jardins, *Women and the Historical Enterprise in America*, 145–76. Historian Earle Thorpe uses the term "historians without portfolio," but he mentions only one black woman. See Earl E. Thorpe, *Black Historians: A Critique* (New York: William Morrow, 1971 [1958]), 150.

32. Susie King Taylor, *Reminiscences of My Life in Camp* (New York: Arno Press and the New York Times, 1968 [1902]), preface, 75–76.

33. Elizabeth Lindsay Davis, *The Story of the Illinois Federation of Colored Women's Clubs* (New York: G. K. Hall, 1997 [1922]), foreword.

34. Elizabeth Ross Haynes, *Unsung Heroes* (New York: G. K. Hall, 1996 [1921]), foreword.

35. White, *Too Heavy a Load*, 21–55, quotation on 36.

36. See Sieglinde Lemke, "Introduction," in Elizabeth Lindsay Davis, *Lifting As They Climb* (New York: G. K. Hall, 1996); Floris Cash, *African American Women and Social Action: The Clubwomen and Volunteerism from Jim Crow to the New Deal, 1896–1936* (Westport, Conn.: Greenwood Press, 2001); and Cynthia Neverdon-Morton, *Afro-*

*American Women of the South and the Advancement of the Race, 1895–1925* (Knoxville: University of Tennessee Press, 1989).

37. Charles Lement and Esme Bhan, eds., *The Voice of Anna Julia Cooper: Including "A Voice from the South" and Other Important Essays, Papers, and Letters* (Lantham, Md.: Rowman & Littlefield, 1998), 51–52, 63, 112–17.

38. Smith, *Gender of History*, 58–61.

39. Des Jardins, *Women and the Historical Enterprise in America*, 145–76, quotation on 147. This interpretation is slightly different from Des Jardins's. See also Dagbovie, "Black Women, Carter G. Woodson, and the Association for the Study of Negro Life and History." Jacqueline Goggin adds perspective in her argument that black men faced terrible discrimination. Goggin also details Woodson's desire to give professional black historians a place to publish and, through careful and objective study, counter negative images of blacks. See Jacqueline Goggin, "Countering White Racist Scholarship: Carter G. Woodson and the *Journal of Negro History*," *Journal of Negro History* 68, no. 4 (Autumn 1983): 355–75. See also Carter G. Woodson, *The Miseducation of the Negro* (Washington, D.C.: Associated Publishers, 1977 [1933]), esp. 20, 85, 136, 139, 146–47, 154–55, for Woodson's views on how black education, including black history, damaged black people and hindered racial progress.

40. Depending on whom one reads, this list varies. Des Jardins and Dagbovie list some of the same people, but their lists differ. See Des Jardins, *Women and the Historical Enterprise in America*, 141; Dagbovie, "Black Women Historians," 251–56; and August Meier and Elliot Rudwick, *Black History and the Historical Profession, 1915–1980* (Urbana: University of Illinois Press, 1986), 125n, 130–31.

41. Goggin, "Countering White Racist Scholarship," 356–60. Meier and Rudwick discuss this issue at length in *Black History and the Historical Profession*, 117, 119–20, 123–36.

42. Goggin, "Countering White Racist Scholarship," 359.

43. For a more complete picture of the discrimination that white women faced, see Smith, *Gender of History*, 185–212.

44. Goggin, "Challenging Sexual Discrimination in the Historical Profession," 770, 802. See also Francille Rusan Wilson, "Black and White Women Historians Together?," *Journal of African American History* 89 (2004): 267. For a description of this world, see Smith, *Gender of History*, 190.

45. Smith, *Gender of History*, 67.

46. Des Jardins, *Women and the Historical Enterprise in America*, 122, 130.

47. Ibid., 151–76; Dagbovie, "Black Women, Carter G. Woodson, and the Association for the Study of Negro Life and History," 27. See also Wilson, "Black and White Women Historians Together?," 268.

48. White, *Too Heavy a Load*, 118–19.

49. Thorpe, *Black Historians*, 4, 8–9.

50. Beverly Guy-Sheftall, "Black Women and Higher Education: Spelman and Bennett Colleges Revisited," *Journal of Negro Education* 51, no. 3 (Summer 1982): 281; Linda M. Perkins, "Lucy Diggs Slowe: Champion of the Self-Determination of African-American Women in Higher Education," *Journal of Negro History* 81, nos. 1–4 (Winter–Autumn 1996): 98–101; Wilson, *Segregated Scholars*, 90–114.

51. Louise Daniel Hutchinson, *Anna Julia Cooper: A Voice from the South* (Washington, D.C.: Smithsonian Institution Press, 1981), 67–84, 131–54; Lement and Bhan, *Voice of Anna Julia Cooper*, 1–43, 307.

52. Hutchinson, *Anna Julia Cooper*, 323 (emphasis added).

53. Ibid., 67–84, 131–54; Lement and Bhan, *Voice of Anna Julia Cooper*, 320–30.

54. Lement and Bhan, *Voice of Anna Julia Cooper*, 333.

55. Information on Wright is scarce. This information is drawn from Margaret Smith Crocco, "The Price of an Activist Life: Elizabeth Almira Allen and Marion Wright Thompson," in *Pedagogies of Resistance: Women Educator Activists, 1880–1960*, edited by Margaret Smith Crocco, Petra Munro, and Kathleen Weiler (New York: Teachers College Press, 1999), 61–76; Dagbovie, "Black Women Historians," 252–54; and telephone interview with Clement Price, March 22, 2007. Price is Board of Governors Distinguished Service Professor and convener of the Marion Thompson Wright Lecture Series at Rutgers University.

56. Crocco, "Price of an Activist Life," 63–64; Perkins, "Lucy Diggs Slowe," 98–99. See also Martin Summers, *Manliness and Its Discontents: The Black Middle Class and the Transformation of Masculinity, 1900–1930* (Chapel Hill: University of North Carolina Press, 2004), 257–60.

57. Meier and Rudwick, *Black History and the Historical Profession*, 105–6, 113–14, 153–55.

58. Crocco, "Price of an Activist Life," 74.

59. Walter G. Daniel, "A Tribute to Marion Thompson Wright," *Journal of Negro Education* 32, no. 3 (Summer 1963): 308–10.

60. Anne Firor Scott, ed., *Unheard Voices: The First Historians of Southern Women* (Charlottesville: University of Virginia Press, 1993), 5.

61. Eugene Genovese, "Black Studies: Trouble Ahead," *Atlantic Monthly* 223 (June 1969): 37–41; John Blassingame, "Black Studies: An Intellectual Crisis," in *New Perspectives on Black Studies*, edited by John Blassingame (Urbana: University of Illinois Press, 1971), 149–66.

62. John Blassingame, "Black Studies and the Role of the Historian," in Blassingame, *New Perspectives on Black Studies*, 220–23.

63. Vincent Harding, "Responsibilities of the Black Scholar to the Community," in *The State of Afro-American History: Past, Present, and Future*, edited by Darlene Clark Hine (Baton Rouge: Louisiana State University Press, 1986), 277–84.

64. John Hope Franklin, "The Dilemma of the American Negro Scholar," in *Soon One*

*Morning: New Writing by American Negroes, 1940–1962*, edited by Herbert Hill (New York: Alfred Knopf, 1963), 60–76; August Meier and Elliot Rudwick, "On the Dilemmas of Scholarship in Afro-American History," in Meier and Rudwick, *Black History and the Historical Profession*, 277–308; Constance Carroll, "Three's a Crowd: The Dilemma of the Black Woman in Higher Education," in *All the Women Are White, All the Blacks Are Men, but Some of Us Are Brave: Black Women's Studies*, edited by Gloria Hull, Patricia Bell Scott, and Barbara Smith (Old Westbury, N.Y.: Feminist Press, 1982), 115–28.

65. Carroll, "Three's a Crowd," 116.

66. Ibid., 120, 124.

# Nell Irvin Painter

I write as an almost-former historian, someone who retired from teaching history and who will be, by the time this volume is published, a full-time undergraduate student in the Mason Gross School of the Arts at Rutgers University. Even though some historians' contributions and honors remain—two more books to be published and presidencies of the Southern Historical Association and the Organization of American Historians—I think of myself these summer days as pretty much past the conventions of academic history. I write to you personally, looking back on a gratifying part of my life. History has given me much pleasure and, as a bonus, much success. Although I won't be teaching history any longer, history will remain in my life as a bountiful source of subject matter. I write my title in French because French expresses an essential part of the freedom at the foundation of my identity and my survival. The genre of historians' writing autobiographically also first came to me in French.[1] Having lived so much on the periphery of everything American, French has anchored me for nearly half a century.

## Having Just Sent Off Most of the Manuscript

The clock thermometer on the porch says 88 degrees, 12:59 P.M., Monday, July 17. I know it knows 2006. I have just sent my editor 335 pages of a very strange book. He won't know what to make of it, but he'll publish it anyway because he's waited for it for a long time; because it's interesting and original; because he paid good money for it. I won't tell you how much, just that for someone whose day job was teaching history at a university, it was a pretty good deal.

The book, *The History of White People*, comes out of my thinking and teaching, but I wrote most of it after retiring, wrote it up here in the Adirondacks, pretty much by myself. Over the last couple of weeks, I revised and re-revised the twelve chapters my editor will presently be receiving. Lumpy, but most intriguing. And you know what? I like it a lot, lumps and all. A prince of a friend in New Jersey has been cheering me on. He thinks the book will be brilliant, but he has only seen bits and can't realize how lumpy the whole thing really is.

Like all my writing, it sounds like me. Themes, diction, narrative story line all original, all phrased in my own voice. Chapters 1–12 (of 15, maybe more) of *The History of White People* send me back to my experience more than twenty years ago writing *Standing at Armageddon*.

That book had originally been intended for a series in the A. A. Knopf college department. I started writing with the history-professor-editor of the series. (I ended up with a different, more imaginative editor at a different publisher, subsequently my regular publisher, W. W. Norton, after Knopf sold the college department and the series folded.) The history-professor-editor wanted my book to look more like regular history books at the time, the early 1980s. He said I should engage historians' controversies and contribute to the historiography of the turn-of-the-twentieth-century field, such as it was.

I confess historians' controversies didn't interest me very much. They were arguing about the meaning of what they assumed had taken place, trying to interpret the larger significance of their assumed events. Was it the spread of the market economy? Was it status anxiety? Urbanization? Industrialization? Those controversies failed to attract me because I harbored doubts regarding historians' accounts of the facts. I had to go back to the primary sources myself and find out what actually happened—to my own satisfaction. My quest after the fundamental events, as opposed to the historiography, dismayed my history-professor-editor. I bet he heaved a sigh of relief when the series collapsed and he didn't have to figure out what to do with my book.

My new editor at Norton liked my vision and made sure *Standing at Armageddon* came out okay. Well, sort of okay. My editor, suffering from depression, didn't manage to get my corrections into the first edition. It came out full of typos. Thank heaven the typos didn't prevent the *New York Times* from reviewing it positively, meaning that on a certain level it had succeeded. Many years later, the Knopf history-professor-editor admitted publicly that I was right and he was wrong. *Standing at Armageddon* is an engaging book; it tells readers what happened in a coherent manner. It never entered the historiography as a major contribution, but it stays in print as a useful text in advanced placement history courses. Every few years, a graduate student or young professor writes me after having just discovered it on his own (it's always been a man who writes). What a great book! Why didn't someone tell him about it before??!! My book, an underground classic. Such will probably turn out to be the fate of *The History of White People*. Some people will love it, some will ignore it. That's okay with me.

Back in the 1980s, radical historians' disregard of *Standing at Armageddon* dismayed me a lot, just as the refusal of the *Women's Book Review* to review my *Sojourner Truth: A Life, a Symbol* hurt in the 1990s. Both experiences distanced me from communities I had thought I belonged to. This was disappointing but, ultimately, not devastating because even my belonging had been contingent. Too many prior discussions had alerted me to our differences. I like my books more than I like radical historians or narrow-minded feminists, and enough other people agree with me to keep up my spirits. I'm still writing, hardly feeling I've failed as a historian. I do fault the radical historians and feminist organs for failing to recognize original work that shares their values.

I think part of their problem lay with me and their difficulties fitting me and my work into their stereotypes. As another editor said about Hosea Hudson as he turned down the manuscript that would become *The Narrative of Hosea Hudson*, I don't tug at one's heart strings. Meaning I don't tug at one's heart strings the way the right kind of black person does. Hudson, the feisty, mouthy, unrepentant Communist, didn't, and neither do I.

The qualities unfitting me for their stereotypes are the very qualities that have kept me productive for more than thirty years. Though clearly and proudly a black woman, I don't inspire pity, and I'm not grateful enough for what American institutions have done for me. I'm also not dead. Not having triumphed over adversity, I can tell no tragic stories. My health is excellent, and I just keep on doing what I want to do, despite the various history-professor-editor kinds of people telling me I'm doing it wrong and I need to do it their way.

I've long suspected some of the advice was intended—consciously or unconsciously—to shut me up. I know the criticism came with that intention. But I just keep on writing my strange books, year after year after year. Now enough readers agree with me that the naysayers sound pretty silly. Two historical organizations have voted me president: the Southern Historical Association and the Organization of American Historians. These honors say my work enjoys a wider constituency than just myself, something the historian in me appreciates deeply. (The honors may be saying something further, which I'll get to in a moment.)

There's always been more than a historian in me, which is why I have kept on writing the way I want to. Sometimes people express surprise on learning I haven't been particularly ambitious, never had goals I wanted to reach as a historian. I just kept writing what I wanted to write the way I wanted to write it. I feel lucky the rewards came along in due time.

This isn't to say all has gone along smoothly and painlessly. Some insults I never have forgotten or forgiven, for instance, the refusal of the Institute of Advanced Study in Princeton to let me use an office there to complete *Sojourner*

*Truth: A Life, a Symbol,* even though I requested no money (I had an NEH fellowship) and such a courtesy appointment is routine for Princeton University professors on leave. No, all has not run smoothly in this career of mine. Some angry sores remain, festering occasionally.

However . . . not having an office in the institute one year a long time ago doesn't begin to compare with real insults and real losses like not getting a job or not getting tenured or promoted, not getting published, contracting a deadly disease, making a bad marriage, or being orphaned early in life. I have lived a charmed life.

### Where I Came From

My family's roots reach back into Louisiana, South Carolina, and Texas. My mother's mother and father, Nellie Eugenie Donato and Charles Hosewell Mc-Gruder, were Louisianans at Straight University in New Orleans when they married. He was a professor; she was a student. My father's parents were Edward Irvin, a skilled locomotive engineer, and Sarah Lee, a housekeeper. She was from the Low Country of South Carolina; he was a Texan born and bred. My parents, Frank and Dona, fell in love at first sight in the library of the then Houston College for Negroes (now Texas Southern University). They married and moved to Oakland, California, in 1942. For their migration, I remain eternally grateful. I never was meant to be a southerner.

Always a voracious reader, I could read before going to school. I excelled right through the University of California, Berkeley; the University of California, Los Angeles; and Harvard. At Berkeley, I slid around, majoring in art, French, and, ultimately, anthropology. I spent a year in Bordeaux, France, before undergraduate graduation, then two years in Ghana teaching French and studying African history before going to UCLA for an M.A. At UCLA, I studied African history; at Harvard, U.S. history. Ramblings diverted me from a straight track, so I didn't finish my Ph.D. until ten years after my first degree from Berkeley.

During the 1960s, I spent a lot of time outside the United States, time I count as a prime source of my sanity. Absence not only protected me from much of the craziness of those exciting times but also kept me peripheral. I occasionally attended various meetings and signed assorted manifestos, without joining the leadership or going all the way down the line. Somehow the manifestos seemed never quite to apply to me. Most things seem not quite to apply to me, in the sense that I'm not the person anyone seems to have in mind, manifesto-wise. The one great exception lies in "African-American Women in Defense of Ourselves" in 1991.[2] I also haven't thought the right things at the right time, finding it difficult to follow an established line of thought just because it's the established line of thought. This characteristic of mine has occasionally proved not particularly endearing.

After the 1966 coup d'état in Ghana scattered us Afro-Americans, I continued my graduate study of African history at UCLA. I noticed there that certain questions were the right ones, as established by prevailing works of history by prevailing historians. Other questions, some mine, not stemming from prevailing history, seemed to be wrong questions. It seemed forbidden to pose a question from one part of African historiography about another African region. In history classrooms at UCLA, I realized three things in 1966–67: there exist acceptable and not-acceptable questions, with acceptability resting on opinion and personal identity as well as science; experience shapes what questions one wants to ask—this is the knower/known equation William James and later poststructuralists recognized; finally, I, as a young black woman, lacked sufficient intellectual prestige to make my questions and answers count. My personal identity—my personal body—seemed to render my smart questions and even excellent answers inaudible. Feminists recognized this phenomenon and rightly generalized it to women's utterance.

After I received my M.A. in African history, I thought of continuing for the Ph.D. Fatuousness delayed that undertaking, pushing me eventually into teaching history at San Jose City College. I no longer recall much about the teaching, but I do remember what sent me back into the university after just one year. I had several self-proclaimed Black Panthers in my classes. I got along well with some of them; the older and more settled struck me as dedicated students. Some others took a more instrumental approach—they threatened to beat me up if I didn't give them good grades. Somehow the threats didn't intimidate me. I gave them the grades they deserved. Perhaps the older Panthers restrained the less mature. Certainly their often-proclaimed pro-black ideology didn't guarantee my personal safety. I wasn't the right kind of black person for the little Black Panthers to love. Such was my experience of the upheavals of the 1960s: being threatened by small-time Black Panthers in San Jose, California.

An actual beating wasn't necessary to convince me to move on from San Jose. I applied to several Ph.D. programs, got into all of them, should have gone to Yale, but followed advice recommending the better university library. I envisioned a library dissertation on Angola, and Widener Library offered richer research resources. At Harvard, I slid out of African history and into U.S. history, then a job at the University of Pennsylvania slotted me in on the bottom rung of the tenure track. At Penn, the scuttlebutt said I wouldn't get tenure, even though I did my work, had a book contract with A. A. Knopf, and received more postdocs after two years than I could accept. One day at the community pool one of my assistant-professor colleagues asked me how it felt to know I owed my academic career to affirmative action. I was surprised to learn that, having acquired most of my education before the invention of affirmative action—something to be said for having been born in 1942. In any case, a Harvard Ph.D. and a book contract kind of took the sting out of that kind of accusation. The mean-spirited colleague later quit academia. His wife left him, and he made a lot of money in finance. I got tenure in three years. That didn't stop the unpleasantness at Penn, so I left for the National Humanities Center in North Carolina. I stayed on at the University of North Carolina at Chapel Hill. Things went well through my first two books, then I started feeling really crummy.

## Faltering in the 1980s

Only once did I seriously falter, in 1984–85, when I felt like a hack trapped in a mediocre career. My research and teaching no longer interested me; I had way too many chores to attend to; I was forgetting things all the time. My professional life seemed to have reached a dead end. I wanted to chuck my career and go home to Oakland.

My parents had held on to a little house for me in Oakland, a kind of security blanket in case I should want to throw it all over and come home. Knowing all along I *could* throw it all over and come home, needing to earn only enough to feed myself and my cats, had permitted my lack of careerism. I didn't have to be a historian. I didn't have to stay a historian. I could survive if academia expelled me or I just wanted to quit. This fallback should have saved me in 1984–85. It didn't. At the point I wanted to quit and go home, I felt trapped. My commitments, my students, even my Chapel Hill mortgage nailed me in place. I couldn't get free. There I was, condemned to life as a mediocrity.

Part of the problem was my ugly-baby book, *Standing at Armageddon*, still in process and getting stranger and stranger every day. Chapter by chapter, I would do some research on an event or significant person, write it up, and ask a relevant colleague to review the part pertaining to his specialty. He'd read it, assure me I'd gotten the facts right, but that was all. His silence said to me: This book is weird. I felt I was writing my way ever deeper into a cul-de-sac.

The greater part of my malaise I share with legions of women: utter exhaustion. A dear friend dragged me off to a smart therapist. The therapist recognized the signs: my depression, my forgetfulness, my lack of interest in the work I usually felt passionate about, all that stemmed from exhaustion.

LESSON ONE

Recognizing exhaustion, I went around to the various people I owed things to, apologizing profusely and explaining I wouldn't be able to do what I had promised. Doctor's orders. The response taught me something. Several people didn't miss a beat, saying no problem, can you just suggest someone else, meaning another black woman academic (it didn't even need to be a historian). Realizing for many purposes I function as just an educated unit of black + female, I resolved then not to accept assignments unless only I could fulfill them, me, with my own particular interests and my own particular knowledge. If someone else could do it, let someone else do it.

My late dear friend Nellie McKay operated differently. She would speak openly as black woman, as black woman scholar, even on topics outside her own interests. I decided not to exhaust myself trying to fulfill our culture's insatiable appetite for hearing from (then forgetting the message of) black women. The appetite still seems too large for me to even begin to satisfy it, so why not do the things only I can do? Addressing race and gender wrongheadedness is like throwing a stone in a lake. After a momentary and visible disturbance, the surface of the lake closes over the stone as it sinks into the hidden depths. Enough stones would ultimately pile up on the bottom and break through the surface, but that would require a hell of a lot of stones, more than I could throw in my lifetime. I do throw a stone into the lake from time to time, especially when I think my seniority adds weight to my stone. To switch metaphors, I quote a French historian speaking of "a debt, constantly paid but never extinguished." That about sums up what a fortunate black woman owes "the Race."[3]

I will speak out as a black woman scholar when I think my professional standing meaningfully amplifies my words. After all, I've been a senior scholar for more than a quarter century. (I was promoted to full professor at the University of North Carolina at Chapel Hill in 1980 and chaired at Princeton in 1991.) Sometimes someone with a long track record can get through better than someone just starting out. Not always, though. In our youth-obsessed culture, young people can speak with more authority than we older folk, especially we old women, we older black women. (My first book benefited from our culture's obsession with youthful freshness.) This world we live in is racist, yes, sexist, yes, and ageist, yes. Black people, women, and people of a certain age, though targets of bigotry, can sometimes do some pretty mean things. I wish I could say their insults don't hurt, but they do, more even than those of white men. I like to think people like me are savvier than others, partly out of just having lived on the qui vive for so many years. But it isn't just us older black women who see how the world works. Others, rare though they be, can be just as perceptive. And people like us can be pretty thick-headed—but not too thick. A dumb black woman will soon stumble into the snares in our paths.

So one lesson of my crisis of 1984–85 was to do only what only I could do— as much as possible. That isn't always possible, of course. The other lesson: seek refuge.

LESSON TWO

My first refuge was a lakeside camp in western Maine we called "Armageddon" because I used my advance royalties from *Standing at Armageddon* to start paying for it. As ever, my dear parents offered essential financial support. Armageddon lay way off the beaten path, so far away no one could find it without specific directions. The fact that the name of the main road kept changing made up-to-date directions absolutely essential. Only people I (later we, after Glenn Shafer and I married in 1989) invited could come there.

The remoteness of Armageddon kept the incessant, insidious messages of the big world at bay, the messages questioning my competence and my professional worth. In the foothills of the White Mountains (where Marsden Hartley painted his early landscapes), I escaped the hierarchies of my workaday world. In Armageddon I lived and swam in a bubble of safety and cool weather. I never have been able to deal with heat and humidity—part of my Bay Area inheritance.

Camps in northern New England—Maine, then Vermont—and now in the Adirondacks of northern New York State afford me shelter from the stresses of my everyday life. I like being alone (alone includes my dear husband) because strangers seem more and more of a drain.[4] For the most part, our solitary summers protect us from the intrusions of public and professional life, an escape absolutely essential to my mental and physical health. I finished *Standing at Armageddon* and *Sojourner Truth: A Life, a Symbol* in Maine. Although *Southern History across the Color Line* began in Vermont, I finished it in Berlin. I began *Creating Black Americans* in Vermont and finished it in the Adirondacks. *The History of White People* will have an Adirondack dateline. This list makes me sound pretty peripatetic, which may actually be the case. As I think about it, being in places other than the United States and, in the United States, other than my work site has saved my mental health. And good mental health has made possible my work as a historian.

### Being Elsewhere

I started being elsewhere in 1962, with a summer in northern Nigeria with Crossroads Africa, followed by an academic year at the University of Bordeaux as part of the University of California's first year of education abroad. After graduating from Berkeley in 1964, I joined my parents in Ghana for two years. I can't imagine how I would see the world—past and present—without these early experiences outside the United States, with its invisible/hypervisible color line. I've said it before: living in a racist culture drives you crazy. It wears you out and wrecks your mind. Not that other countries are unracist, but other countries have their own forms of bigotry that don't make me the token, the target. Bordeaux, then Ghana afforded me the opportunity to refocus my eyes from U.S.-style racism and see things differently. In Bordeaux, I discovered I really do like history and am very good at it. I studied French medieval history there, one of the fields in my general exam at Harvard years later. I just love the study of history. If I hadn't been born black when I was, I probably would have been a historian of medieval France.

In Ghana for two years, I discovered a whole new world of issues, problems, and ways of sorting out the world. I learned the meaning of class, for instance, along socialist lines. Even though I'm from the relatively enlightened San Francisco Bay Area, I grew up in the 1950s in the United States. Without my realizing it, my world was so racialized I took my bearings according to the North Star of race. France dimmed the star's brilliance without obscuring it completely. In Ghana, where everyone who counted was black, I lost sight of my American lodestar. Loss of meaning sent me first into political confusion. In Ghana, the pressing issues were economic, questions related to development and how it worked out in a political arena where all the players were black. (As I write "black" again, I need to acknowledge how meaningless the American term is in a West African context where so very much besides race matters—every day and fundamentally.) I had to learn to figure out the Ghanaian political economy according to colonial history, contending political ideologies, and party lines. Americans might be tempted to rearrange colonial relations along a more familiar color line. But imperialism is so much more than race and color, even though a color line nearly always accompanied twentieth-century imperialism. Colonial relationships don't need race and mean so much more than color that to try to explain them through race is to lose most of the meaning. It took me a while to figure that out.

I recognized the need to readjust most clearly on the everyday level of essential class relations. The rich and the poor and the middle were all people of the same race (so to speak), but their lives played out according to their relative wealth and connections. Working people who couldn't afford powdered milk for their children saw the self-proclaimed socialist, Pan-African Nkrumist regime very differently from those of us in easier economic circumstances. We with money loved the historical resonance of, say, the Black Star Line, the national shipping line named for Marcus Garvey's own company. Those short of cash went hungry, Marcus Garvey or no.

In San Jose, I glimpsed the limits of ideology. Those limits appeared with utmost clarity in Ghana. As someone outside the political class, I wasn't privy to the details. (My jobs were broadcasting in French for Ghana Radio and teaching French to the telephone operators for the upcoming African summit in Accra.) But I could see enough to discern the gaps between professed socialist ideals and class relations on the ground. I'm still not cynical about politics in general, but experience in Ghana taught me not to take political speech at face value. There's theory, but then there's also praxis to be taken into account. In Ghana, the interests of the people sometimes called the "national bourgeoisie" diverged from those of ordinary folk. I took what I had learned from my Ghanaian and French educations into my work as a historian.

### Notice sur les Travaux de Nell Irvin Painter

My Harvard dissertation became my first book, *Exodusters: Black Migration to Kansas after Reconstruction*. In response to my own peripatetic habits, the book deals with migration. It answers my wondering why black southerners stayed in the South after the end of Reconstruction. Answer: They did not all stay put. In *Exodusters*, I wanted to show how ordinary people lived after the end of Reconstruction, why they stayed, and how they left. I described both everyday life and the frightened migration of victims of racial terrorism in Louisiana and Mississippi and Kentucky. *Exodusters* compares their search for safety with educated commentary from the "national bourgeoisie" in northern cities. Frederick Douglass, by 1879 a Republican elder statesman in Washington, D.C., lectured the Exodusters who ran for their lives. Douglass told them to stay in the South and stick up for their rights. I saw Douglass as more in touch with ideology than with sympathy for poor southerners. Reviewers scolded me for portraying Douglass in an unflattering light. But I thought it important to say there was no single black position on conditions in the South or on the Exodus.

I still don't know whether to date *Exodusters* from its copyright year (1976) or its actual date of publication (January 1977). Publication coincided with the initial broadcast of *Roots* on television and a trip to Atlantic City with a friend in his unheated Volkswagen to see Hosea Hudson. Hudson seemed of more import at the time than *Exodusters*. The *New York Times Book Review* published a full-page review of *Exodusters* by a leading historian, the kind of treatment reserved for heavyweights and the very young. Penn granted me tenure that spring. Subsequently a white woman colleague threatened to sue because she was refused tenure after I had succeeded. I was in North Carolina for the duration when my second book came out in 1979.

Though I like rereading all my books, *The Narrative of Hosea Hudson: His Life as a Negro Communist in the South* is still my sentimental favorite. The notion of a working-class black Communist living in Birmingham, Alabama, in the 1930s intrigued me enough to start me taping Hudson's memoir in 1976. I was still on the lookout for the experience of ordinary, working-class people. The book was Hudson's idea; he wanted a new biography. I hope the book fulfills both our aims. I certainly learned a lot and enjoyed the process, which Nellie McKay shared. She was staying with me in Philadelphia while conducting dissertation research and came along when I visited Hudson for the first time. Her visit marked the beginning of a regular correspondence lasting until 2005, when she lost the strength to write.[5] Nellie died in January 2006 of colon cancer, leaving an astonished group of friends and colleagues. We thought she was about sixty—she had given us that impression—but she was actually seventy-five. She had been keeping even more secrets than that from even her very best friends.

After the publication of *Hosea Hudson* in 1979 and *Standing at Armageddon* in 1987, I returned to the project I had begun when Hosea Hudson and *Hosea Hudson* entered my life: "American Views of the South." I had conceived this project as discourse history: what various people had to say about the South and southerners. Research in the Duke University Libraries changed my course. I was looking around for meaty material when an archivist showed me a 1,380-page typescript of the journal of a Georgia plantation mistress, Ella Gertrude Clanton Thomas. What a rich document from what another historian has called the mind of the master class! I wondered why such a resource had not been published. The answer lay with a controlling descendant, a woman of literary pretensions. After much work and negotiation, Gertrude Thomas's journal finally appeared from the University of North Carolina Press in 1990 as *The Secret Eye*. My introduction taught me a great deal about women's history, feminist theory, psychology, and descendant avoidance. *The Secret Eye* took me away from "American Views of the South" but made me attend to the psychology of historical actors. I still believe that the key to late-nineteenth-century political upheaval in the U.S. South relates to competition over women, a point that still has not been grasped, perhaps because it makes black and poor women crucial historical figures. Issues of psychology, power, and sexuality permeate my work on Harriet Jacobs and Sojourner Truth.

The disjunction between visual and verbal depictions of Sojourner Truth intrigued me. Knowing no more than anyone else about Truth at the outset of my research, I contrasted the angry black woman emerging from the utterance then mistakenly said to be "Ar'n't I a woman?" with the composed and ladylike image in Truth's photographs. I knew from the beginning that representation and discourse history would play major roles in my biography, *Sojourner Truth: A Life, a Symbol*. Only by the middle of my research did I realize I would need to educate myself in the rhetoric of the image (to quote Roland Barthes) in order to read meaning into Truth's photographs. I'm still disappointed by historians' disregard of my chapter on Truth's photographs, but at least art historians have made excellent use of it.

People sometimes ask me whether I like Sojourner Truth. No, I don't like her, in the sense of liking a friend. She was too deeply religious a person for me to get along with, and, living in such a white-supremacist era of American history, she tended to disregard black people, especially other black women. No, I don't like her, and she wouldn't see any reason to spend time with me. But I deeply respect Sojourner Truth for her ability to use the power of the Holy Spirit to heal the wounds of enslavement and remain a public figure over the course of four decades, for her intelligence and wit and ability to put her thorough knowledge of the Bible to excellent rhetorical ends. People still misquote Sojourner Truth, whether or not they have read my book. As Strong Black Woman, she plays a far more usable role than I, a mere academic historian. I showed her as a person whose individual psychology counts alongside her role as a symbol. But many people just want a symbol, unchanging and undisturbed by psychological development.

At the end of the twentieth century, I edited two Penguin Classics: *Narrative of Sojourner Truth* and *Incidents in the Life of a Slave Girl*. Both introductory essays stress the individual psychology of the protagonists. I'm not sure how influential these essays have been because I'm not sure how ready American readers are to see black figures as singular individuals rather than units of race. But black people as individuals populate the fine and thoughtful dissertations of graduate students working with me at Princeton.

During the late 1980s and 1990s, I published several essays with racially mixed casts of characters. Scattered in journals and in books under other people's names, these pieces eluded those trying to track them down. I collected several biographical pieces, which the University of North Carolina Press published in 2002 as *Southern History across the Color Line*. I still have uncollected essays on history and memory.

More recently, I have written about art. Art increasingly occupied my narrative history of African Americans, *Creating Black Americans*, published in 2005 (but with a 2006 copyright, another book I'll never know when it was published). In this book, I wanted to balance the horrific history of African American racial trauma with the enormous achievement of survival and creativity. Visual art offered a means of capturing the beauty of black history. I'm happy to have produced such a book by myself, but once again I learned a valuable lesson: not to write anything else requiring elaborate permissions. Securing permissions nearly did me in, even with the help of a consultant and the generous financial support of Princeton University.

You see from my account that advising graduate students plays only a small large part in my sense of myself as a historian. Others may not view my career in similar terms. In 2001, for instance, after the American Historical Association had given me a gratifying award for mentoring graduate students, a colleague came up to inform me that mentoring was my vocation as a historian. I reminded him I also write books. He contradicted me: mentoring constitutes my "real" vocation. Were I prone to violence, I would have socked him in his fat little jaw. Nowadays I ask people not to talk about my mentoring. I ask them not to gush over me as a wonderful person so good to the youth. One of my former graduate students has promised to prevent people from carrying on like that at my funeral. It's just too easy to reenvision a woman, a black woman, an older black woman as a nurturing figure. Too stereotypical. Too easy to disregard the scholarship, especially when the scholarship asks the reader to overcome established habits of thought.

### Next Steps

For the first time in my life, I have a plan and I have ambitions: first a B.F.A. from Mason Gross, then an M.F.A. from the most demanding art school I can get into, then making art worth serious recognition. My father first taught me to draw many, many years ago and always encouraged my art. My mother, who taught me to write, also showed me how to start over at retirement. I had intended to start over at sixty-three, last fall instead of this. But my current book project took longer than expected—fancy that! I begin again this fall at sixty-four. Wish me luck, and save your money for a painting.

NOTES

Many thanks to my esteemed and beloved colleague Deborah Gray White for this opportunity to speak candidly about my experiences as a historian. Wiser but no more temperate than I, Deborah sees the historical profession with more than my patience. Thanks, too, to Dona Irvin and Thadious Davis for helpful readings.

1. The term "ego-histoire" comes from Pierre Nora, who collected a series of brief autobiographies from French historians born between the two world wars. Nora's anthology is *Essais d'ego-histoire* (Paris: Gallimard, 1987). See also Jeremy D. Popkin, "Ego-Histoire and Beyond: Contemporary French Historian-Autobiographers," *French Historical Studies* 19, no. 4 (Autumn 1996): 1139–67.

2. On November 17, 1991, 1,600 educated black women placed a full-page ad in the *New York Times* in support of Anita Hill and in protest against pernicious stereotyping of black women in American culture. The ad gave rise to a conference at the Massachusetts Institute of Technology in January 1994, "Black Women in the Academy: Defending Our Name, 1894–1994."

3. Annie Kriegel, *Ce que j'ai cru comprendre* (Paris: R. Laffont, 1991), 195, quoted in Popkin, "Ego-Histoire and Beyond," 1159. Kriegel is speaking of the French Communist Party, of which she was a leader in the 1960s.

4. We've always had a few dear friends around our northern homes: Leo and Jane Marx in Maine; Hazel Carby, Michael Demming, Priscilla Barnum, and the late Ted Draper in Vermont; Russell Banks and Chase Twitchell plus newly acquired good people in and around New Russia, New York; and my dear friend Thadious Davis and my parents when they would visit all three places.

5. Our correspondence now resides with my papers in the John Hope Franklin Collection in the Duke University Rare Book, Manuscript, and Special Collections Library.

# Darlene Clark Hine

## BECOMING A BLACK WOMAN'S HISTORIAN

Imagine my surprise and delight when I learned that I was to be inducted as a fellow into the American Academy of Arts and Sciences on October 6, 2006. The letter indicated that my work in the history of black women was the primary basis for this honor. I never entertained any thoughts of receiving such a distinction. To be named a fellow in the AAAS represented, along with my earlier presidential tenures of the Organization of American Historians and the Southern Historical Association, the academy's recognition and acceptance of black women's history as an integral and legitimate area of study essential to a fuller understanding of American and African American history. Then, to compound my amazement, I heard from University of South Carolina historian Wanda Hendricks the wonderful news that the Organization of American Historians had approved the establishment of the Darlene Clark Hine Prize for the best book in African American women's history and gender. I was deeply touched and virtually speechless. After almost three decades of my engagement in myriad efforts to create and to institutionalize the field of black women's history, this new area of study, considered marginal by early skeptics, had moved to the center. I am pleased to have been part of the collective intellectual struggles of black women in the academy that achieved this transformation and opened new opportunities for advanced study and professorships in the ivory tower for future generations of black women.

My decades-long study of the professional lives of black women during the era of legal segregation commanded a considerable portion of my academic career, especially the last two decades of the twentieth century. Therefore, it is perhaps inevitable that I should employ the understandings thus derived from the pursuit of the history of black women nurses, physicians, and lawyers to the contours of my own academic odyssey in the ivory tower. Informal learning combined with structural academic and professional training is an essential determinant of professional success. Equally important are networks, family support, and academic and intellectual mentors who open doors of opportunity. When Deborah Gray White invited me to contribute an essay to this volume, I was reticent, believing that the details of my career are readily available in a number of previously published autobiographical essays and that students should be more invested in history than in the lives of historians. White was persistent, arguing that students may not need to know my story but that they would perhaps derive benefit from learning about my intellectual evolution. Persuaded, I accepted the challenge to explain the forces that converged to shape my work as a historian of the lives and experiences of African American women who, since the beginning of their tenure in this nation as indentured and enslaved Africans, embarked upon a relentless quest for freedom and human dignity.

How did I become an African American women's historian? What were the strategies African American women historians deemed essential and effective in the launching of a field of intellectual inquiry that scarcely existed in the late 1960s and early 1970s? What were some of the major impediments to the development of black women's history? In my case, I must confess that I "learned on the job." In other words, never in the course of my undergraduate years at Roosevelt University in Chicago (1964–68) or during graduate training at Kent State University in Kent, Ohio (1968–74), did I have the pleasure or inclination to study black women's history. Did black women have a history? To be sure, a young dynamic cohort of East Coast–based black women graduate students were concentrating on the history of black women. Rosalyn Terborg-Penn, Sharon Harley, Evelyn Brooks Higginbotham, and Bettye Collier-Thomas, to name a few, were quite advanced in their academic study of black women's history. Back then, however, this middle westerner firmly believed that to do— meaning research, write, and teach—African American history meant that I must focus on the more important experiences and exploits of black men. In other words, I did not question the implicit assumption of my teachers, all of whom were men, that whatever was said about black men applied with equal validity to black women, who apparently rarely, if ever, ventured beyond the domestic sphere. With the exception of Phillis Wheatley, Sojourner Truth, and Harriet Tubman, black women were voiceless and faceless in history texts. To be sure, the black women's literary renaissance of the 1970s, which catapulted writers Maya Angelou, Alice Walker, and Toni Morrison into national prominence, and the arrest and trial of Angela Davis and run for presidential nomination of Congresswoman Shirley Chisholm brought black women national attention. Still, my lack of a nuanced and sophisticated feminist consciousness left me ill equipped to connect these contemporary women's creative expressions and political activism with a black past in which significance was gendered and raced black male and all women were considered marginal in intellectual matters.

In 1980, my ignorance of black women's unique and distinct history held little purchase against the fiercely determined Shirley Herd, president of the Indianapolis chapter of the National Council of Negro Women. Herd demanded that I write a history of black women in Indiana, and when I demurred, she, like Deborah Gray White, refused to take "No" for an answer. My work in collaboration with Indianapolis black women schoolteachers Shirley Herd and Virtea Downey and the members of the Indianapolis branch of the NCNW signaled the beginning of my transformation into a historian of black women. In 1993, were it not for the intellectual and material support of white male publisher Ralph Carlson, the encyclopedia of black women's history of which I am very proud, *Black Women in America: An Historical Encyclopedia* (New York: Carlson Publishing, 1993), would never have been prepared or published. Black women historians Elsa Barkley Brown and Rosalyn Terborg-Penn shared the immense co-editing labors involved in the creation and production of this two-volume reference work. The three-volume second edition published by Oxford University Press in 2005 benefited enormously from the expertise and energy of an advisory board consisting of Deborah Gray White, Rosalyn Terborg-Penn, Wilma King, Brenda Stevenson, Wanda Hendricks, Jacqueline McLeod, and Daina Ramey Berry. My co-author of *A Shining Thread of Hope: A History of Black Women in America* (New York: Random House, 1998), Kathleen Thompson, served on the editorial board while coordinating the work of assigning the biographical entries to hundreds of scholars and writers. Photo researcher Hilary "Mac" Austin did a splendid job of tracking the extraordinary images that adorn and enrich the new edition. Each editor wrote numerous article-length interpretative essays, making this the most definitive and comprehensive compilation in our field.

As a student and professor in the American academy, I have been affected personally and professionally by the interconnection of race, class, region, and gender dynamics. Today's generation of young scholars readily employ analyses of these key concepts. They embrace and manipulate the theoretical concepts to construct frames essential to deepening understanding of the historical and present experiences, activities, and belief systems of America's black women. This essay separates easily into two parts: the first chronicles the early phase of my intellectual development and training as a historian, and the second focuses on the scholarly, theoretical, and popular historical writings and the archival and reference works produced to institutionalize the study of black women's history.

Born on February 7, 1947, in Morley, Missouri, I spent my formative years living with my grandparents, Robert and Fannie Venerable Thompson, on their farm in Villa Ridge, Illinois, an area referred to as Little Egypt. My parents, Levester and Lottie Mae Thompson Clark, had migrated to Chicago, where my father worked as a truck driver and my mother worked at home attending to my brother Orlando and younger sisters Barbara Ann and Alma Jean. The entire family made frequent visits to Villa Ridge to see me and the large extended family until I relocated to Chicago when I was to enter the third grade. It was my good fortune to spend every summer with my grandparents until age seventeen. These summers were such a wonderful gift of quiet time and solitude, full of hours of reading and listening to the stories told by my grandfather.

My grandparents left indelible impressions on my consciousness. A veteran of World War I, my grandfather recounted in vivid detail his exploits in the Great War and, with equal passion and dramatic effect, his encounters with white landowners in Mississippi, Arkansas, and Missouri. Grandfather and Grandmother had worked as sharecroppers for two decades before they were able to purchase the farm in Villa Ridge. His abiding passion was land. He preached the virtue and necessity of landownership at every opportunity. His self-constructed masculinity and manhood were inextricably connected to landownership and armed resistance to any white encroachment on or threat to the family's land. Grandmother preached a different gospel, fervently espousing the importance of education. While Grandfather's often-repeated stories concerned white encroachment on his land, Grandmother vehemently asserted that education was the only thing that the white man could never take from you.

I was obsessed with my grandmother and shadowed her every move, listened to everything she said, and always tried to be her perfect grandchild. Although she had given birth to fifteen children, eleven of whom had survived, she treated me with special gentleness. I was the one to whom she would read her Bible, and in the evening before I got into bed between her and Grandfather, she would listen to me recite my prayers. I doubt that any of the other family members harbored envy of my "privileged" position in bed between Grandfather and Grandmother, but at least I was never cold.

Two memories, one about praying and the other about reading, linger still. My grandmother silently prayed after reading the Bible. One night, she remained in a kneeling position for such a long time that I thought she had fallen asleep. I made a mistake that I never repeated: I gently shook her shoulder and asked why she was taking so long. To my amazement, she was annoyed with me. She told me that I was never to interrupt her while she was talking to God. When I asked why, she explained that with a family as large as hers, it took a long time to pray for the souls of everyone. The other memory revolves around the Bible-reading sessions. I had enough sense not to ask Grandmother why she read from the Bible every night month after month and yet never seemed to be able to finish it. I was eager to learn how to read, as much for the sheer joy as for the prospect of helping Grandmother finish reading the Bible so we could move on to other books.

Reading, storytelling, hard work, education, family solidarity, religion, obedience, and landownership were the foundations of my belief system and the core values inculcated during a childhood and adolescence spent between rural and urban midwestern homes. My formal intellectual development began in high school (Crane on the West Side of Chicago) and escalated during undergraduate study at Roosevelt University in downtown Chicago. The civil rights and black power movements provided the more vivid and consequential background.

I was the valedictorian of my high school graduating class (1964), and my address was entitled "Education Is the Key to the Door of Opportunity." Roosevelt University granted me a full scholarship, as it did to all valedictorians of the area's high schools. The topic of my address and my choice of biology as a major reflected Grandmother's teachings and the influence of my Uncle Dennis Perry, a professor of microbiology at Northwestern University Medical School. Uncle Dennis and Aunt Fannie (my mother's sister) lived upstairs in the family compound. Throughout my high school years, Uncle Dennis worked with me on various science fair projects and was especially generous with help on algebra, geometry, and trigonometry problems. His interests became my own, and I was determined to become a biological scientist. I admired the precision, silence, and relentless quest for answers that science and Uncle Dennis represented. Within a year of entering Roosevelt, however, I had abandoned dreams of test tubes and embraced history. The civil rights movement was in full throttle, and I was at a loss to explain, much less understand, why African Americans were angry and white Americans seemed so scared.

My first year in college was full of transitions, the most profound of which was personal. On August 10, 1965, I gave birth to an adorable baby girl, Robbie Davine. My family, especially my mother, was understandably upset with me, all the more so because I refused to marry my baby's father. Unmarried motherhood was not respectable or acceptable. Only the timely and welcome intervention of my grandmother dispelled the tension. She advised my mother to take care of Robbie and suggested to me that I eschew further childbearing and concentrate on completing my education. Now that we all had our respective instructions and since Robbie was such a beautiful and joyful child whose presence enriched our family, I pursued knowledge with a strong motivation that everyone, except my father and grandmother, found difficult to understand. Even with her father's support, I realized that I would have to provide for

Robbie and help my family in the years ahead. When I went away to graduate school, I left Robbie in the care of my parents, just as they had left me with my grandparents when they migrated to Chicago in the early 1950s. (Fast forward: A graduate of Indiana University in Bloomington, Robbie earned a master's degree in organizational psychology at Roosevelt University, specializing in human resources. Robbie was promoted to second vice president of Northern Bank and Trust in Chicago, then was quickly recruited to work at People's Energy. I admire her integrity, humor, and impressive skills as a computer systems designer and analyst. She also somehow finds the time to be a caring and generous godmother to three young girls. When her father died in 2000, I delivered the eulogy at his funeral.)

The years between 1965 and 1970 were spent in search of understanding the "multiple dualities" of identity. I embraced an internal agenda to learn who I was and to find a way to fit into the world, especially intellectually. I had to discover the talents and gifts I possessed in order to develop them so as to make a contribution to society and earn a living. There were few role models of public black women who commanded respect in the academy or in most arenas, with the exception of popular music. There was always Aretha Franklin and Mahalia Jackson! My mother and aunts all believed that teaching, nursing, and social work were respectable professions that, when combined with marriage and family, made for a good life and the epitome of personal fulfillment. The larger society stereotyped black women either as welfare queens and matriarchs responsible for the "breakdown" of the family or as superreligious, mindless followers of black ministers. Therefore, it was very important for women in my family to be circumspect. The men in my family seemed to possess a larger array of professional role models and opportunities. While they universally applauded the successful entrepreneur, they also imagined themselves capable of becoming doctors, lawyers, musicians, and, most important, property owners. I wanted to roam in their dreamscape. Why did men have more of everything than women? I became a close observer of male behavior, of how men are represented in the larger society and how they fashion positive identities for themselves.

The civil rights and black power movements framed the 1960s and the 1970s and provided me ample opportunity to study and learn about black men, including, for example, Muhammad Ali, Malcolm X, Martin Luther King Jr., Huey P. Newton, Bobby Seale, and Eldridge Cleaver. During an era rampant with negative images and caricatures of black men as lazy, clownish, or hypermasculine, these real-life black men were a powerful antidote. These leaders were vibrant, captivating, occasionally perplexing representatives of black manhood. Articulate, handsome, fiercely self-conscious freedom fighters, these men garnered massive media coverage with their demands for black political rights, education and economic opportunities, and curricular transformation in colleges and universities. The fear they engendered among some white Americans was as palpable as the anger that pulsated in black communities across the continent. The tumultuous sixties with the Watts Riot, the assassinations of Malcolm X and Martin Luther King Jr., and the urban rebellions in Chicago, Detroit, Newark, and Washington, D.C., inflamed my desire for understanding. Why were these things happening?

I decided to become a historian, to study the past to understand the relations between black and white people and the meaning of the strange phenomenon of racism and race. Science had taught me that there was only one race, the human race, and I knew that skin, regardless of color or shade, was a biological organ with a specific function and as such was neither good nor bad. Skin protected the body from disease and injury. Thus, the social, cultural, and political meanings of race and practice of racism must have been constructed in the past. History, therefore, as opposed to biology, seemed most likely to hold the key to understanding this American dilemma.

To be sure, before making the change from biology to history I met with an academic counselor. During the course of our conversation about my major, he asked me what subject I performed well in with minimum effort: "What subject do you receive the highest grades in without trying too hard?" That was easy— history. He speculated that I probably could do even better if I concentrated my effort. So history became my major, with a minor in English. I enrolled in a series of courses, gravitating to those taught by African American professors, including historian Hollis Lynch and linguist Lorenzo Dow Turner. I made a point of taking a wide range of history courses to acquire familiarity with English history, Russian history, and African history. I augmented my formal course work by attending all, or as many as my schedule allowed, the public lectures of sociologist St. Clair Drake, University of Chicago historian John Hope Franklin, editor of *Ebony* Lerone Bennett, and political scientist Charles V. Hamilton. I took careful notes and read the books they authored or mentioned.

One of my great good fortunes was to secure a work-study assignment in the Roosevelt University Library, where I helped to process new books and to return volumes to the stacks. It was while thus employed that I discovered and read the works of many black male scholars, three of whom would make lasting impressions: Carter G. Woodson, the father of African American history; W. E. B. Du Bois, the founder of modern American sociology; and Booker T. Washington. Woodson once said, and here I am paraphrasing, that every person is entitled to two educations, one that he receives in formal institutional settings and one, even more important than the first, that he gives to himself. It was such a simple declaration, one that I internalized. Woodson's most popular polemic, *The Mis-Education of the Negro* (1933), drove home his message about the necessity for self-education when living in a racist society. I reckoned that I owed it to myself to acquire the best possible self-education and resolved to never stop learning as long as there was a degree to be had.

W. E. B. Du Bois's most often quoted passage about "double consciousness" resonated as much as Woodson's exhortation to self-educate. I committed to memory Du Bois's observation in *The Souls of Black Folk* (1903): "It is a peculiar sensation, this double consciousness, this sense of always looking at one's self through the eyes of others, of measuring one's soul by the tape of a world that looks on in amused contempt and pity." Du Bois insisted that he simply wanted to ensure the possibility that a man could be both a Negro and an American "without being cursed and spit on by his fellows, without having the doors of opportunity closed roughly in his face." At this stage in my development, I recall that what I most appreciated about Du Bois was his language. The final member of my intellectual male trio was Booker T. Washington, whom I admired for his successful development of Tuskegee Institute as a major educational center and community resource during the formative years of Jim Crow racial segregation.

When I wasn't reading history or academic texts, as part of my self-education I read the novels, essays, and autobiographical writings of Richard Wright, Ralph Ellison, and James Baldwin. The titles of their books give some indication of the depth of masculine preoccupation: *Native Son* (1940); *Black Boy: A Record of Childhood and Youth* (1945); *Invisible Man* (1952); and *Notes of a Native Son* (1963). At the insistence of fellow male students, I read John A. Williams's *The Man Who Cried I Am: A Novel* (1967); Sam Greenlee's *The Spook Who Sat by the Door: A Novel* (1969); Claude Brown's *Manchild in the Promised Land* (1965); and *The Autobiography of Malcolm X* (1965). The artists, musicians, and community activists with whom I became friends introduced me to the music of John Coltrane, Miles Davis, and Pharoah Sanders, and I developed an abiding appreciation for the drawings and paintings of visual artists Murry N. DePillars, Jeff Donaldson, and John Lockart.

Perhaps I am being too hard on myself, but the point is that I was oblivious to the lack of attention that I and others paid to black women's experiences. By the time I left Chicago for Kent, Ohio, my sharpened black masculine consciousness mirrored the academic world. My woefully deficient feminist perspective remained underdeveloped as I studied under the guidance of August Meier (*Negro Thought in America, 1880–1915: Racial Ideologies in the Age of*

*Booker T. Washington* [Ann Arbor: University of Michigan Press, 1963]) and the other professors, all white males with the exception of African historian Felix Ekechie, at Kent State. Intense course work left little time for general reading. Meier, a demanding major professor, leaned heavily on me to master the historiography, to carry my weight in seminar discussions, and to get the facts right and always prepare perfect footnotes. There were only a couple of black male students in the program. Christopher Robert Reed was there with his family until he completed his course work. John Bracey, whom I had met in the library at Roosevelt University, came to Kent occasionally to work with Meier on editing projects. I returned home as often as possible to visit Robbie and my family.

I became close friends with one of the white students who, on leave from his teaching position at South Carolina State College, a historically black school in Orangeburg, South Carolina, arrived in 1969 to study with Meier. I did not know that William C. Hine had witnessed the Orangeburg Massacre until we stood next to each other on the grassy hill that fateful day, May 4, 1970, when the Ohio National Guard killed four students just as the South Carolina state troopers had done two years earlier at State College. In August 1970, William and I were married. What happened? I reached the point at which I would never judge another human being on the basis of skin color, hair texture, or facial features. In the aftermath of the South Carolina State College and Kent State University state-sanctioned carnage, I knew that the internal qualities of goodness and commitment to help others live better lives were what mattered. In 1972, I accompanied William back to what was later renamed South Carolina State University, where I was appointed an assistant professor of history and coordinator of African American studies. Teaching five courses that attracted large numbers of students and working on a dissertation was fun but more than a little taxing. In 1974, I accepted an offer to join the history department at Purdue University. It was here that I met and became friends with a colleague, Harold D. Woodman, who became my mentor. Woodman was especially helpful when I was searching for a publisher for my first book.

I recall that selecting a dissertation topic had been a challenge. Through a process of elimination of my suggestions of a biography of T. Thomas Fortune or a history of the Black Populist Party movement in the Middle West, August Meier and I agreed that I would write a history of the NAACP's legal struggle to persuade the U.S. Supreme Court to declare unconstitutional the Democratic Party's white-primary disfranchisement laws. At the time, Meier and Elliott Rudwick were researching a history of the NAACP, so this topic was of considerable interest to him. In the one-party South, the most important elections were the Democratic Party's primaries. Membership in the Democratic Party was a prerequisite to voting in its primaries, and only white people could become members. General elections merely rubber-stamped the choices that the electorate determined in the primaries. Black men and women excluded from participating in the primaries remained politically powerless. In a series of U.S. Supreme Court cases beginning in the 1920s, black members of local Texas chapters of the NAACP developed test cases later argued by national NAACP attorneys that challenged the constitutionality of this blatant disfranchisement strategy. In 1944, in the case of *Smith v. Allwright*, the Supreme Court declared the white primary unconstitutional. The Democratic Party was not a private organization, like the Masons or Odd Fellows, and it did not have the right to restrict membership, with the attendant privilege of voting in primaries, to whites. The decision paved the way for millions of African Americans to vote, but it would take a civil rights movement to make suffrage a reality.

The point to underscore here is that in my dissertation I omitted meaningful discussion of black women's involvement in the campaign to overthrow the white primary. I would later revise the dissertation while working toward tenure and promotion in the Department of History at Purdue University, and still leave them in the shadows. I spent a lot of time in Texas researching this study and focused exclusively on the activities of male leaders. When I encountered documents that revealed the massive community mobilization and fundraising work of black women, I put them aside. Because I possessed no framework or perspective from which to evaluate or interpret the significance of their efforts to the success of the larger objective, I left black women on the periphery. Two decades after *Black Victory: The Rise and Fall of the White Primary in Texas* (New York: Kraus Thomson Publishers, 1979) appeared, a black woman historian at Texas Southern University, Merline Pitre, would write a splendid biography of Lulu White (*In Struggle against Jim Crow: Lulu B. White and the NAACP, 1900–1957* [College Station: Texas A&M University Press, 1999]) and thus give voice to this amazing black woman.

Throughout the 1970s, I was consumed by a desire to master the historian's craft. Meier was equally as determined that my dissertation reflect thorough research, logical arguments, and perfect footnotes. While I learned how to do history, it never occurred to me to question him about the absence of black women, and thus I, as is probably the case with most historians-in-training, wrote history that reflected my training. Little did I anticipate the drastic shift that my scholarship would take after my dissertation was published and I achieved tenure at Purdue University.

When I joined the Purdue history department, I was the only black historian and one of only a few black women professors on campus. Thus, when two women graduate students, Thavolia Glymph and Kate Wittenstein, asked me to teach a reading seminar in black women's history in 1978, I agreed only on the condition that they help identify the books to be read and discussed. I fully anticipated that they would not be able to find enough books and was surprised when they selected Anna Julia Cooper's *A Voice from the South* as our first text. From there we read Gerda Lerner's *Black Women in White America: A Documentary History* (New York: Pantheon, 1972); Harriet Jacobs's autobiography, *Incidents in the Life of a Slave Girl: Written by Herself*, edited by L. Maria Child (1861); and some works of fiction. We also read the first anthology of scholarly essays written by young black women historians, *The Afro-American Woman: Struggles and Images* (Port Washington, N.Y.: Kennikat Press, 1978), edited by Rosalyn Terborg-Penn and Sharon Harley. In short, Kate, Thavolia, and I taught each other. Kate (now a professor at Gustavus Adolphus College), who had prepared a research paper on plantation mistresses, submitted a panel proposal that was accepted by the Association for the Study of African American Life and History. When it proved impossible for Thavolia (now a professor at Duke University) to present her paper, I was asked to pinch-hit and within an incredibly short period to prepare a paper. I had read the contemporary slavery studies and decided to address the largely omitted experiences of slave women who struggled to control their reproduction through the use of abortion, abstinence, and infanticide. What I intended to be a food-for-thought piece aroused the ire of many black male historians who chastised me for suggesting that black women would ever engage in such behavior. Undaunted, Kate and I revised the essay and published it in Filomina Steady's *Black Woman Cross-Culturally* (Cambridge, Mass.: Schenkman, 1981). Kate went on to Boston University to pursue her doctoral degree.

It was the August 1980 request of Shirley Herd, president of the Indianapolis chapter of the National Council of Negro Women, that I write a history of black women in Indiana that forced me to use my professional training to think seriously about black women as historical subjects. Initially, I had tried to convince Herd that her request exceeded my expertise and that the absence of abundant documentation made it impossible to write a creditable history of black women in any state. Herd and her best friend, Virtea Downey, both teachers in the Indianapolis public schools, overcame my objections by delivering to my house a roomful of boxes containing every conceivable type of primary document that illuminated the multilayered dimensions of black women's lives in the Hoosier state. Acting under the directive of Dorothy Height, president of the National Council of Negro Women, each group of state officers had been challenged to prepare its own history. Herd, Downey, and other members had begun collecting the paper records of hundreds of black women. By 1980, they had determined that I was the only black woman historian in the state of Indiana, so they had decided to approach me. I spent six months reviewing the materials they had collected and then wrote the pamphlet *When the Truth Is Told: Black Women's Culture and Community in Indiana* (Indianapolis: National Council of Negro Women, 1981). Later in the year, I published an essay entitled "Lifting the Veil, Shattering the Silence: Black Women's History in Slavery and Freedom" in my edited volume *The State of Afro-American History: Past, Present, and Future* (Baton Rouge: Louisiana State University Press, 1986).

It was while working with Herd and Downey on the Indiana black women's history study that I began to fully appreciate the rich legacy of community-building work of black women. I was enthralled by the entrepreneurial genius of Madam C. J. Walker as she made her fortune manufacturing hair and beauty products and training and inspiring thousands of black women to join her sales force and acquire economic autonomy. (I wrote an essay entitled "Booker T. Washington and Madam C. J. Walker" in my book *Speak Truth to Power: Black Professional Class in United States History* [New York: Carlson Publishing, 1996].) When I learned that the materials they had collected had been returned to their owners, I invited Herd and Downey to join me in creating a permanent archive of sources on black women. This collaborative effort became the Black Women in the Middle West Project. With the assistance of white male historian Patrick Biddleman, an adjunct professor at Purdue, we developed a proposal and secured funding from the National Endowment for the Humanities to train black women to identify and facilitate the collection of primary sources in their communities that were deposited with the Indiana Historical Society and the Chicago Historical Society. The NEH had stipulated that the funds be used to collect the records from black women in two states instead of the five we had proposed, so we decided to concentrate our efforts in Indiana and Illinois. My graduate student, Wanda Hendricks, would become the first to use these materials when she consulted them as the basis for her dissertation on the social and political history of black women in Illinois. Indiana University Press would later publish her book, *Gender, Race, and Politics in the Midwest: Black Club Women in Illinois* (Bloomington: Indiana University Press, 1998).

The need for a network of mentors was one of the impetuses for the creation of the Association of Black Women Historians under the leadership of Rosalyn

Terborg-Penn and Eleanor Smith. I became the first editor of the association's publication, *Truth*, and used it to share news about job opportunities, fellowships, research projects, and the publications and activities of women in our field. The ABWH was also committed to recognizing the work of scholars in black women's history inasmuch as we knew that the larger profession still questioned its value. Jacqueline Jones's *Labor of Love, Labor of Sorrow* (New York: Vintage Books, 1995) would receive one of the earliest ABWH awards for the most significant book in black women's history published in a particular year. I was enormously impressed with Deborah Gray White's pioneering monograph on the history of enslaved women in the plantation South, her first book, *Ar'n't I a Woman?: Female Slaves in the Plantation South* (New York: W. W. Norton, 1985). It was as if my essay on female slave resistance had been on the right track. White's work and that of Jacqueline Jones helped anchor the monographic foundation for this emerging field. My study of black women in the nursing profession further demonstrated the potential for research and study. By the end of the 1980s, there was no turning back. Black women's history was ready to explode.

In the early 1990s, I began thinking about theoretical frameworks. I had been reading the burgeoning production of black women novelists, catching up on all the works they had published while I had been engaged in the Black Women in the Middle West Project. I sought a way to connect the historical scholarship with the literary outpouring. This was the impetus for my writing the essay that has resonated across the years and influenced both black and white women historians. In a piece initially presented at the Southern Association of Women Historians convention at Converse College in Spartanburg, South Carolina, I historicized rape as a fundamental factor in black women's lives and analyzed their reaction to a legacy of sexual abuse, secrecy, and silence as a "culture of dissemblance." The essay has been reprinted several times and has generated a great deal of scholarship in the past two decades ("Rape and the Inner Lives of Southern Black Women: Thoughts on the Culture of Dissemblance," *Signs* 14, no. 4 [Summer 1989]: 912–20).

Influenced by black women I met while working on various projects and lecturing to groups across the country, I became a black women's historian. The decisive moment came when I decided to shelve my project on the history of black men in the legal and medical professions and write instead a history of black women in the nursing profession. A timely fellowship at the National Humanities Center facilitated the writing of what became *Black Women in White: Racial Conflict and Cooperation in the Nursing Profession, 1890–1950* (Bloomington: Indiana University Press, 1989). The book joined a growing list in the Blacks in the Diaspora Series that John McCluskey, Barry Gaspar, and I co-edited for Indiana University Press. Over the course of seventeen years, the series produced over forty titles, many of them tenure books by black women scholars writing on topics in black women's studies. I have always thought of my work on this series as one aspect of the larger objective to institutionalize black women's history. Many women historians and social science and literary scholars, such as Wanda Hendricks, Rosalyn Terborg-Penn, Irma Watkins-Owens, and Lillian Williams, published books in the Blacks in the Diaspora Series.

By the time I joined the Department of History at Michigan State University in the fall of 1987 as the John A. Hannah Professor of History, my work in black women's history was attracting considerable attention both inside and outside the academy. The *New York Times* even published a story about the Black Women in the Middle West Project, as did the newsletters of several professional organizations. It would be inaccurate to suggest that there was widespread celebration. Some of my male historian colleagues still questioned the value of black women's history, deeming it a fad, a waste of time. Others may have deflected feelings of threat or fears of displacement with criticism of this new field. That male colleagues believed black women's history was in competition with black men's history deserved more analysis. Clearly any opposition reflected, to a degree, the underlying assumption that the only valid perspective was one that accepted men's rightful privilege to occupy the intellectual center of black life and thought. A white male colleague did suggest to me, as a friend, that I was committing professional suicide to switch from studying the white primary or male professionals to writing the history of the most marginalized people in America. He later apologized and admitted he had been wrong in making these comments.

I remained affiliated with Michigan State University for twenty years. During these two decades, I concentrated on the teaching and training of a generation of young historians, many of whom have published monographs based on their dissertations and all of whom have found positions as assistant professors in the ivory tower. Among the black women historians for whom I have served as major professor are Jacqueline McLeod, Carmen Harris, LaTrice Adkins, Chantalle Verna, Kennetta Hammond Perry, and Marshanda Smith (A.B.D.). The black men include Felix Armfield, Pero Dagbovie, Randal Jelks, Matthew Whitaker, John Grant, and one Japanese student, Yasuhiro Okada. I have served on scores of other committees of students of diverse ethnic backgrounds in history, literature, and the social sciences. Regardless of field of study, I impress upon the students the imperative to do exhaustive and meticulous research; engage the analytical constructions of race, gender, class, and region whenever possible; and, most important, prepare perfect footnotes. As their revised dissertations begin to appear as monographs, I feel vindicated.

Throughout the 1990s, while training graduate students, I had the good fortune of working with a white male publisher, Ralph Carlson, on two projects that helped to cement the intellectual foundation of African American women's history. The first project was the editing of a sixteen-volume set of articles and dissertations, and the other was the co-editing of *Black Women in America: An Historical Encyclopedia*. The sixteen volumes included four dissertations in black women's history and studies by Beverly Guy-Sheftall, Dorothy Salem, Adrienne Lash Jones, and Beverly Johnson. Later in the decade, I co-edited with Duke University historian David Barry Gaspar two anthologies of original essays on enslaved and free black women in the Americas: *More Than Chattel: Black Women and Slavery in the Americas* (Bloomington: Indiana University Press, 1996) and *Beyond Bondage: Free Women of Color in the Americas* (Urbana: University of Illinois Press, 2004). Finally, I co-edited with black women historians Wilma King and Linda Reed *"We Specialize in the Wholly Impossible": A Reader in Black Women's History* (New York: Carlson Publishing, 1995). I emphasize the edited works because I value collaboration and also because so much of what later appeared as monographs in African American women's history was first published in essay form. The anthologies make important developments in the evolution of this field accessible not only to an academic audience but also to a larger general population. Moreover, they are very effective for use in graduate seminars because they help teach students to engage in theoretical discourse and help identify topics that need elaboration.

I could not have imagined a more exciting and rewarding academic odyssey. It has been exhilarating to labor in the creation and development of a field of study that has reclaimed the histories of so many ignored, negatively stereotyped, and marginalized black women. The field of African American history has been invigorated by the questions asked and debated about the intersections of race, class, and gender in the inventions and reinventions of the complex multilayered identities of black women and men across time and place. Today we ask new questions about manhood, masculinity, and femininity and how they are constructed in relation to one another. The vitality of the field and the proliferation of fresh new studies show no signs of subsiding. Black women have moved from the margins to the center of intellectual discourse in the academy and do not intend to relinquish this ground or moment without taking full advantage of the opportunities now available to create new knowledge. Black women's legacy is one that accords equal weight to service and sacrifice. I have embraced the lessons drawn from the lives of our amazingly resilient foremothers to challenge assumptions about who counts in American society and history and to rewrite the past. There is much more work to be done if we are to truly transform the ivory tower and make it a welcoming place for black women scholars and historians.

# Merline Pitre

## A JOURNEY THROUGH HISTORY

My path to becoming a historian was not inevitable or preordained. Perhaps nothing more effectively put me on a path toward this endeavor than the insidious combination of poverty and racism. Growing up in the segregated South profoundly shaped my worldview and my work as a historian in two basic ways. It gave me a reverential view of education, and it instilled in me a determination to struggle incessantly against racism, sexism, and social and cultural ostracism. Different people have used various strategies to cope with or fight against such evils. Some accommodated, others became openly defiant, and still others simply endured. I chose to fight via education and became a student of history. This action was based on the premise that historical ignorance begets racial ignorance.

A review of my upbringing provides intriguing glimpses into the influences that prompted my actions and shaped my views later in life. I came of age in south-central Louisiana, a region noted for its segregationist laws and customs and its French Acadiana culture. While Louisiana was not unique in its legally sanctioned oppression of blacks, its reputation for such oppression was equal to that of other former Confederate states. Segregation was the order of the day, and many of Louisiana's white residents viewed violence and intimidation as tools essential for maintaining the subordinate position of blacks. African American citizens were also effectively banned from voting in some parts of the state until 1965. Perhaps most oppressive of all was sharecropping, which often kept blacks under the yoke of white landowners for life.

As the daughter of a sharecropper, I grew up in the small rural community of Plaisance, which is located in St. Landry Parish, six miles north of the parish seat of Opelousas. Aside from Native Americans, the first settlers of St. Landry were white slave-owning farmers who had come from France. Although the French language, culture, and religion appeared to have been dominant in southern Louisiana from 1720 to 1860, the influx of other people into the state produced a new culture. This means that even today one can find Catholics as well as Protestants, French-speakers as well as non-French-speakers, descendants of free people of color as well as descendants of slaves in St. Landry Parish.[1]

When my parents, Florence White and Robert Pitre, entered into holy matrimony, and when I entered the world in the early 1940s, the political and social condition of black citizens in St. Landry Parish had not changed markedly from what it had been at the turn of the century. For instance, African Americans could not vote; they had to enter the back doors of most public places, especially country stores; and violence was frequently inflicted on them. My parents spoke of two incidents that were tantamount to lynching. The first occurred in 1939 when a black man from Plaisance, Louis Rideaux, was riddled with bullets for allegedly sicking his dog on a white man's cow. Another episode occurred in 1948 when Edward T. Honeycutt, a black man, was arrested and placed in the Opelousas jail for allegedly raping a white woman. Before Honeycutt could be tried, a white mob dragged him out of the jail and took him to the Atchafalaya River with the intention of hanging and then drowning him. Before they could execute their plan, Honeycutt escaped, but he was captured the next day. He was subsequently placed on trial and found guilty. His lawyer appealed the case but to no avail; Honeycutt was retried, found guilty, and finally electrocuted in 1951. At issue had been the fairness of the trial. My parents vividly remembered the Honeycutt episode. Even three decades later, blacks of Opelousas could recount with accuracy this tale of terror, for this event shaped their thinking and informed their actions for generations to come.[2]

Although St. Landry Parish had a large number of black landowners in the early 1940s, my parents did not belong to that group. For the Pitres, as well as other sharecroppers, hard work, poverty, and exploitation were stark realities. As sharecroppers, all of us worked the land, which in turn enabled us to live in the farmhouse that was on it. For seeds, fertilizer, and farm equipment, we had to negotiate with the owner of the country store or some other white businessman who charged exorbitant interest rates. Cotton and sweet potatoes were the main cash crops in the parish. Although we produced on average ten to twelve bales of cotton per year, we still had problems making ends meet. Because there were no factories or industries in the parish, any drop in cotton prices sent financial shivers through the black community. And when cotton season ended, we dug sweet potatoes, graded them, and sold them for a dollar a crate, only to discover that on the open market they were being sold for three times that amount.

Despite these unpleasant realities, as my siblings and I grew into adulthood, we were given strong institutional support from our family, church, and school. We had a close-knit immediate and extended family, a family where everyone looked out for each other and met each Sunday at my grandmother's house to discuss politics. My father, a hardworking farmer, had only a fourth-grade education and was quite reserved in his demeanor. Yet he embodied a spirit of responsibility and was supportive of his family in every way. My mother was then and is yet soft-spoken, but at the same time, she could be aggressive and assertive. Caring, nurturing, and openhearted, my mother always stressed, through examples and precepts, the importance of church, school, and hard work. She and my father took us to church and Sunday school each week. Later, after we had graduated from high school, she went to adult school and earned a General Educational Development (GED) certificate. Her perseverance in acquiring two years of college afterward speaks volumes to the importance that she placed on hard work, education, and the benefits she believed could accrue from the two.

No matter how hard my parents encouraged us to seek education or how insulated my siblings and I felt in the separate black world of Plaisance, the indelible marks of segregation remained. In Plaisance, as in many rural areas in the South, blacks could not very easily obtain an education. When I started school, I attended a white frame Rosenwald School that had been built by my grandfather and other black men in the community. I had to walk for miles to school, while white schoolchildren rode school buses. To be sure, separate was anything but equal in Opelousas and the surrounding areas. Whites went to vastly better schools. At Plaisance Elementary, there was no gymnasium and no running water. We had to use an outhouse that had been constructed behind the school. Desks, books, and other supplies were passed down from the white schools. Moreover, the school board did not provide enough cooks and workers to manage the kitchen at our school, so each class, starting with the seventh grade, had to wash dishes and serve on the lunch line for a week at a time throughout the school year.

Despite these hardships, we had caring teachers who strove to nurture and develop the whole student. One of the teachers who made a lasting impression on me was Josie Ruth Hammond. Mrs. Hammond was a great teacher and a strict disciplinarian, one who would stand up to any man. It was in her class that I became aware of the great contributions that African Americans had made to American society. She brought the *Pittsburgh Courier* to class each week and gave it to me to read. This was an enlightening experience. Reading the *Pittsburgh Courier* not only made me more conscious of race relations in the United States but also inspired me to read more on all subjects. My hard work paid off, and I graduated from the eighth grade as valedictorian of my class.

Upon completion of the eighth grade, I began to dream of going to college. At the time, I knew that my parents' economic condition did not allow for such an expense, but I continued to dream because I knew that my only ticket out of the field was education. Moreover, role models in the community had made it to college despite hard times. My aunts, uncles, and cousins had come out of similar social and economic settings and had become teachers and leaders in the community. Also, O'Neil Ray Collins, the first African American from St. Landry to receive a Ph.D., was a graduate of Plaisance High. Given these realities, I chose to continue to work hard in order to achieve my goal.[3]

The political and social conditions for blacks in the state had begun to change by the time I entered high school in the late 1950s. The civil rights movement was sweeping the state and nation. Blacks in St. Landry were not only voting but voting with the blessings of some whites, including Sheriff J. D. "Cat" Doucet. Local whites were beginning to entertain the issue of integration as a result of *Brown v. Board of Education*. In an attempt to forestall integration, the St. Landry Parish school board (as was the case in many other parishes in the state) decided to build a number of new schools for "Negroes." But these new physical structures did not necessarily offer a stronger curriculum. What counted most were the caring and innovative teachers who encouraged us to work and be competitive with the current curriculum. Thus, we competed in academic decathlons, in 4-H Club, and in forensic tournaments. In the academic areas, students excelled in English, history, and science at the local, district, and state levels. I participated in the American History Competition during my junior year and placed second in the state. My interest in and love for history were piqued by that experience. As I prepared for my senior year, I was now confident that I could compete with the best, especially in history.

My senior year was one of the defining moments in my life. By that time, I had excelled academically. I had been selected as one of two black females to represent St. Landry Parish at the Bayou Girls' State Leadership Conference in Baton Rouge and was almost certain that I would graduate at the top of my class. Yet I was very unsure about being able to attend college. Not having a high school counselor, I was especially uncertain about how to overcome the economic obstacles. As I got closer to graduation, I posed the question to my mother: "Do you think I can go to college?" Tears rolled down her cheeks as she said, "We'll see." A few weeks later, I learned of the National Defense Education Loan. I filled out an application for a loan and one for admission to Southern University. Within a few weeks, both of my applications were approved.

When I left for Southern University, I moved from the secure and somewhat sheltered environment of home and embarked on a journey to adulthood against the backdrop of a rapidly changing and increasingly dangerous world. In the midst of the civil rights movement, the meaning and ideals of American democracy seemed elusive as they applied to African Americans. The students at most historically black colleges had left their respective campuses to protest Jim Crow laws and confront the power brokers downtown. One year prior to my arrival, twelve students had been expelled from Southern University for demonstrating at the state capitol. The students' actions made my parents, especially my mother, nervous. She knew that their cause was just, but she also knew that if I got involved in the student movement and was put out of school, I might not get another loan and she could not afford to pay my tuition. She, therefore, cautioned me to be careful and not to get involved in anything that could get me expelled. Before I left home, Selina Pitre, the matriarch of the Pitre/White clan and my mother's older sister, had called me: "Look, you are going to college. You are going to uphold the family's name. You are going to help your family when you return." My family internalized and constantly inculcated the notion that "from those to whom much is given, much is expected" oand that if you go to college, your motto should be "lifting as you climb."

I matured socially and intellectually while living on Southern's campus for four years. At the end of the first year, I had to declare a major and a minor, which became French and social studies, respectively. Recognizing that my best subject was history but still wanting a challenge, I selected French as my major and specialized in the gender-specific career of teaching. Although French was spoken in the St. Landry/Opelousas/Plaisance area, the parents of my generation never spoke French to their children because when the latter went to school, they were stigmatized, ostracized, and looked down upon because they did not speak "proper" English. What I was soon to discover was that the patois spoken at home was, in many instances, a mispronunciation of French. Although I had not had a formal French course in high school, I excelled in French, in part because of nurturing teachers such as Helen Little, a patient, kind, and caring person who made us "country folks" feel at home.

Regarding my minor, social studies, I was most impressed with Henry E. Cobb, a history professor who taught a course on the Civil War and Reconstruction. Cobb was also concerned about his students, and he could rattle off history facts as if he were simply telling a story. Cobb had a profound impact on my thinking and on my becoming a historian years later. A meticulous scholar and a prolific writer, he demanded perfection from his students and despised mediocrity. His high standard of scholarship really impressed me. But there was another side of Cobb that was equally striking. Cobb was a sensitive man committed to racial equality and community service. He quite often spoke out against all types of racial discrimination and against the second-class status imposed on African Americans. He was also involved in a number of projects in the community.

Southern University opened new intellectual horizons for me. Above all, it offered me the opportunity to discuss and explore the world of ideas. My curiosity about the larger world deepened as I was exposed to new ideas. I discovered some of these ideas while attending lectures, seminars, and vesper services on Sunday and during midweek. It was at a vesper service that I heard Benjamin Mays, president of Morehouse College, recite one of his famous maxims: "Poverty is not a sin, but low aim is." After listening to this speech, I was firmly convinced that if my aim was high enough, the sky would be the limit. My aim was still to beat poverty and racism through education.

While Southern's faculty members worked hard to provide a nurturing and supportive atmosphere that encouraged students to think critically, like their counterparts at most historically black colleges and universities, they held fairly conventional notions about gender. For instance, the faculty and administrators were committed to training females for their middle-class roles in society, and the female students were expected to exhibit traditional female behavior—behavior reflecting high morals, spirituality, and self-sacrifice. Accordingly, women were not allowed to wear pants or to leave the dormitory without permission. But these conventional notions would be challenged by female students who became activists in the civil rights movement. For black females of the 1960s (including myself), as well as those of the past, race was always more important than gender.

While Southern did a great deal to transform my life, I experienced more overt sexism at my graduation than I had encountered during my entire four-year tenure at the university. Prior to the commencement exercises, university officials decided to allow the student with the highest average to lead the line of march in his or her respective school or college. Since I was graduating magna cum laude and had the highest average in the College of Education, I knew that I would be accorded that signal honor. This practice, however, was applicable to every school or college except the College of Education. A former army major had convinced the male dean that the class marshal for the College of Education need not be the student with the highest average. While this decision was disappointing to me, I remembered what my parents had taught me—"Whatever you learn, no one can take it away from you." So despite this setback, graduation was a shining moment in my life. My proud parents sat in the audience, beaming at what I and they had accomplished.

By the time I graduated from Southern, I had carved out my own path, contrary to my mother's wishes, that took me first to Atlanta University and then to St. Augustine's College. After receiving the baccalaureate degree, I matriculated at Atlanta University, where I had received a fellowship to pursue a master's degree in French. There, I was joined by two other Southernites, Brenda Stewart and Thadious Davis. Each of us pursued a different course of study, and at the end of one year, each was awarded the M.A. degree. Before I graduated from Atlanta University, I had received an offer to teach French at St. Augustine's College in Raleigh, North Carolina. St. Augustine's was a small, predominantly black liberal arts college supported by the Episcopal Church, and it had an enrollment of approximately 2,000 students. The social and intellectual atmosphere of St. Augustine's was enhanced by the occasional visits and lectures of such activists as Stokely Carmichael and Robert F. Williams, as well as by its location in Raleigh, the birthplace of the Student Nonviolent Coordinating Committee (SNCC). My three-and-a-half-year stint at St. Augustine's provided me a wider window from which to view the world. I was now a professional, teaching domestic and international students, and an active observer and participant in the civil rights movement.[4]

During my first year at St. Augustine's, Martin Luther King Jr. was assassinated, and his death became a defining moment for me, as it was for many people throughout the country. This act of violence against King sparked a march by St. Augustine's students and faculty (myself included) from the campus to the capitol. It also led to similar demonstrations and riots in other states and gave rise to students' demands that black studies programs be established at various colleges and universities. As I observed this movement's effect around the country, I began to look at my own education. I realized that although I had received a master's degree, I knew very little about African American history. As I continued to ponder this issue, during the summer of 1968, I was informed by the vice president of academic affairs at St. Augustine's that Columbia University was recruiting faculty members from HBCUs (historically black colleges and universities) to attend an Intensive Study Summer Program. Faculty members in this program attended lectures and read extensively in academic disciplines of their choosing. Naturally, I decided to attend and chose African American history.

Needless to say, these readings opened up new vistas and whet my thirst for more African American history. The next summer, I enrolled in an African American Institute at the University of California, Berkeley, taught by Nathan Huggins. The following summer, 1970, I attended an Institute on African History at Hamline University. These three summers made me consider pursuing a master's degree in history. So I began applying to graduate schools in history for the fall of 1970. I was accepted at the University of California, Berkeley, beginning in the spring of 1971, but when I arrived, I discovered that I would have to wait a couple of weeks before my financial packet would be ready. Upon hearing this news, I had an important decision to make. I could stay and wait with little or no money, or I could return home and apply to another university. I chose the latter. I returned to Opelousas and engaged in substitute-teaching ventures.

A pivotal experience occurred in the summer of 1971 that made me think even more seriously about becoming a historian. I enrolled in Clarence Bacote's history class at Atlanta University and was inspired not only by this erudite professor but also by the connection between his lectures and those of the Institute of the Black World (IBW). The Institute of the Black World (1968–71), organized by Vincent Harding and his colleagues, advocated the integration of scholarship and activism in the community. In the summer of 1971, Harding, via the IBW, brought to Atlanta University such notables as C. L. R. James, St. Clair Drake, John Hendrik Clark, Harold Dotson, and William Strickland. Listening to lectures by these individuals was intellectually invigorating. They provided exceptional cultural and political stimulation. Of all the lectures, it was Harding's "Responsibilities of the Black Scholar" that had the greatest impact on me. In this speech, Harding discussed the vocation of the black scholar vis-à-vis the struggle of the black community. He argued that the primary responsibility of those who are called scholars in the black community is to "direct as much of their writing, their speaking and their teaching to the life and heart and growth of the community of pain and hope. [But in the process] they should never forget the source—the people."[5]

I left Atlanta that summer with a newfound sense of responsibility and a determination to pursue further studies in history. Meanwhile, I returned to Opelousas and secured a teaching position in French at my alma mater, Plaisance High School. Once I became settled in Plaisance, I repeated the process of applying to graduate schools at various universities. By the spring semester of 1972, I had been accepted at several universities, but I chose Temple University in Philadelphia, in part because of the financial packet. This aid was supplemented by an interest-free loan from the Hattie M. Strong Foundation.

When I arrived on Temple's campus, I was almost as intimidated as I had been as a freshman at Southern University. But I was quickly put at ease by the cordial reception I received from my prospective adviser, Lawrence D. Reddick. Reddick, the first biographer of Martin Luther King Jr., had been a participant in the Montgomery bus boycott and subsequently had been fired from Alabama State University for his active role in the civil rights movement. When I first met Reddick, I told him that I was interested in pursuing a master's degree in history and then continuing for the Ph.D. I indicated to him that my interest was in African American political history. He gave me a list of readings and helped me fill out a schedule but told me that I should not stop with the master's degree. So after earning my master's degree, I applied for admission to the Ph.D. program and was accepted. Reddick continued as my adviser, inasmuch as my primary field of interest was social and political history. My interest in this aspect of history was driven by newly published works on the Civil War and Reconstruction, by changes that were occurring in the political landscape of the South, especially in St. Landry Parish, as well as by the civil rights movement. When Reddick later asked me to present him a topic for my dissertation proposal, I chose the political career of Frederick Douglass—"Frederick Douglass: A Party Loyalist, 1870–1895."

Reddick's lectures deepened my understanding of African American history. He exposed his students to numerous outstanding scholars of the history and culture of African Americans and encouraged us to get involved in professional organizations. It was in his class that I was first introduced to the Association for the Study of African American Life and History (ASALH). I attended my first ASALH meeting in Atlanta in 1974. I was impressed with and pleasantly surprised by the work of African American scholars whom I met at this conference. Moreover, as I networked with these scholars, I soon realized that although a lot of work had been done, still more was needed. This realization was reinforced when I took a class from Vincent Harding in which he reiterated his view that black scholars should focus on the community.

It should be noted that there were other professors at Temple who helped to mold and shape me into the historian that I would become. These included Allen F. Davis, Donald L. Wiedner, and Clement T. Keto. Unfortunately, I did not have a female Ph.D. history professor in graduate school, nor did I have one at the undergraduate level in history or French. Despite this lack of gender diversity, I persevered and the hard work paid off. In May 1976, I received the Ph.D. in history.

A few months before I graduated from Temple University, I received an offer to teach history at Texas Southern University (TSU), a historically black university. I would have preferred to stay on the East Coast, but since TSU was located in Houston, at that time the fifth largest city in the United States, and it was near home, I accepted the offer. The youngest of the HBCUs, TSU was only thirty years old, and, as was typical of most other HBCUs, the workload was twelve hours per semester. Most of the survey classes in history that I taught averaged over sixty students. This did not leave much time for research. But if I were to become a scholar, I would have to make time for research. With the cooperation of my chair, I carved out a research schedule and immediately began to review, revise, and craft articles from my dissertation. Additionally, I began presenting papers at various professional meetings. One of my most memorable presentations was made possible by an invitation from John Blassingame to participate in the Frederick Douglass International Scholars' Colloquium held at Howard University in 1979. There, I presented a paper entitled "Frederick Douglass and American Diplomacy in the Caribbean." The invitation to this conference gave me a great deal of confidence because it meant that I was recognized by my peers.[6]

I soon realized that if I was going to continue to pursue research and teach twelve hours per semester, I would have to tailor my research to a subject area with accessible sources. Thus began my interest in Afro-Texan history. Following my course of study on the Reconstruction and Post-Reconstruction period, I first perused the literature on blacks in the Reconstruction era in Texas and discovered that very little had been written on this subject. Consequently, I published "A Note on the Historiography of Blacks in the Reconstruction of Texas," in which I argued that "the history of blacks during Reconstruction in the Lone Star State was left to the not-so-tender mercy of Bourbons or Bourbons sympathizers." This literature search prompted me to do a study on black Texan legislators during Reconstruction. Despite my flexible schedule, my heavy teaching load did not permit me the time to conduct research for a new study. I needed time off, so I applied for and received an independent fellowship from the National Endowment for the Humanities (NEH). Fortunately, the year that I received the fellowship, the stipend was commensurate with the salary that I was getting from the university.[7]

Armed with an NEH fellowship, I spent the school year of 1983–84 doing research on black legislators, most of which was done in Austin. Afterward, I returned to my teaching job and continued to write. My book *Through Many Dangers, Toils, and Snares: The Black Leadership of Texas, 1868–1898* was finally completed in 1985. The purpose of this study was twofold: to examine the role of the black political leadership cadre in Texas from 1868 to 1898 and to fill a void in the history of Afro-Texans. This work explores the complexities and contradictions that led to the emergence of black legislators in Texas; examines the nature and degree of these lawmakers' influence on their constituents, as well as on their white colleagues; and analyzes whether or not blacks participated in the overthrow of Reconstruction and whether the black leadership formulated or manifested a clear, unifying ideology.

Until the publication of my work, the only piece written on these men was the one by black folklorist J. Mason Brewer in 1935. Yet my work did not receive much acclaim from white male Texas historians until 1987, when Barry Crouch acknowledged it in his article, " 'Unmanacling' Texas Reconstruction: A Twenty Year Perspective." In fact, I met one white male historian at a professional meeting who complimented me on the book and indicated that if it had been written by a white male and published by a university press, it would have received many more accolades.[8]

The publication of *Through Many Dangers, Toils, and Snares* meant that I had turned a corner, that I was on my way to becoming a scholar. Moreover, I had increased my network and visibility in the field. To be sure, the network that I established through the publication of my book proved to be very helpful. I could always turn to a number of colleagues and friends for assistance, especially Darlene Clark Hine, Howard Jones, Jacqueline Rouse, Alton Hornsby, and Wilma King. For example, not only did Hine critique my manuscripts and write letters of recommendation for me, but when she organized a conference entitled "The State of Afro-American History: Past, Present, and Future" in 1985, she sent me a special invitation. Much to my surprise, when I returned from the funeral of my father, I received a letter from Hine offering me and two of my students an all-expenses-paid trip to the conference. Everybody who was somebody in the field of African American history was there. My confidence had now risen to another level. I had arrived in the field. More important, Hine understood the need to mentor, prepare, and produce prospective historians for future generations. Yvonne Frear, one of my students who attended, is currently a Ph.D. candidate at Texas A&M University and has published a number of articles in professional journals. Additionally, Howard Jones, an undergraduate classmate of mine and a master at networking, prodded me to work with him to establish the Southern Conference on African American Studies. Today, the organization is thriving and has a professional journal of its own, and I am currently serving as its president.[9]

After publication of my first work, I began to do a little soul-searching. I was a member of the Association of Black Women Historians, the aim of which is to perpetuate the history of black women, but I had not done any research on women—I had completed a study of forty-two men of color. Now I felt it was time to examine the role of African American women in Texas. When I studied the political history of women, I frequently came across the name of Lulu B. White. Not only was she an intriguing figure, but she was the "workhorse" of the NAACP in Texas during the 1940s and 1950s. Further research led to my second book, *In Struggle against Jim Crow: Lulu B. White and the NAACP, 1900–1957*. Writing *In Struggle against Jim Crow* was more than an intellectual enterprise for me. It put me in touch with feelings I had experienced as a child growing up in segregated southern Louisiana, where I learned that to be black was "to struggle, to struggle—to struggle to salvage the self," to struggle against racial and gender stereotypes in order to struggle against prejudice, injustice, and hatred. Lulu B. White's life story reflects this collective memory of Jim Crow.[10]

I firmly believe that one cannot be a scholar without being a teacher or a teacher without being a scholar. Also, I take seriously my responsibility as an African American scholar to transfer to students what I have learned through research and at conferences. When I arrived at TSU, not all students were required to take African American history. In fact, African American history was taught only as an upper-level course. So if a student did not take this course as part of a major requirement, it was possible to graduate without knowing anything about African American history. To remedy this situation, I incorporated African American history into my survey classes and supplemented students' knowledge by sponsoring black history programs and bringing noted lecturers to campus. Because the university had earmarked no money for black history programs, I began to write proposals to the Texas Committee for the Humanities (now Texas Humanities) (TCH). I was funded almost yearly until 1990, when I was selected to serve on the board of the TCH.[11]

At about the same time that I became a member of the TCH board, William H. Harris, a prominent historian, became president of TSU, and he asked me to serve as dean of the College of Arts and Sciences. As rewarding as I found this administrative role, my first love was still scholarship. Although it was a challenge to balance administrative and scholarly duties, I was determined never to allow my scholarship to suffer even as my public commitments and duties multiplied. During my tenure in the dean's office, I decided to write a proposal to the NEH for funding a workshop for college teachers entitled "Salvaging the Self: Black Southerners' Response to Jim Crow." I was able to convince the agency that this workshop should be restricted to TSU faculty because many of them had been born in the South during the era of Jim Crow and had lived through this dreadful era, but their heavy workloads had not allowed them time to read about, analyze, or reflect on it. The argument apparently was compelling, for the NEH agreed to pay the faculty members a stipend to take part in an intensive interdisciplinary workshop on Jim Crow. The participants claimed that the workshop was one of the most enlightening experiences of their careers. As was expected, they incorporated the literature on Jim Crow in their respective disciplines and were invigorated by the lecturers of the seminar. These individuals included Henry L. Suggs, John Bracey, Mack Jones, Thadious Davis, Jeff Donaldson, Howard Harris, John Boles, Joseph Pratt, Luci Fultz, Kenneth Hamilton, Linda Reed, and Cynthia Flemings.[12]

William Harris left the TSU presidency in 1994, and I stepped down from the dean's office the same year. This exit was a blessing in disguise, for between 1994 and 2000, I finished my work on Lulu B. White, revised *Through Many Dangers, Toils, and Snares* for use as a reference work for a traveling exhibit, and continued other scholarly pursuits. During that time, I also worked with Richard Blackett and his colleagues at the University of Houston on a black history workshop for graduate students. This workshop was unique in the academy. Students from the United States and abroad who were in their final stage of writing dissertations on topics on the black experience were invited to read a chapter from their work. Workshop scholars would critique the chapters and give the students input. This was a learning experience for everyone and gave us a sense of helping to build a cadre of black scholars. Unfortunately, after Richard Blackett left the University of Houston, the workshop he had worked so hard to establish fizzled out.

In 2000, I once again agreed to serve as dean, but again I continued to be active in the profession. I was nominated by Stephanie Shaw to run for a position on the nominating board of the Organization of American Historians representing HBCUs and was elected. I also continued to do research and write about black women. For example, I wrote an essay in Darlene Clark Hine's 2003 revision of her book *Black Victory: The Rise and Fall of the White Primary in Texas*, because Hine realized that when the book was first published in 1979, she had omitted the role that black females had played in helping to destroy the Texas white Democratic primary. My essay detailed the efforts of Lulu B. White and other black women to secure the ballot. In that same year, I was invited by Quintard Taylor and Shirley Anne Wilson Moore to contribute an essay to their edited book, *African American Women Confront the West, 1600–2000*. Taylor shares my view that Texas is both western and southern; therefore, an essay on Texas women was in order. Currently, with Bruce Glasrud, I am editing *African American Women in Texas*.[13]

To be sure, there is much work to be done, and I intend to continue to use my knowledge, ingenuity, and research in the teaching and creation of new knowledge. From my entry into the academy, my goal has been to use my knowledge and training to improve my community and ultimately society. My journey into and through history has provided me with an opportunity to speak to a wider American audience. I, therefore, subscribe to John Hope Franklin's credo: "Every generation has the opportunity to write its own history and indeed must do so in a way that can provide its contemporaries with material vital to understanding the present and planning strategies for coping with the future."

NOTES

1. "Some History of St. Landry Parish from the 1690s to 1962," *Opelousas Daily World*, July 29, 1982, 52, 112–82.

2. Interview by author with Florence Pitre, July 20, 2006; "Transcript of Trial of Edward Honeycutt, 1949," Criminal Record Book 30, Case Numbers 14193 and 141412, Parish Records, St. Landry Parish, Opelousas, Louisiana.

3. At the time, Louisiana had the highest illiteracy rate in the nation, second only to Mississippi. A graduate of the University of Iowa, O'Neil Ray Collins went on to become chair of the botany department at the University of California, Berkeley.

4. My mother cried when I left for Atlanta University but was soon reminded by my grandmother that I was "going away to get what she could not get and what my grandmother could not give her." Brenda Stewart Birkett is former vice chancellor of academic affairs at Southern University and now dean of the Business College at McNeese State University in Lake Charles, Louisiana. Thadious Davis is professor of literature at the University of Pennsylvania.

5. Vincent Harding, "Responsibilities of the Black Scholar to the Community," in *The State of Afro-American History: Past, Present, and Future*, edited by Darlene Clark Hine (Baton Rouge: Louisiana State University Press, 1986), 281.

6. See program for "The Frederick Douglass International Scholars' Colloquium," Howard University, October 22, 1979, in possession of the author. See also Merline Pitre, "Frederick Douglass and American Diplomacy in the Caribbean," *Journal of Black Studies* 13 (June 1983): 457–76.

7. Merline Pitre, "A Note on the Historiography of Blacks in the Reconstruction of Texas," *Journal of Negro History* 66 (1981–82): 340–45; "Grants," *Chronicle of Higher Education*, February 2, 1981, 2.

8. Merline Pitre, *Through Many Dangers, Toils, and Snares: The Black Leadership of Texas, 1868–1898* (Austin, Tex.: Eakin Press, 1985); Barry A. Crouch, " 'Unmanacling' Texas Reconstruction: A Twenty Year Perspective," *Southwestern Historical Quarterly* 93, no. 3 (January 1990): 275–302.

9. See also program for "A Comparative History of 'Black Peoples in Diaspora': A Symposium," Michigan State University, April 13–15, 1995, in possession of the author.

10. Merline Pitre, *In Struggle against Jim Crow: Lulu B. White and the NAACP, 1900–1957* (College Station: Texas A&M University Press, 1999).

11. See Executive Meeting Minutes, 1993–95, Texas Committee for the Humanities, Austin, Texas.

12. "Grants," *Chronicle of Higher Education*, February 2, 1981, 2. See also program for "Salvaging the Self: Black Southerners' Response to Jim Crow," Texas Southern University, 1994, in possession of the author.

13. See Merline Pitre, *In Retrospect: Darlene Clark Hine's "Black Victory"* (Columbia: University of Missouri Press, 2003), 25–40; and Quintard Taylor and Shirley Anne Wilson Moore, eds., *African American Women Confront the West, 1600–2000* (Norman: University of Oklahoma Press, 2003), 293–308.

# Rosalyn Terborg-Penn

## BEING AND THINKING OUTSIDE OF THE BOX

### A BLACK WOMAN'S EXPERIENCE IN ACADEMIA

*Memory tells me that blackness is in my essence as surely as blood is in my veins. It is an antenna I do not always know I am wearing, but which is surely there, identifying me as a woman who belongs to a group different in particularities from women who are Asian, Latina, Chicana, Native American, or Jewish. It is a way of seeing myself and seeing others like me through a lens that never closes.—Gloria Wade-Gayles, 1996*

Reading poet and scholar Gloria Wade-Gayles's personal essay, "When Race Is Memory and Blackness Is Choice," made me understand why we get along so well and why we both have functioned outside of the box. We are from a generation of black women intellectuals who have been trained, for the most part, outside of black institutions. However, unlike many of our sisters who remained in mainstream institutions, we chose to teach in historically black colleges and universities (HBCUs). In so doing, we opted to practice outside of the box. As a result, Gloria and I share the frustrations and rewards of committing our professional lives to educating primarily black students yet also functioning among academics in mainstream associations and institutions. Relying on my memory—as well as a few published pieces that address aspects of my life as either a student or a scholar—I bring you my story. It is based on my over forty years as a student, a faculty member, or a scholar in higher education. My memories reflect interactions with peers, as well as interactions with the stalwarts who guard the doors to the ivory tower.

I present my remembrances in three stages of my development as an academic. The first stage is the 1960s, when I was an undergraduate at Queens College of the City University of New York and later a master's degree student at George Washington University. The second stage is the 1970s, when I became a junior faculty member at Morgan State College and then a Ph.D. student at Howard University. The third stage is the 1980s and the 1990s, when I decided to remain at Morgan State University, became the coordinator of graduate programs in history, and developed as a published scholar.

In the past, I have likened my development as an academic to "a black history journey."[1] Even in the 1960s, in the eyes of traditionalists in the so-called ivory tower, taking this journey meant being outside of the box. At the time, traditional history departments where I enrolled had not quite acknowledged the legitimacy of black history as a field of study.

Majoring in history at Queens College was fine because in this male-dominated department nobody noticed women. This ultimately worked to my advantage because I did not stick out as a "colored" student activist as I had when I majored in biology as a freshman, then sociology as a sophomore, and experienced discrimination that I was not prepared to meet. Faculty in biology and sociology at Queens College expected black students not to succeed, and our grades often reflected these negative faculty expectations. This pattern did not appear to exist in the history department. We were taught primarily Western culture with a sprinkling of European colonial history. If you performed well, as I did, you were rewarded. However, in this environment, students did not learn about non-Europeanized societies. For the most part, I followed the traditional path since I had changed my major two times and needed to graduate.

Learning beyond the norm was not uncommon for me since knowing about black life and culture was part of my family upbringing, but I realize it was not customary for others. However, there was a disturbing dichotomy in the two communities where I was raised. I spent my first ten years in a middle-class black neighborhood in the Bedford-Stuyvesant community of Brooklyn, where some of our neighbors were history makers. Then we moved to an integrated working-class neighborhood in South Ozone Park, Queens, where the community was turning over as whites fled the blacks moving into the area. In Bedford-Stuyvesant, being "colored" was normal, but in South Ozone Park, being "colored" meant being an outsider. This reality was exacerbated when I attended Queens College. Luckily, I could return home every evening.

Fortunately, the sixties witnessed a radical student movement at Queens College, and as odd as it now seems, those of us who joined the campus chapter of the NAACP were considered radicals. One semester, the so-called radical student associations pooled their resources and invited Malcolm X and Herbert Aptheker to give lectures on campus. Their impact on my growing black consciousness was unforgettable. I discovered black history as a legitimate field of study, not just a narrow discourse that I heard from my father at home. As a developing intellectual, I began to probe and ask questions, but only one of my professors responded—Solomon Lutnick, who taught early-nineteenth-century U.S. history in a traditional way that did not include the role of blacks. Yet he did know a Negro historian, John Hope Franklin, who had chaired the history department at Brooklyn College in the 1950s. Lutnick assured me that there were others who researched and wrote about so-called Negro history, and he encouraged me to find them. As I was drawn into this field, I found that it was not a new one as I had presumed, just one hidden from my view.[2]

After commencement, I went on to graduate school as my parents expected me to do. I wanted to go to Howard University, but I also applied to other universities in Washington, D.C. I was accepted at George Washington University (GWU). Disappointed that I had not heard from Howard in time to apply for my guaranteed loan, I enrolled at GWU, not knowing that the admissions staff apparently assumed that I was a white student. They saw my last name of Dutch origin, my undergraduate college with its low minority enrollment, and my black-and-white photo, which made my skin appear to be lighter than it is. When my new adviser assumed I was in the wrong office and asked if I needed directions, I realized that I was in the South and the graduate school had made a mistake by accepting me. Having been undaunted by Queens College, I was hardly going to let GWU intimidate me. I worked hard my first year, majoring in U.S. history and diplomatic history, yet I could not find courses that would allow me to study black life. In spite of my hard work, I earned only Bs the first semester. This was a problem for a full-time M.A. student because I needed to earn two As in order to graduate from the program.

Timing was everything in the mid-1960s, when history departments were being pressured by civil rights activists to accept black students into graduate programs. I learned from a sympathetic white teaching assistant at GWU that the senior professors in the history department realized that it was a good thing to have a black student after all, and they changed their strategy of trying to make me fail. I earned two As in my second semester and went on to research and write my thesis while working as an activist with an organization called D.C. Students for Civil Rights.[3]

My thesis adviser was Wood Gray, whose specialty was nineteenth-century U.S. social history. Gray was the first professor to teach me that no historian is truly objective because we all bring our prejudices to the table. I also learned that he had a difficult time accepting my blackness. Although he and black historian Elsie Lewis, who chaired the history department at Howard University, had been fellow students at the University of Chicago, Gray still wanted me to be something other than ethnically black and refused to let me use the term "black" in my thesis. Nonetheless, he allowed me to take Lewis's black history course at Howard University. She became my first black professor. Gray agreed to the thesis topic of my choice, but he titled it "A Study of Negro Demands for

Equality, 1800–1877" and provided little mentoring. Fortunately, I had gotten a taste of it in the course I had taken with Lewis.

Earning my M.A. degree did not land me a job in the profession. I remained outside of the box. Wood Gray would not write recommendations for me to teach at any college in the Washington, D.C., area, so for a few years, I worked in private and public social service agencies, happy to be employed. Finally, I heard of an opening, applied, and began my college-teaching career in Baltimore at Morgan State College in the fall of 1969—the beginning of the second stage of my life in academia.

Roland C. McConnell, who chaired the Department of History, Political Science, and Geography, hired me. I was familiar with the college because most of my black friends in high school who left New York State to go to college went to either Howard University or Morgan State College. In 1969, Morgan was primarily a liberal arts college with about 3,000 students and a new graduate school offering master's degrees in disciplines such as history, math, and education. About one-third of the students came from northeastern states and Caribbean and African countries. The campus was diverse and had a recent history of civil rights activism.

The environment was welcoming, but teaching in Baltimore meant moving away from Washington, D.C., primarily because we could not afford to buy a house in a nice neighborhood in the de facto segregated District of Columbia. Consequently, my husband and I decided to move to Columbia, Maryland, a new planned city located between Washington, D.C., where he worked, and Baltimore. We were sold on the idea that as black people we should not have to pay a premium to live in a community free of housing discrimination, a phenomenon prevalent throughout the 1960s in most of the nation.

Working at Morgan State was a dream come true because I did not have to convince my colleagues that teaching and researching black life was worthwhile. In addition, I had mentors who truly wanted me to succeed, including Benjamin Quarles, one of the authors whose works I had read as an undergraduate when I searched for historians who wrote about black life. Although my mentors at Morgan were men, I soon learned that some of the most influential professors on campus were black women, an unusual occurrence in academia. I was awed by Iva Jones in the Department of English, Gladys Bradley Jones in the Department of Education, and Irene Diggs in the Department of Sociology and Anthropology. These were radical women who spoke their minds, influenced college policies, and ultimately became my role models. They were truly acting outside of the box.

However, my task as an instructor was to teach general-education courses to undergraduates. Fortunately, we were mandated to integrate the black experience into our U.S. history courses. The required supplement to the textbook was Quarles's *The Negro in the Making of America*, a short history that included black women, which was eye-opening to me. Some of the black women in the book, like Jenny Slew, a slave who sued Massachusetts for her freedom, I had not heard of before. We were also encouraged to integrate writing across the curriculum, so I assigned students topics on which they did research and wrote papers. Including the black experience was truly outside of my experience, but I relished the challenge. However, finding topics about black women for my students to research became a major challenge. By the 1970–71 academic year, I began to research data about black women on my own, not realizing how frustrating my efforts would be because secondary sources were so limited.

In the meantime, my senior colleagues—McConnell, Quarles, G. James Fleming, and Isaiah Woodward—encouraged me to go back to graduate school to earn my Ph.D. They wanted me to remain at Morgan, but I could not, they argued, if I was not tenured. At Morgan State in those years, tenure required passing your Ph.D. comprehensive exams. It took me until 1972, when I was on maternity leave, to find the time to enroll at Howard University in the history Ph.D. program. My major field was U.S. history before the Civil War, with a concentration in black history.

I knew I wanted to write a dissertation on some aspect of black women's lives, and I naively believed that I could just pick a topic, find a dissertation adviser, and do my research. Little did I know that I was the first person in Howard's history department to declare a topic concerning black women's history and that I would have an uphill struggle because I had to convince the faculty that black women's experience was viable. I did not realize until later that I was truly thinking outside of the box.

Although women's history had been rejuvenated in 1970 because the year marked the fiftieth anniversary of the ratification of the Nineteenth Amendment, proponents of African American history did not take much notice. On the other hand, there had been discussions in the press and among feminist scholars about black people's lack of support for woman suffrage fifty years before. I was familiar with the argument, but I found these discussions to be at odds with what I experienced as a child growing up in Brooklyn, a place where black women like Lena Horne's grandmother had been politically active two generations before. Also, Shirley Chisholm recently had been elected to Congress to represent the Bedford-Stuyvesant area of Brooklyn. Besides, my mother and both of my grandmothers voted consistently. I was challenged by what appeared to be untrue. As a result, whenever possible I researched and wrote about black women and their lack of civil and political rights. At Howard, I finally narrowed my research topic to women's rights issues, focusing on black views on the subject.

At first, some faculty at both Howard and Morgan State discouraged me from pursuing my topic. The professor for whom I worked as a graduate assistant at Howard called my topic "Mickey Mouse" and suggested that I study something more serious, such as Eleanor Roosevelt. When I gave a talk at Morgan State about a paper I was researching on black men and their views on women's rights, one of the male professors criticized me mercilessly for focusing on such an "unimportant" topic until Benjamin Quarles reminded his colleague about the article on Frederick Douglass and the woman's movement that Quarles had published in the *Journal of Negro History* over thirty years before.

Others encouraged me to submit my paper, "Black Men in the Struggle for the Rights of Women, 1833–1863," to the 1973 Rayford W. Logan Prize Committee of Howard University's history department. I submitted the paper and won the prize. The occasion was the fourth annual Rayford W. Logan Lecture, delivered by C. Vann Woodward. In Logan's closing remarks, he talked about the significance of Mary McLeod Bethune, Eleanor Roosevelt, and Mary Church Terrell.[4] I had few problems with my professors at Howard or my colleagues at Morgan State after winning the Logan Prize.

Aside from one year when I accepted an assistantship and became a full-time student on leave from Morgan, I was a part-time student at Howard University and paid for my own tuition while teaching four three-credit courses each semester at Morgan State. I learned from my fellow students at Howard and at mainstream universities that my status was unusual. Most of the black women graduate students I knew during the 1970s were full-time students with fellowships or assistantships. I remained outside of the box as a part-time student because I needed to keep my position at Morgan State.

Nonetheless, some of my most meaningful experiences occurred at Howard University, where Lorraine Williams, chair of the history department; Harold Lewis, director of graduate programs in the department; and Okon Uya, who taught historiography and oral history, mentored me. However, it was my cohort of graduate students, primarily at Howard University, who provided the majority of my intellectual and moral support. Some of the key people in this group were Elizabeth Clark-Lewis, John Fleming, Gerald Gill, Sharon Harley, Sylvia Jacobs, Debra Newman (Ham), Bernice Reagon, and, at Georgetown University, Janice Sumler-Lewis (Edmond).

During the early 1970s, I joined my fellow students in attending conferences such as those held by the Association for the Study of African American Life and History (ASALH), the Berkshire Conference of Women Historians (the Berks), and the American Historical Association (AHA). These conferences became springboards for my professional development and allowed me to network with well-known individuals in the discipline. In addition, I interacted with scholar-activists such as John Henrik Clarke, who introduced me to a black nationalist conceptual framework for analyzing my work.

Testing my analysis required presenting my work at conferences. The first conference I attended that addressed black women's history was held in 1973 at the University of Louisville. Several of us from the history department at Howard University submitted paper proposals and applied for travel grants. Lorraine Williams saw to it that those of us who wanted to attend received funding. It was at this conference that I presented the paper "Discrimination against Afro-American Women in the Woman's Movement, 1830–1920," which I later published in the anthology Sharon Harley and I edited in 1978. Little did I know that as a result of this book Harley and I would become pioneers in developing black women's history.

We conceived the idea for the anthology for practical reasons. Like me, none of my fellow students who were college faculty could find scholarly books and articles on African American women's history short of a few biographies and documentary collections. Our first step was recruiting colleagues to write essays with historical themes for the manuscript, "The Afro-American Woman: Struggles and Images." Editing essays was not as difficult as finding a publisher to agree to read the manuscript. We began in 1974 by sending letters to numerous university presses. The only one interested was the newly established Howard University Press. However, the press kept the manuscript for two years, then returned it and said it was not interested.

In the meantime, Howard faculty members had mixed reactions to our project. Lorraine Williams was supportive. She had been my dissertation adviser, but her promotion to vice president for academic affairs forced her to step down as my committee chair. Although Williams remained on the committee, Martha Putney became my new dissertation adviser and committee chair. She admonished me for taking time away from my dissertation to give papers at conferences and trying to have them published. She predicted that no publisher would ever accept our manuscript. On the other hand, Arnold Taylor, another member of my dissertation committee, joined Williams in encouraging Harley and me to publish the anthology.

Finally, one of the Howard history faculty members, Al-Tony Gilmore, recommended us to his publisher, Kennikat Press. I had never heard of the press, but what choice did we have? Fortunately, the publisher understood our vision and reviewed our manuscript. Harley and I both wrote two essays each. I defended my dissertation in the summer of 1977, while the press narrowed down the essays we had submitted to those written by Gerald Gill, Daphne Duval Harrison, Evelyn Brooks Higginbotham, Cynthia Neverdon-Morton, Andrea Benton Rushing, Harley, and me. *The Afro-American Woman: Struggles and Images* came out in 1978, shortly after Howard University conferred my Ph.D.[5]

The year 1978 was a transitional one for me. I was promoted to associate professor at Morgan State and was invited to become a member of the AHA's Committee on Women Historians (CWH), which mandated that one woman of color be a member. I replaced the member in that slot, Marie Perimbaum from the University of Maryland, who had nominated me to the committee. As the first member of the CWH from a historically black university, I came to the AHA as an outsider. Nonetheless, membership on the CWH allowed me entry to the mainstream profession, including the Program Committee of the Berks, where I replaced the outgoing member of color on the committee, Nell Irvin Painter from the University of Pennsylvania. Soon after, I was invited to integrate the editorial board of the journal *Feminist Studies*. As the 1980s began, I marked a new stage in my academic life as I continued to function outside of the box.

Propelled outside of the black academic world, I soon realized that members of the mainstream profession sought my advice primarily about African American history. When I insisted that my degree was in U.S. history and that to know African American history one had to study U.S. history, many of my new colleagues dismissed me politely. They ignored the fact that I could evaluate proposals, manuscripts, and other academic projects involving U.S. history. Furthermore, several of my white "socialist feminist" colleagues in women's history challenged the argument in my dissertation that white women discriminated against black women seeking to join the nineteenth-century women's movement. They argued that patriarchy united all women and that sexism trumped racism. In their view, white women were powerless while white men were the agents of discrimination. We debated this position for several years.

In the meantime, I continued to be involved in the ASALH, where the prevailing attitude among many of the black men who attended conferences was sexist. Many of them argued that women's history was feminism and that it distracted us from the struggle to legitimize black studies. Several of my black female colleagues noted this phenomenon—racism from white feminist scholars and sexism from black nationalist male scholars—and we tried to develop strategies to overcome the prejudice we discerned. The debates over sexism went on for several years also.

These conflicting positions left me and many other African American women historians in the cross fire. In 1979, Elizabeth Parker from San Francisco, Eleanor Smith from Cincinnati, and I decided to divide up the nation and put out an organizational call to black women in the profession. Parker's sudden death left the task to Smith and me. We asked our colleagues to join us in developing an association to promote black women in the historical profession that would be affiliated with one of the professional organizations that we frequented. After caucusing at several conventions, we realized that most of our cohorts attended the ASALH conferences. The group settled on the Association of Black Women Historians (ABWH) as the organization name, then Smith and I met with ASALH executive director J. Rupert Picott. We signed an agreement to allow us to meet with the ASALH and have a member of the ABWH serve on all forthcoming program committees. Our steering committee was pleased as we set out to elect officers for an executive board. I was elected the first national director.[6]

Unfortunately, challenges came from some men in ASALH who felt that black women stepped out of their place in taking leadership roles in the profession. Some men came to sessions where papers on black women were being presented just to criticize the authors. Our supporters, however, came to our defense, including longtime ASALH members John Henrik Clarke, Dorothy Porter, and Benjamin Quarles. One very important supporter, *Journal of Negro History* editor Alton Hornsby, opened the doors of the journal's suite so that we could host the first ABWH reception at the ASALH conference. Soon afterward, the protests against the ABWH subsided and our organizational activities gained national recognition. As a result, in 2001 we celebrated our twentieth anniversary in Washington, D.C., at the Bethune Council House National Historical Site.

Throughout the 1980s and 1990s, I continued my work as scholar-activist, primarily because I taught at an HBCU. Many of us felt compelled to challenge "benign neglect" in state funding and program approval, as well as negative views from mainstream institutions about so-called unprepared black students. I was honored for my work as a pioneer in developing African American women's history and, by the mid-1980s, African Diaspora women's history. However, my colleagues in mainstream academia seemed to herald me more as an activist who promoted black women historians than as a scholar of black women's history. I often felt excluded—outside of the box.

Nonetheless, during these crucial years in my career development, I had to acknowledge that being a scholar was difficult. My husband and I had separated in 1979, and besides being a single parent (Jeanna was born in 1972), in 1986 I became the coordinator of graduate programs in history at Morgan State. I administered two graduate programs, plus I taught three three-credit courses each semester, and I had limited travel funds to attend conferences outside of the region. Nonetheless, I published several articles and was the principal investigator for a National Endowment for the Humanities–funded research grant for a conference entitled "Women in the African Diaspora: An Interdisciplinary Perspective," sponsored by the ABWH. Writing a theoretical essay about African feminism and co-editing the anthology that resulted from the conference seemed to enhance my reputation as a scholar-activist rather than as a serious scholar.[7]

Nonetheless, I repeatedly received invitations from history departments to apply for a position as chair of a department or, in one case, the director of the Bunting Institute. After being interviewed at several places during the late 1980s, for various reasons I decided to remain at Morgan State.

There were also times when I felt that my invitation to key scholarly events was an afterthought. Sometimes I was not invited at all or I was invited as a representative of an HBCU, not as a black history scholar. A sad example of this scenario was the initial planning symposium for the "Behind the Veil" project in 1990 at Duke University, which offered special funding grants so faculty at black colleges could come and hear the ideas of their colleagues from mainstream institutions.[8] I attended because I felt we at black institutions should ignore organizers' patronizing attitudes and become involved. Some of the organizers seemed surprised that I provided innovative ideas and analyses during the symposium discussions. Unfortunately, the Duke University experience was one of many similar experiences.

Some of my friends in mainstream institutions suggested that I needed to finish my book in order to earn more respect. I agreed but needed a block of time away from Morgan State so I could work without distractions. Since writing my dissertation, I had done additional research on African American women who had been woman suffragists and had published several articles focusing on them. I had found significant information during my first sabbatical leave from Morgan State during the 1978–79 academic year. However, my heavy teaching load and service to the profession left me little time to write a book.

My first opportunity came with my 1984–85 sabbatical leave and a Berkshire Conference–Bunting Institute summer fellowship at Radcliff College. By September 1984, I had revised my dissertation and changed the title to "African American Women in the Struggle for the Vote." I sent it to the University of

Michigan Press, whose editors were seeking manuscripts on women's history. In January 1985, I received comments from two readers who liked my findings, made suggestions for revisions, and recommended the manuscript for publication. However, the editors were waiting for another reader to respond. The evaluation did not arrive until July. The press requested that I revise my work according to the suggestions of the third reader, who maintained that I should write a study different from the one I had authored. The new theme proposed was a comparative study of white and black women in the suffrage movement, which I declined to pursue.

My frustration nearly stymied me; however, Martha Vicinus, one of my fellow editors at *Feminist Studies*, explained that the press reflected the view of white middle-class scholars who, unable to see beyond their own experiences, needed books about women to be placed in the context of their own lives. She encouraged me to give the press a bit of what they wanted to read, then proceed with my focus on African American women. The strategy was a wise one, but by summer's end, I was back to teaching full-time, doing committee work, and raising my teenage daughter.

Fortuitously, while waiting for the press to respond, I had researched and discovered new primary sources that corroborated my revisionist thesis that African American women had fought racism and sexism simultaneously in their struggle for the right to vote. These findings kept my hope for a book alive as I wrote more essays for publication.

Another decade passed before I could get another sabbatical leave. In 1994, I accepted the AHA's invitation to chair the CWH and returned to my book project with a fellowship from the Smithsonian Institution's National Museum of American History. While at the museum, I researched extant copies of the National Woman's Party newspaper and the museum's collection of anti–woman suffrage data. Again, my findings confirmed my argument about barriers against black women's involvement in the woman suffrage movement, primarily during the early twentieth century.

Fortunately, the 1990s saw university presses' fear of black women's history wane. As researchers purchased copies of my dissertation in microfilm, new studies of the woman suffrage movement interrogated issues of race. In addition, black women historians were developing more theoretical analysis of African American women's experiences. New questions were being raised about interpretative voices and multiple levels of consciousness and oppression, and additional venues appeared for examining race, class, and gender.[9] In light of these new theories and research, I reexamined and expanded my woman suffrage study. I switched from a revisionist interpretation to what I called a black nationalist feminist theory for analyzing black women's voices and finding alternative meanings from inside black communities and organizations for their participation in the suffrage movement.

During my sojourn at the Smithsonian Institution, I rewrote my manuscript again. In 1995, I submitted it to Indiana University Press, where my colleague Darlene Clark Hine was senior editor of the Blacks in the Diaspora Series. This time, I had no need to defend writing an exclusive history of black women's experiences. The reviewers supported my work, and the press offered me a contract. *African American Women in the Struggle for the Vote, 1850–1920* was published in 1998, and the following year it won the ABWH book prize.[10]

As the twentieth century drew to a close, I continued to be invited to lecture about African American women's political and social history because many in the profession tried to place me in a sphere defined only by the woman suffrage movement. However, since the 1980s, I had been moving in other women's history directions defined by themes in the African Diaspora, where cross-cultural studies require comparative approaches. As African Diaspora studies began to become recognized by scholars in mainstream institutions, those of us at HBCUs like Howard University, Spelman College, North Carolina Central University, and Morgan State University seemed to be pushed aside. This was disturbing because we had been in the trenches early in the struggle for field legitimization. The cycle seemed to continue. More often than not, HBCU scholars were overlooked for keynote speaking slots unless one of their colleagues at the mainstream table intervened to nominate them for a chance to present at a major conference. On a few occasions, this happened to me.

As I entered the twenty-first century as a scholar who remained at a historically black university, I had spent thirty years teaching primarily black students and interacting with ivory tower doorkeepers in professional associations. My name was recognized in many professional circles. However, aside from my work at my university and the primarily black professional associations, I seemed to remain outside of the box in being and in thinking.

NOTES

1. Rosalyn Terborg-Penn, "A Black History Journey: Encountering Herbert Aptheker along the Way," in *Nature, Society, and Thought: A Journal of Dialectical and Historical Materialism* 10, nos. 1 & 2 (1997): 189–200.

2. Ibid., 191.

3. Ibid., 192.

4. Michael R. Winston, *Howard University: The Department of History, 1913–1973* (Washington, D.C.: Department of History, Howard University, 1973), 147.

5. Sharon Harley and Rosalyn Terborg-Penn, *The Afro-American Woman: Struggles and Images* (Port Washington, N.Y.: Kennikat Press, 1978).

6. Janice Sumler-Edmond, "The Association of Black Women Historians," in *Black Women in America*, 2d ed., edited by Darlene Clark Hine (New York: Oxford University Press, 2005), 1:37–38.

7. Rosalyn Terborg-Penn, Sharon Harley, and Andrea Benton Rushing, eds., *Women in Africa and the African Diaspora* (Washington, D.C.: Howard University Press, 1987).

8. William H. Chafe, ed., *Remembering Jim Crow: African Americans Tell about Life in the Segregated South* (New York: New Press, 2001).

9. For theoretical constructs for analyzing black women's history during the mid-1990s, see the works of Adele Logan Alexander, Elsa Barkley Brown, Bettye Collier-Thomas, Sharon Harley, Wanda Hendricks, Evelyn Brooks Higginbotham, Darlene Clark Hine, Nell Irvin Painter, and Deborah Gray White.

10. Rosalyn Terborg-Penn, *African American Women in the Struggle for the Vote, 1850–1920* (Bloomington: Indiana University Press, 1998).

# Deborah Gray White

## MY HISTORY IN HISTORY

Before the Southern Historical Association meeting of 2003, I never gave much thought to how and why I became a historian. But the meeting was a sort of turning point for me because a session on the impact of my first book, *Ar'n't I a Woman?: Female Slaves in the Plantation South*, was on the program.[1] I was deeply honored, in fact humbled, by the recognition, but in writing my response to the papers on that panel, I was forced to reflect on how I came to write and feel about the book. Two years later, I was again forced to reflect on my life as a historian as *Ar'n't I a Woman?* was again honored with a two-day conference at the Huntington Institute in Los Angeles and a session at the Berkshire Conference of Women Historians.[2] Something curious began to happen to me as I accepted these tributes—fully twenty years after *Ar'n't I a Woman?* had been published. They certainly filled me with pride and joy and a sense of accomplishment, but they also left me feeling angry and the anger did not pass quickly. With the help of a very gifted professional, I had been dealing with my past, but I had always seen my work as an oasis of sorts, disconnected from my personal life. I felt lucky to make a profession out of what had always been my passion—history. But the sessions and conference on my book brought certain things to light, made me notice things I had not noticed before, and, in classic midlife-crisis style, cast me adrift in a wash of emotions that I am only now getting a handle on. Truth be told, this volume, *Telling Histories*, my first edited volume, is part of the "work" I needed to do to move through this peculiar patch of life.

I always loved history. It was my favorite subject in elementary school, junior high, and high school. It was the subject I could always depend on to boost my overall grade point average. In the early grades, social studies was my forte. In junior high, it was history—any kind of history. In high school, I was good in political science and economics, but history, especially American history, was my favorite subject. I can only guess at why and how that happened.

For sure, I was embarrassed by the bits and pieces of black history I learned. Every Black History Week (it was only a week back then), we learned about

George Washington Carver and Booker T. Washington. As I look back, I am appalled at the New York City social studies/history curriculum of the 1950s and 1960s. I always wanted to crawl under the desk in my elementary school class of mostly black and Puerto Rican students when we discussed slavery and black life. My mother was a domestic worker. I—though not my mother, who was proud that she set her own hours and chose her employers—was embarrassed by the fact that she cleaned white people's homes. When my classmates talked about their factory-working mothers, I fell silent. Somehow I associated the history of slavery with my mother's work. I hated and was jealous of her care for the white children of her employers. I hated going to work with her on my days off. I hated going to their country homes when she helped clean them out at the beginning of the summer. I just hated that she was a maid.

But I loved history and the social sciences. I remember reading Lenin's *Imperialism: The Highest Form of Capitalism* on my crosstown bus ride to and from Julia Richman High School. And I remember the astonishment on my political science teacher's face when I, one of the few "colored girls" in his honors class, explained the book to the entire all-girl class (Richman was single sexed at that time). To this day, I believe he called on me because he thought the reading was above my comprehension. Boy was he surprised.

Thank God my American history teacher, Ms. Rothman,[3] embraced my interest in this area. She did all she could to satisfy my craving for something other than the stale history offered up in our high school textbook. One day after class, she handed me a few books that were part of a series on problems in American history. They opened a whole new window of learning and discovery. I devoured the edition that explained slavery, the Civil War, and the decisions made by Lincoln and the Republicans. An article on African Americans in the military helped me understand my father's bitterness about his naval experiences in World War II and my brother's opposition to the Vietnam War. I didn't know then that I would become a historian, but I did make up my mind to be a history teacher, not only because history helped me make sense of my world but also because it was the one subject that made school tolerable, that made my average soar, and that I enjoyed doing the homework for.

I received many honors at my high school graduation, but I was truly disappointed when I did not get the history award. I thought I deserved it, and I believed that the three white girls who got it only received it because the advanced-placement teacher liked them and I was black. We had not received the grades from our AP course by the time of graduation, but I believed I had studied harder and knew more. But the recipients had worked on an independent project with the teacher (not Ms. Rothman), and I, being the silent type, was not one to "kiss up." Despite the recognition I received as president of the student body of over 3,000 girls, at the graduation ceremony for more than 700 students, what I remember most is that I did not receive the history award that I thought I deserved.

A phone call one Sunday morning in the early spring of 1967 made all the difference. Until that call, I had reconciled myself to attending Hunter College, one of the city colleges of New York. My brother had taxed our family's finances by attending Grinnell College in Iowa. During the years that they scraped enough money together to make up the difference between his scholarships and loans and the tuition, I watched them struggle and argue and silently vowed never to ask my parents for a dime. Hunter was a logical choice because it was near Julia Richman High. I was already familiar with that side of town and had gotten used to a female environment (Hunter had been a woman's college until 1964). I had gotten into Hofstra and Binghamton (Harpur College), but both had given me only limited financial aid. The call changed everything. It was from the New York Bank for Savings informing me that I had been chosen to receive a four-year scholarship—the Clifford Alexander Scholarship—of $1,000 each year to go to the college of my choice.[4] Subsequently, some of my mother's "friends" complained that I should not have received the scholarship because it was meant for a student in Harlem and I lived in midtown, but neither I nor my mother, the motive power in our household, paid them any mind. I never looked back; I had my freedom paper. Until this day, I think the scholarship changed the direction of my life. Like my brother, I wanted to get as far away from home as possible. I chose Binghamton over Hofstra because it was farther away, and with the scholarship and the other financial aid, I actually had more money than I needed for tuition, room and board, and books.

Though I came to regard Harpur College as a refuge and affectionately called it Camp Harpur, the four years I spent there were not easy. During freshman orientation, a dean announced the new program that brought minority students into the college under a different set of admissions criteria than the rest of the student body. Hence, from the very first day, I was stigmatized as a "special admissions" student, as were all of the minority students, whether they entered under the new program or not. Boy, did I feel my color. There were only a handful of us (I remember 6) out of a student body of about 3,000, and we were singled out from the beginning as somehow less qualified than the other students.

To me, the original criteria were unfair. My high school grade point average was in the nineties; I had been in student government since elementary school; I had been a member of Arista, the honor society, since junior high school; and I played the violin (second violin actually) in the Manhattan Borough-Wide Orchestra. As a kid who grew up in the projects, I was an overachiever, a nerd by everyone's standards, and had excelled despite the odds. I had done so well in seventh grade that I was one of three black students to leave the general classes that held all the black and Spanish kids to integrate the all-white special-progress classes in the eighth and ninth grade. In high school, I was one of the few black kids to enter the Country School, Julia Richman's honor school. Presumably, the only things Harpur's white students had on me were higher SAT scores, and many let me know they thought I was inferior to them. It was really hard to confront these students, but deep inside, I remembered the lesson that I had learned in eighth grade when I integrated the all-white "8spe3" class of William J. O'Shea Junior High School: the white kids were separated into the smart class not because they were any smarter than me or my friends but because they were white. It was a heart-stopping and painful lesson for a kid from the mostly colored Amsterdam Projects to learn, and unless I had to, I did not speak in school for most of the eighth grade. At great emotional cost, I acquired this insight early enough to use it to protect myself against some of the mean-spirited and ignorant students at Harpur.

By my second and third years, more minority students were admitted, but this was a double-edged sword. The first year, 1967, there were too few blacks to organize a black student union, but there were enough black and Puerto Rican students to form a small organization that we called the Afro-Latin Alliance. My student-government service and prospective history major seemed to qualify me to head the organization, which I enthusiastically did. One of the first things we did was lobby the administration to bring in more minorities. In those days, everyone was lobbying the administration for something, and it usually caved in to demands. The next year, 1968, more blacks and Latinos came in than we could have hoped for. There were enough to successfully pressure the university to offer black studies courses, but the increased number also spawned divisions. In a very short time, there was a call for a black student organization that was separate from a Latino one. Some of the more nationalist black students called those of us who wanted to keep the Afro-Latin Alliance names like Oreo and Uncle Tom. I felt particularly set upon as president of the Afro-Latin Alliance because the new students demanded masculine representation. Also, my name, Gray, and my straight nose came in for more ridicule than I could bear. I moved off campus after my sophomore year, and though I never got used to being the only black in most of my surroundings or being a moderate among black nationalists, I persevered.

If success is the best revenge, then I had mine. A "special admissions" student, I played on three varsity women's athletic teams, including the tennis team, and when I lived on campus, I represented my dorm on the student council. I graduated Phi Beta Kappa and magna cum laude. Upon graduating, I won the Henrietta A. Pitler Harpur College Foundation Award for the most outstanding graduating woman in leadership and scholarship. Maybe I achieved much and got those awards because of affirmative action, but I don't think so. To this day, I support and defend affirmative action and thank God that I was one of its beneficiaries.

I have always said that Harpur gave me the two most important things in my life: tennis and a diploma, in that order. More than I could ever have predicted, tennis changed my life. It provided an alternative social network at Harpur, including more than a few boyfriends, and no matter where I lived, I could always show up on a tennis court or at a tennis club and make instant friends. It was an entrée that I came to depend on again and again. It also gave me a new lens through which to view my birthplace. I learned to hate New York City because there were so few tennis courts and it was too expensive to play in the city. I reluctantly returned to New York City after graduation, frustrated by the overcrowdedness and my craving for time (to play tennis) and open air.

That I became a history professor had more to do with the fact that I could not get a job teaching high school history when I graduated than with any particular planning. In September 1971, I started teaching fifth grade in the Southwest Bronx. By November, I had made up my mind that I would go back to graduate school, and by March 1972, I had a fellowship in Columbia University's history Ph.D. program.

Not getting a high school history job was only one of the reasons I didn't stay in the New York City school system. First, I could never get my lesson plans in on time, and I could not get my class of 22 boys and 8 girls to walk in two straight lines through the hallways. I saw why the students needed to walk in lines, but I also thought too much stress was placed on orderliness and not enough on learning. I especially chafed under the rigidity of the fifth-grade curriculum. The textbooks were dated, and to me they were irrelevant to what was going on in my students' daily lives. I substituted the *New York Daily News*, which my students bought every Monday. We took our spelling and vocabulary words and our science and social studies lessons from the paper. My students loved it, but the assistant principal did not. She started making surprise visits to my classroom to make sure I was covering what was in the curriculum and what I had put in my lesson plans. She was not pleased when she found us reading the newspaper, and more than once, I was "written up." I didn't stay in the system long enough to learn the consequences of those write-ups, but I can't imagine that I would have fared well.

As it was, not only was I chafing under the system's inflexibility, but I had landed in the New York City school system right in the middle of the community-control crisis. Everybody was fighting each other: blacks, Jews, Puerto Ricans, whites. No group was happy. I gleefully left for Columbia, though I substitute taught during my year there.

And I got married. I think my family and especially my mother's friends were surprised by this because most people thought that all I did was read books and play sports and that I had no interest in boys. Despite the women's movement, or maybe because of it, many questioned my sexual orientation and wondered out loud where I had found this guy. In fact, I had found him one summer while employed in SUNY Binghamton's Upward Bound Program (something else I brought home besides tennis and a diploma). A friend and I were giving a party and two men walked in wanting to know where the black students hung out. We informed them that the few who were on campus would be arriving soon to party in our room. The rest is history. I married one of them, and my friend married the other.

The marriage brought together two black people with very distinct cultures. I was the child of southern migrants who left their sharecropping families as soon as they could—my mother with a degree from the Colored High School of McColl, South Carolina, and my father with less than a sixth-grade education from a small town near Dothan, Alabama. My husband had immigrated from Jamaica, leaving his mother, a teacher, and his father, a successful businessman. I was brought up in one of the largest cities in the world; he spent most of his childhood in a small country parish before moving to Kingston for high school. I was accustomed to cold weather; he was not. I had a New York accent with a pinch of southern that I picked up during summers spent in Clio, South Carolina; he spoke the Queen's English in formal settings and a patois when with his friends and family. I was used to southern-style food and the Motown sound; he was used to pepper, calypso, and reggae. My father, who as a short-order cook had to compete against immigrants on the job, didn't like West Indians; his mother didn't like African Americans (especially women). Having grown up in a black and brown country, he was more confident around whites than I was. Despite and because of these differences, we fell in love and stayed together for twenty-five years.

My first year of marriage coincided with my first (and only) year at Columbia. It was really rough going, not because the work was hard but because I had no academic network and everyone seemed so smart. I felt very lonely and isolated. Students in the history program seemed to have networks outside the university in the greater New York area, as did I, but I could not connect with anyone, and as usual, being the only black person made me very self-conscious. Everyone talked the talk, and I did not learn to trust my intellect. I remember sitting through classes, wanting to make a comment but being afraid to say anything. When the professor (I took courses with James Shenton, Nathan Huggins, and Herbert Klein) would say that he wondered why no one thought of this or that, I would kick myself for not having said what I was thinking since it was along the lines of the professor's comment. But for the entire year, the cat ate my tongue. It was like being back in eighth grade again. Throughout my college years, I had often retreated to my world of silence, but my year at Columbia was a longer visit than usual. When my husband got a job in the Chicago area, I was disappointed that I would not complete my degree at Columbia, but it was easy to leave, at least emotionally.

On the anxiety side, in order to receive the master's degree, I had to pass the French test. I wrote my master's thesis ("Mulattoes in the United States") under the guidance of Nathan Huggins, who was very supportive of my work. But all the time I was working on it, I was fretting about the French test. All I had to do was translate a few paragraphs, but it loomed so large. I had started French in high school and took it through college, but I failed my first two attempts at the test. To make matters worse, the last test of the year was given during finals week, after I handed in my thesis (and before my birthday, which ironically is July 14, Bastille Day). I had completed all of the requirements but needed to pass this one test in order for the year not to be a total wash. I bought a book explicitly designed for people like me, with paragraphs that went from easy to hard to harder. I spent as much time studying for the French test as I did for my thesis. It's a terrible feeling to be taking a test that you know you are failing, and that is what I did for the first two. The third, however, was a dream. I have had reason to look back and wonder what my career would have been like, what my life would have been like, if I had gotten a Columbia Ph.D. I have wondered but have not regretted.

I chose to go to the University of Illinois, Chicago Circle (now the University of Illinois at Chicago), because it was cheaper than the University of Chicago. The decision to move from New York came too late for me to apply for financial aid, so despite the fact that John Hope Franklin was at the University of Chicago, going there was out of the question. Besides, I was confident that Circle would work out since Gilbert Osofsky was there and his books, especially *Harlem: The Making of a Ghetto*, were brilliant. I arrived there in September

1973. Before the beginning of the next year, Osofsky died. Since we had not had many conversations, I was sort of set adrift.

If it hadn't been for an astute associate dean at Circle, I would have drifted right out of the history program. My husband had led the way to Chicagoland, and I became part of his network of corporate ladder–climbing engineers. Bell Laboratories was paying him to work and attend Northwestern for an M.A. and Ph.D., so both of us were in school, but my social circle in Illinois was made up of the newly recruited African American employees at the Bell facilities in Naperville, Illinois. They and their spouses (not all of the new recruits were male) were all employed and making money, and I was the only academic among them. Not only was I unemployed, but I missed my network of friends in New York. Again I was the only black person in the history program, and my longing for more company, combined with my desire to make money, drove me to apply for an assistant dean position at Circle. When I arrived for the interview, I was asked why I wanted to leave the history Ph.D. program. I explained that I needed the money and that I didn't think I fit in well in the department. The dean's response was to call the history department and inquire about a teaching assistantship. I received it and a desk in a T.A. office. I began interacting with other graduate students, most of whom I still communicate with today. I still use the notes from our study groups for lectures in my survey courses.

Being a T.A. had its ups and downs. It certainly was a learning experience. As I look back on it, I realize that age, race, and gender played a big role. Having had teaching experience, I was not afraid to be in front of a class. My fifth-grade teaching and then substitute teaching in a junior high school in the heart of the South Bronx had given me a lot of experience in holding a class's attention and getting students engaged. I was not prepared, though, for the subtle racism of white students who purposely asked questions they thought I could not answer and who challenged every grade but an A or the sexism of black male students who made obscene gestures in class and who saw me as an emasculating matriarch (they had obviously read the Moynihan Report). I was not much older than the black women in my classes, and many of them treated me like a sister, friend, or competitor. I didn't know it then, but these problems would continue for a long time. I eventually worked them out but not before I was well into my middle-age years and not before I got my Ph.D. and tenure.

Being a T.A., finishing my course work, even taking both my written *and* oral (on any question the committee could think to ask) preliminary exams were a cakewalk compared to writing my dissertation and getting tenure. Although

*Ar'n't I a Woman?: Female Slaves in the Plantation South* is today regarded as a classic and a pioneering text in African American women's history, it barely escaped the trash heap. I had no idea what I was getting into or what I was taking on when I chose my dissertation topic.

I had not intended to write a dissertation on female slaves. During one of the few meetings I had had with Osofsky, we had settled on a study of black women athletes because Althea Gibson was one of my heroes. The publication of multiple books on slavery and a graduate paper I did on the black family changed my mind. I remember reading works by sociologist Robert Staples and noting the veiled hostility toward black women that seemed to jump off every page. Obviously, the Moynihan Report left me feeling the same way, but so too did works by historians.

Although John Blassingame, Eugene Genovese, and Herbert Gutman inserted black agency into slavery historiography, their works gave me an uncomfortable feeling. There was a present-mindedness, a very black nationalist feeling in their works, particularly when they covered black men. I was certainly more attuned to this than my fellow graduate students, who were mostly white and male, and it was a challenge to try to explain (I was talking again) in a graduate class that Blassingame had not identified all plantation stereotypes when he said that the major slave characters were Sambo, Jack, and Nat or that Genovese's constant references to slave women's deference to black men missed the mark. It was the mid-1970s, and I was still smarting from encounters with black male co-eds at Harpur and my male students who demanded "deference" from me. The works on slavery, while in many ways brilliant, still left me feeling like the nun in the Madeline children's books—"Something is not right."

And so I had a dissertation topic. I thought I could just go to the sources, to the archives—to plantation records, to slave narratives, diaries, etc.—find what had been left out, and make things right. Obviously I was wrong. Black women were everywhere but nowhere. In the sources, they were in everybody's background. This was not only a source problem but *the* problem. That I did not rely on traditional plantation sources became a major criticism of the dissertation and then the book manuscript. I had not, it was said, done enough work. I had not examined enough plantation records. I had not combed through enough diaries, court records, wills and probate proceedings, southern journals and newspapers. I had relied, it was said, too much on the WPA narratives.

In retrospect, the criticism puts me in mind of enslaved women who, after working from dawn to dusk, were described as lazy shirkers of work. In reality, I was being told that by relying so heavily on the WPA narratives—the black sources—I was taking the easy way out, that I was shirking the hard work presented by the traditional white sources. The fact is that I had spent over a year with plantation records and other traditional sources, and finding information had been like getting blood from a stone. I was not a quantifier or a genealogist, and my adviser, though very supportive and helpful with the writing, was not an expert on slavery or women or African Americans. Neither he nor I thought that the WPA narratives were the easy way out. Uncataloged, not indexed, arrayed in a totally nonsensical unending series, they were, in those days, thoroughly unwieldy and in many other ways problematic.

I took this criticism as a personal assault without seeing the larger political picture. Encoded in the criticism was a piercing message. Enslaved women were invisible in the historical record, and I was being told that to make them visible I would have to abide by the rules and regulations of those who had rendered them invisible in the first place. I was being told that enslaved women's voices, as they came through the WPA narratives, would not be heard unless filtered through white and black male-authored sieves. I was being told that my objectivity was suspect because I was a black woman doing black woman's history, and underneath all the critiques of the innumerable "problems" that existed with the WPA narratives (as if they are the only sources on slavery that present problems) was the message that I was a lousy historian.

I realize now that it was good that I took the criticism personally. Had I seen myself at the intersection of racist and sexist gatekeeping, I might have judged the barriers insurmountable. But I was foolish and did the typical female thing—I internalized the criticism, and I promised to do better. Truth be told, what became *Ar'n't I a Woman?* got better. But it was a very painful process because I was rewriting in response to critiques that alleged that I had not done enough work in the proper sources, and I knew that I could spend a lifetime and still not be able to do what was being demanded. It was painful because I was rewriting without a language that expressed the interdependence of race and gender. And I was rewriting without guidance from someone who had done this before and in a climate that at best was benevolent disinterest.

The rejections came fast and furious. A date in November 1977 had been set for my dissertation defense, but at the eleventh hour, three weeks before the defense, my dissertation was rejected. I was devastated. I had never failed at anything; it took three tries, but I had eventually passed even my French qualifier. I had even passed calculus in high school. My hair turned gray and large clumps fell out. For the most part, I kept this rejection to myself. I couldn't tell family and friends that after all these years of schooling, I had failed. They already thought that history was a waste of time, that I was spending way too much time in school and the payback would be minimal. My in-laws, who devalued everything that did not have to do with the sciences, were maintaining a contemptuous amusement toward my chosen profession. Based on a tip from historian Daniel Scott Smith, I turned to the burgeoning anthropological literature on women. I rewrote the dissertation, and it was accepted fully a year later. I told almost no one about this, nor did I let escape the fact that most of the articles that I sent out kept coming back. Very few knew about the serial rejection of the book manuscript.

I did get some encouragement during the next six years, mostly from women historians. My female colleagues were incredibly supportive. "Put it in another envelope and put another stamp on it," said Margo Anderson. At one point, I was invited to a series of conferences by a professor who was setting up a project on black women. At the first meeting, I was asked to give a paper but was among the last to speak. At first, I was upset because what I had to say was being said by everyone before me. But the feeling evaporated as I heard so many others testify to the source problem inherent in doing black women's history. It was the first confirmation that I was not wrong about the source problem. This conference —part of the Black Women in the Middle West Project—was part of an effort to address the problem. It was the late 1970s, and for the first time since I had begun my project on enslaved women, I received affirmation not only about the source problem but also about the importance of inserting black women into American historiography. And it was the first time that I laid eyes on a living, breathing, functioning black female professor—Darlene Clark Hine, who has since become a dear friend and colleague.

For the most part, however, the six years after I finished the dissertation were survived in unbelievable anguish, not all of it stemming directly from my problems with the manuscript. I was commuting to the University of Wisconsin– Milwaukee from where I lived in the Chicago area. Under the best of circumstances, the two-hour one-way trip would have drained anyone's energy, but in the wintertime, especially in the late seventies and early eighties, I-94 was treacherous. (I learned how to use a tape recorder and even write during the long stretches of nothing between Chicago and Milwaukee.) On top of this, I had two children during this ordeal. Since I wanted to tuck them in at night, I only occasionally stayed over in Milwaukee. The juggling act between work and mothering proved so difficult that I began to question those in the women's movement who claimed that women could have it all. When I was working, I felt guilty because I was not spending time with my children; when I was with my children, I felt that I would never be able to compete with peers who had nothing to take them away from their work. Until the birth of my daughters, I had not given much thought to sexism. Race was my primary concern. Motherhood, in particular, changed my perspective. Not only did I become acutely aware of the ways society is structured to make women perform most of the work of parenting, but I got an up-close object lesson in male privilege. I lived with it, and my periods of silence returned.

The problems I was having with my manuscript only increased the stress. I had my first daughter before I began my commute, so the severe preeclampsia that caused her to be born prematurely was not associated with that, though I can't say the same about the difficult research for my dissertation. Four and a half years later, in 1981, after the normal birth of my second daughter, my blood pressure went sky high and until this day must be controlled by medication. I can only speculate on the relationship between my work and my health.

Looking back, I think I might have done it differently, but I don't know how; it was just hard. I got two articles published—one in the *Journal of Family History* and one in the *Journal of Caribbean Studies*. But two articles do not tenure make. I needed a book. Most of my colleagues in the history department were sure that I needed to scrap the manuscript on female slaves and start another project on which to base my tenure. The Department of African American Studies, where 49 percent of my line rested, presented a different problem. When I told the chair what I was working on, he rubbed his chin and frowned. When he lightened up and smiled, I thought he had found a reason to appreciate my work. His response was disheartening. "Oh, I guess that will be useful," he mused. "Black women need to learn how to raise black men for the twenty-first century."

Sadly, his response was not atypical. I remember being a respondent on a panel that reviewed a certain author's work on slavery and nationalism. I praised the work but added that it would have been enriched by a gendered approach and by adding the experience of enslaved women. For the next twenty minutes, I endured what could only be described as an unrestrained verbal thrashing, the likes of which no scholar should have to endure. When I left the session, I headed straight for the bar, where I downed several straight-up brandies. It was not the first or the last time that my subject would drive me to drink.

I had no reason to be optimistic about finding a publisher because publishers' critiques were similarly dismissive. "It was not complete, there was not enough work, the proof wasn't there." And then, almost universally, publishers added, "There is no audience for this book."

What did they mean? Nobody wants this in the historical record; black women's history is not interesting enough for people to pay for it; black women, black people don't read; nobody will believe this because it's about black women coming from a black woman? Was it just about making money? In those days, university presses published esoterica that never went beyond university libraries.

To make a long story short, I was up against the tenure wall. With every year, the ticktock of the tenure clock pounded ever more loudly. I prepared for another career and studied for the LSATs. I even scheduled an interview with the Nuclear Regulatory Commission. I prepared for the end of my life as an academic.

And then everything changed, just like that. While walking across campus—my assistant professorship slipping away with every step—I opened a letter that had come from North Carolina. I had carried it around for a couple of days, shoring up my defenses for another rejection. It was really cold and really dreary that day, and it must have been the adrenalin that propelled me from one end of the campus to the other that gave me the courage to open this by-now crumpled letter. I froze in my tracks as I read it. I had been told that I was wrong for so long that I had begun to believe it. But here, right in front of me, in black-and-white print was a letter that said I was right. It was from Anne Firor Scott. She explained that she and Jacqueline Hall were writing a review essay in black women's history (or women in slavery) and had come across my dissertation. Having read everything on the subject, they thought that "Ain't I a Woman?" (the title of my dissertation three revisions ago) was the best work they had read on women's slavery and wanted to know if they could cite it. Scott also wanted to know what my publication plans were. A reader for W. W. Norton, she volunteered to take it to Norton if I had not yet found a publisher. Within a month, I had a contract and reason enough to abandon a career with the Nuclear Regulatory Commission.

*Ar'n't I a Woman?* was published in 1985. It proved to be the first full-length published study of enslaved black women and one of the first post–civil rights histories of African American women. So unique was this volume that when it arrived at the Library of Congress it had no place to go. On February 13, 1985, a subject cataloger proposed that the heading "women slaves" be established. The heading was approved at the subject editorial meeting on March 5, 1985, and books about female slaves were recataloged under the new heading.[5]

That was over twenty years ago. Today, as I ponder whether to accept an offer from Brown University and work for one of the people I most admire, President Ruth Simmons, I look back at the profound changes that have occurred in the profession and in my personal and professional life. For sure, some things are still the same, but so much has changed—for the better.

I thought the 1983–84 academic year was traumatic, but it was just a dress rehearsal for the dreadful nineties. W. W. Norton seemed to seal the deal for tenure, and for the most part, it did, at least in the history department, my tenure home. The chair of African American studies, however, was not convinced that a book on enslaved women was worth much. Moreover, he thought that I was not a good citizen because I repeatedly objected to having to host Friday afternoon socials to introduce students, who never showed up, to the Department of African American Studies. For sure my commute and my children were at the center of my objections, but there was more. I resented the fact that the chair thought this chore particularly suitable for female faculty. I also had objected when I was made the official hospitality hostess when our department hosted the National Council for Black Studies. I simply refused to take on the title or the job. Consequently, I understand that he, alone among the ad hoc committee assembled in African American studies, objected to my tenure. Thank God for the history department, W. W. Norton, and *Ar'n't I a Woman?*

Besides tenure, the year brought another crisis to wrestle with. Everyone associated with AT&T knew that the 1982 decision that broke up the company would have consequences, but no one knew precisely what it meant for them. In the summer of 1983, I found that for me it meant that I would be moving to New Jersey—with or without a job. I was devastated. I had worked so hard and finally would be getting tenure and now it could possibly be for naught since I would be following my husband—who by now was an assistant vice president and primary wage earner of our family—back East. I obviously had mixed feelings since I hated my commute. But in the summer of 1983, I felt defeated. When the fall AHA *Perspectives* announced a job opening at Rutgers, I saw a glimmer of hope. Margo Anderson again came to the rescue. She dried my tears as she showed me the advertisement and told me what a great place Rutgers, her Ph.D. alma mater, would be. Again, thank God for *Ar'n't I a Woman?*, for I believe that it was on the strength of the manuscript and a good interview that I got the job.

And then came the nineties. I still carry the scars of that decade, but I also wonder where I would be, personally and professionally, without the trauma that forced me to re-create myself. It was a decade of losses. I lost my marriage and the twenty-five-year relationship that went with it. As a consequence of the tumultuous split-up, I lost my in-laws, people who had been my family for most of the twenty-five years and whom I had lived among for more years than I had lived with my birth family. In 1993, I lost my gay brother to AIDS. A genius by any standards (he had an IQ of over 160), he never learned how to live among people of average intelligence, and people of average intelligence never quite warmed up to him. Before he passed, my mother was diagnosed with Alzheimer's. The disease progressed fast, and in 1995, when my father realized that she would no longer be able to care for him, he retreated to the back room of their Clio, South Carolina, house (they were both part of the reverse migration back South) and drank himself to death. My mother continued her progress into the land of the walking dead until 2003, when God showed mercy and took her home, but early on, I was forced to decide whether to care for my ailing mother or to care for my two daughters. I could not do both. The circumstances of the divorce, my own health, and my daughters' needs mandated that I choose. And, of course, there was really no choice. I regrettably put my mother in a nursing home, steeled my nerves, increased the frequency of my visits to my therapist, and dug in for what were the hardest years of my life, even harder than getting the Ph.D. and tenure.

I was remade in the process. As I, alone, saw to the internment of each family member, I did more than bury my past. I literally put it behind me. Left for a time without money to pay the mortgage and threatened, in the broadest sense, with the loss of my children, I redefined my work and my relation to it. In adulthood, I had always had a man to depend on. I had even come to think of my work as supplementary. If the court, which treated me in every respect like a single-parent welfare mom, did not intervene, I would now have to support myself and my children. I accepted every invitation to give a talk, whatever the honorarium. I stepped up the work on *Too Heavy a Load* and published it by the end of the decade. I also added two chapters to *Ar'n't I a Woman?* and published a revised edition before the year 2000. In addition, I wrote a small volume for Oxford University Press entitled *Let My People Go*, a history of antebellum African Americans. I played a lot of tennis too. Most important, I learned to follow the rainbows and welcomed God back into my life.

I learned more about myself in the nineties and in the early years of the new millennium than I had learned in all my previous years. I learned to call myself a historian, not just a professor. I learned to value what I do because my work had sustained me and my daughters through some dark times. As I lived the lessons that I taught in history classes, I learned that I am living proof of the strength *and* fragility of African American women. I learned to fight for what I believe in and not retreat into silence. Most of all, I learned how not to be silenced, whatever the odds or the risks.

And while all that happened, the profession transformed itself—sort of. I can still go to AHA conventions and wonder if I am in the right professional place. After thirty years, it still feels alien. I can still open books, even those written by feminists, and not find African American women in places they should be. I can still look across the university world and find senior women making less money than junior male colleagues, African Americans and women passed over for promotions that they should have gotten, and whole historiographies that have resisted race and gender analysis. But unlike when I first entered the profession, I don't have to, and I refuse to, justify my field of inquiry. Though few and far between, there are senior African American women scholars who make a difference in the books that are published, the people who get hired, and the assistant professors who get tenure and other promotions. African American history, women's history, and African American women's history may be ignored, even demeaned, by many. Be that as it may, I am convinced that it will never be eliminated. This volume, *Telling Histories*, may be ignored, but it will not be disappeared. And to me, that is real progress.

NOTES

1. I thank Nancy Hewitt and Steven Lawson, the Program Committee chairs, for conceiving the panel.

2. For the conference at the Huntington Institute, I would like to thank Brenda Stevenson, and for the Berkshire Conference, I extend thanks to Jennifer Morgan.

3. I use the title "Ms." because I do not know her marital status.

4. I only recently learned that the scholarship was named for historian Adele Logan Alexander's father-in-law.

5. Leslie A. Schwalm, "Ar'n't I a Woman?: Rethinking the History of Women, Gender, and Slavery," 3, 5n, unpublished paper presented at the 2003 meeting of the Southern Historical Association.

# Sharon Harley

## THE POLITICS OF MEMORY AND PLACE

### REFLECTIONS OF AN AFRICAN AMERICAN
### FEMALE SCHOLAR

*The same forces responsible for our oppression . . . "also seek to control what we know of the past and the present."—Buzz Johnson, 1985*

Nearly twenty-five years after receiving a Ph.D. in U.S. history from Howard University, I find that writing a personal reflection of my life as an academic offers an extraordinary opportunity to be my own subject—to share *my own history* of being an African American woman historian and university professor specializing in African American women's history. Since writing a personal memoir or autobiographical text is a chance for a scholar to reflexively confront the continual task of the historian—to consciously (and subconsciously) choose the elements to include and exclude—it reveals significant aspects of my mission in life to both my readers and myself.

Furthermore, historians are especially cognizant that such details will likely be scrutinized and (re)interpreted by generations of historians and other scholars. For these reasons, I—like many female historians of color—am drawn to this task because in telling my own story I can try to reduce (although I realize I can never completely eradicate) the strong possibility that I will be misinterpreted or, worse, maligned by scholars and others. As a historian, I am keenly aware of the long and largely uninterrupted history of misinterpretations and outright falsehoods about people of color at-large. In telling my story, then, I hope to set the record straight—or, at minimum, counter dominant racist and sexist stereotypes.

However, this opportunity, like most others one encounters during a long and unpredictable life, is not without its challenges. There is the daunting task of remembering both the joys and pains of academic and personal life and the twists and turns involved in being a member of the first large cohort of black professional historians and the very small group of female scholars in the pioneering field of African American women's history.

Moreover, in a profession that requires its practitioners to analyze and interpret people's lives, thoughts, and values based on the analysis of primarily written data (letters, reports, newspapers, and, yes, autobiographies and memoirs), oral histories, and, increasingly, visual representations, there is the pressure to be balanced and objective. Consequently, a historian given the chance to tell her own story generally feels an even greater obligation than other writers to include aspects of her life that might reflect negatively on herself as well as others. In other words, I know my joys and triumphs have little color or meaning without due attention to my weaknesses and disappointments.

Given the variety of ways that I could construct a narrative of my life up to now, my strategy here is to center this story of a professional historian on my published works and professional activities and interlace it with my personal life. Not surprisingly, it begins with my days as a graduate student in the early 1970s, first at the Washington, D.C., campus of Antioch College, where I focused my work and personal activities on leftist politics and class struggle, then at Howard University, also in my hometown of Washington, D.C., where I shifted my research attention to the brand-new field of black women's history. The end of my current story brings me to 2007, where it seems I have come full circle: my most recent work encompasses black women's lives and work—not only their paid labor but also their cultural, familial, and community work— *and* their radical politics. I have strived both in my scholarship and in my professional work (as a historian, faculty member, college administrator, and principal investigator and director of a series of research seminars) to give black women who were major figures in their lifetimes their rightful place in the annals of history. In the process, I have been constantly amazed, even shocked, by the extent to which they have been ignored and altogether obfuscated by far too many scholars (some of whom I naively believe should know better). Consequently, I have simultaneously engaged in academic and political struggles to unearth the reasons for the often-deliberate neglect of black women's critical roles in black community struggles within and beyond the organized women's club movement, which has been an oft-reviewed subject in African American women's history.

I begin this reflection on my professional and personal life over the past few decades from my current "perch" as chair of the Department of African American Studies at the University of Maryland, College Park (my fourth stint, although not consecutively). Hopefully, this essay will shed light on the development of the scholarship in the field of black women's history, the historians who do work on this important subject, and my professional and personal life.

## In the Beginning...

It would be fair to say my interest in pursuing a career in history began when I was a student in the honors track (then called "Track One") in the Washington, D.C., public schools, where my history and government teachers exposed me to the exciting world of telling the rich stories of people's lives. By high school, I had already decided to major in history in college and most likely become, like my mentors, a social studies teacher in the D.C. public school system. (As it turns out, I held a goal in common with a surprising number of black women scholars, many of whom were public school teachers before pursuing doctorates and becoming college professors.)

By my senior year at St. Mary-of-the-Woods College, a Catholic women's college just outside of Terre Haute, Indiana, my love for history and Catholicism was matched by a strong and growing interest in the struggles and writings of the late 1960s black power movement, especially those of the Black Panther Party (BPP). One of my undergraduate college suitemates was from the West Side of Chicago and knew the murdered Black Panther Fred Hampton. She had been active with the BPP and was the first person to introduce me to the BPP and its principles. But even before that suitemate arrived at St. Mary-of-the-Woods, I had replaced my daily Bible readings with the poetry of black writers Sonia Sanchez, Nikki Giovanni, and Don L. Lee (now Haki Madhubuti); by my senior year, those writings were supplemented by the communist thoughts expressed in Mao Tse Tung's Little Red Book. My concerned parents joined my professors in wondering what had turned a quiet, serious student who had been the first African American from St. Mary's to student teach into a certified *radical*. My twin sister, who matriculated at the historically black Howard University, attributed the shift in my thinking to living in Indiana—a far cry from Washington, D.C., which was known at the time as "Chocolate City"—and the lack of any kind of social life. While I was perceived as too bourgeois by the black students at nearby Indiana State University (ISU), I was regarded as just plain *different* by the white students at St. Mary-of-the-Woods, many of whom allegedly had not seen a black person before except as a maid or on television, and so I lacked personal interaction with all but a few of my white classmates.

Maybe if there had been at least *one* other black student graduating in the class of 1970, no one would have so easily identified the "light-skinned" girl with the large Angela Davis–style Afro and the "Power to the People" BPP button featuring Huey Newton holding a shotgun as belonging to the lone extended black family in the audience. By then, it was no secret to most of my white classmates and several of the college administrators and faculty that I had a keen interest in the growing black power struggles. I had served as president of the thirteen-person black student organization at St. Mary-of-the-Woods, often cosponsoring events with my counterparts at ISU and at Rose Polytechnic Institute (now the Rose-Hulman Institute of Technology), where James Stewart, a black economist who later served as the long-term chair of African American studies at Pennsylvania State University, served as president of a black student organization with only three members.

### My Graduate Years: From Radical Antioch College to the Black "Mecca" of Howard University

My graduate education began at the Washington, D.C., campus of Antioch College, where I received a master's degree in the art of teaching, with a concentration in the social sciences. Since my classmates and my professors were smart and progressive scholars, I loved Antioch for offering the best of two worlds: the academy and radical politics. I studied under Jack O'Dell, Tom Porter, and Bob Rhodes and discussed and wrote papers on political economy. In the evenings and most weekends, I participated in progressive study groups comprised of fellow students and others, met with associates of a Panther-affiliated group on 18th Street NW (in the heart of what is now the Adams Morgan neighborhood), and sold BPP papers on the streets of downtown D.C. In the summer of 1970, I attended the Amiri Baraka–led Congress of Afrikan Peoples in Atlanta, stayed at Paschal's, listened to Louis Farrakhan and others, and met Queen Mother Moore. Despite my frequent participation in BPP activities, nothing to that point had even approximated the euphoria I experienced at the Atlanta event.

Upon graduating from Antioch in August 1971, I taught in the D.C. public school system. Eventually I left, in part because I mistakenly believed that many of the teachers were more interested in getting a paycheck than in educating the inner-city youth we taught. Two years later, I enrolled in the Ph.D. program in the Department of History at Howard University, which was commonly referred to, then and now, as "the Mecca of Negro education."

I am not sure how unusual this was, but I had not selected Howard's graduate school after any sustained fact-finding mission into graduate programs in history; I knew little about its faculty, ranking, or research focus. What it had was the benefit of being local, which meant I did not need to resign (at least not immediately) from my teaching position. Moreover, my twin sister, Sheila Harley, who had graduated cum laude from Howard, constantly reminded me that I was "culturally deprived" for not having attended a historically black college or university (HBCU) for either my bachelor's or master's degree.

### Howard University: The Starting Point of Black Women's History

Before I set foot on Howard's campus as a graduate student, I somehow knew that its reputation as "the Mecca of Negro education" did not exactly indicate it was a hotbed of racial politics, although it had produced its fair share of "radical" student leaders and civil rights lawyers over the years. Still, its academic reputation as a historically black university, its location in Washington, D.C., and its large population of students from Africa and the African Diaspora succeeded in attracting, in the 1970s, a significant cohort of black graduate students who had been active participants in the era's civil rights and black power struggles. Howard, not unlike the majority of HBCUs (largely due to their historically conservative, white financial base), paradoxically promoted conservative middle-class values and beliefs and, at the same time, imbued its students with a sense of empowerment that often conflicted with mainstream political beliefs and practices.

So a large group of black, radically minded graduate students ended up at Howard in the 1970s. Many, like me, had been awarded graduate fellowships from the Ford Foundation (which had given Howard part of a large grant intended to increase the number of black Ph.D.'s in the United States). Their presence and the occasional activist professor continued to foment my leftist understanding of history, if not my activism. Overcoming my initial disappointment that Howard was not like Antioch, I soon came to appreciate the intellect and wealth of experiences of my cohort, which included Bernice Johnson Reagon, Student Nonviolent Coordinating Committee activist and Freedom Singers member; northern student activist Rosalyn Terborg-Penn; and southern activists Janette Houston Harris and John Fleming. There were so many of us that we occasionally occupied two or three tables in the snack bar of the Library of Congress. It was an exceptional experience and a sight to see, one that was virtually impossible before the 1970s and even less likely today!

Among the first people I met at the beginning of my graduate career were future renowned historians Rosalyn Terborg-Penn, Evelyn Brooks Higginbotham, Gerald Gill, Sylvia Jacobs, and John Fleming. Evelyn, who had just completed her master's degree in history at Howard and was working at the campus's Moorland-Spingarn Research Center before she would enroll in the Ph.D. program at the Department of History at the University of Rochester, and I became close friends since we not only shared a strong interest in Marxist analysis but also had many personal circumstances in common: we were both native Washingtonians; her mother, Elaine Wells, had been my social studies supervisor in the D.C. public school system; and we both had been public school teachers. We often laughed about how our mothers, although support-ive, wondered why we gave up *good* teaching jobs to pursue our doctorates. Over the years, we spent long hours at the Library of Congress working on our dissertations. Work was often interspersed with funny stories and excursions to the local High's ice cream store, where we once had to dig in our purses to come up with twenty-nine cents between us to buy a pint of ice cream! (Our lives continue to overlap as we are presently both chairs of African American studies departments—she at Harvard University and I at the University of Maryland.)

Another valued and enduring friendship that grew out of my days as a graduate student at Howard is the one I share with Rosalyn Terborg-Penn. Since my research interests were not shared by most of my history professors at Howard or at other institutions, it was primarily through my friendship with Roz, as she is better known, that I began to shift my focus from leftist politics and class analysis to African American women's history. While working on her dissertation on African American women in the woman suffrage movement in the United States, she shared highlights of her research over lunch. I became fascinated with and inspired by the subject. It was new territory for me, and these women were excellent role models—smart, courageous, and politically active.

In a seminar on the Jacksonian Era, I attempted to write my first paper on black women. I wanted to focus on the New England textile mills but dis-covered that the only documented evidence of black women's presence in such factories was of those who were passing for white! Their absence was symptom-atic of the notion that blackness represented a social threat to the textile indus-try, which promoted itself as a place of moral purity and a "safe" place for white farmers to send their young daughters. (Ironically, under this guise of moral purity, white female textile workers were actually exploited by mill owners, who controlled all aspects of their work and personal lives.) At the mid-semester point, I switched my topic to the general condition of female African American women wage earners during the Jacksonian Era. The resulting paper was reflec-tive of the first stage of black women's history in that it was largely a project in discovery and description; race, gender, class analysis, and a focus on the non-professional working class would later come to play a more important part in my scholarship and in black women's history in general.

Next I wrote a paper about the early black feminist educator Anna Julia Cooper, whose papers were conveniently housed at the Moorland-Spingarn

Research Center. A middle-class professional who earned two degrees from Oberlin College in the 1880s and a Ph.D. from the Sorbonne in 1925, Cooper was committed to feminist struggle and the uplift of the working class throughout most of her adult life. This project helped to define my dissertation, which ended up largely focusing on middle-class black clubwomen in Washington, D.C., who expressed personal and organizational interest in the welfare of the working class. It signaled a turn from focusing on leftist politics and Marxist studies to researching the organizing efforts of middle-class professional and working-class black women. My graduate studies replaced direct political action. Even my personal appearance reflected these changes as my hair style transformed from a large Afro to a short, curly natural style to, ultimately, straight, relaxed hair.

Pursuant to our studies and with the financial support of the Department of History, I joined fellow Howard classmates in attending or presenting papers at several major history conferences, especially those of the Association for the Study of Negro Life and History (now the Association for the Study of African American Life and History) and later the Organization of American Historians (OAH), the Southern Historical Association, and the American Historical Association (AHA). In the mid-1970s, few sessions at these annual meetings focused on women. But the benefit of this dearth, especially the absence of black women's history, was that Rosalyn and I were often invited to present papers at the Berkshire Conference of Women Historians and at the Racine Conference on Women, organized by Gerda Lerner. Throughout the late 1970s and 1980s, I met an array of fellow graduate students and many of the leading white women historians who were the early pioneers in women's history, including Lerner, Amy Swerdlow, Anne Firor Scott, and Joan Scott.

Although Lerner was the major force behind more fully integrating black women into the profession and the scholarship of history, the field at-large effectively made black women invisible or insignificant. Although my mission to "right" wrongs had shifted its location from the streets to the academy, my commitment to it thus remained resolute.

During our frequent walks across the quad at Howard and along Georgia Avenue in Northeast D.C. to buy lunch, Roz and I expressed our anger about the neglect of black women's lives and experiences by far too many of the nation's senior women historians in the burgeoning field of women's history. For example, white women scholars studying the woman suffrage movement more often than not expunged black women from the record of who had been present and who had spoken at the very woman suffrage meetings they recounted in order to correct the historical record. We decided that rather than continue to complain about the eradication of black women from not only U.S. women's history but also African American history, we would publish our own book, an anthology comprised of our work and that of our fellow Howard classmates, including Cynthia Neverdon-Morton (who was later an associate professor and chair of the Department of History at Coppin State College), Gerald R. Gill (who became an associate fellow at the Institute for the Study of Educational Policy at Howard before becoming a Tufts University professor), Daphne Duval Harrison (who was later an associate professor of African American studies at the University of Maryland, Baltimore County), Andrea Benton Rushing (who became an assistant professor of English and black studies at Amherst College), and Evelyn Brooks Higginbotham (who was an assistant professor at Dartmouth College and the University of Maryland and an associate professor at the University of Pennsylvania before attaining her current professorship at Harvard).

I was thus part of a movement of early black women historians who understood that our effort to encourage white women historians to adopt a more inclusive women's historical discourse was too laborious and that we had better do something about it on our own. With the defiant spirit owed to black power struggles and the sense of self-empowerment that often inspires black students at HBCUs (which continues to make them attractive to black college students and their parents today), Roz and I sent out many letters to potential publishers about our proposed book project. As I recall, we received only one favorable response—from Kennikat Press out of Port Washington, New York. As graduate students without prior publishing experience, we were elated that even one publisher was interested and unaware of how privileged we were to be in a graduate-school environment that did not penalize us for being brash enough to publish a book prior to graduation. My essays on Jacksonian Era black female wage earners and on Anna Julia Cooper, along with the co-authored introduction, formed my contribution to the pioneering volume, *The Afro-American Woman: Struggles and Images*, that Rosalyn and I eventually co-edited, three years before receiving my Ph.D.[1] Four of the scholars who contributed to this volume went on to publish pathbreaking monographs in the field of black women's history: Cynthia wrote *Afro-American Women of the South and the Advancement of the Race, 1895–1925* (Knoxville: University of Tennessee Press, 1989); Evelyn published *Righteous Discontent: The Women's Movement in the Black Baptist Church, 1880–1920* (Cambridge, Mass.: Harvard University Press, 1993); Rosalyn produced *African American Women in the Struggle for the Vote, 1850–1920* (Bloomington: Indiana University Press, 1998); and Daphne wrote the pioneering text on black women blues singers, *Black Pearls: Blues Queens of the 1920s* (New Brunswick, N.J.: Rutgers University Press, 1988).[2]

In the 1970s and 1980s, I was also privileged to know and work with some of the early giants of African American history, many of whom were among the first cohort of early-twentieth-century black public intellectuals who labored without the large salaries and public recognition given to their white contemporaries and to many top black scholars today. Among them was Howard University professor Rayford Logan. When I won the essay contest named for him at Howard, fate would have it that Herbert Gutman, labor historian and author of the award-winning *The Black Family in Slavery and Freedom, 1750–1925* (New York: Random House, 1976), was the featured speaker at the award ceremony. Noted historian and former college president Charles Wesley and scholar and renowned librarian Dorothy Porter Wesley became my "adopted" godparents. They worked tirelessly to chronicle and write the history of black people. While I was assisting Wesley, who was in his eighties at the time, in writing a history of the National Association for Colored Women's Clubs, Charles and Dorothy wondered why I had to call it quits at midnight while they continued to work. Dorothy hosted my wedding reception in 1986 at her beautiful home, where the guests were probably more intrigued by her collection of original African American paintings (many by her first husband, James A. Porter), African art, and books than by the fact that I was actually getting married.

### The Life of an Untenured Black Woman Professor: Teaching, Publishing, and Self-Mentoring

While completing my dissertation, "Black Women in the District of Columbia, 1890–1920: Their Social, Economic, and Institutional Activities," I also taught history courses at the University of the District of Columbia, where David Levering Lewis, C. L. R. James, and Janette Houston Harris were my colleagues. In 1980, a year before I completed my dissertation and my doctorate, I began my long teaching career in the Afro-American Studies Program (AASP) at the University of Maryland.

To complete my dissertation and publications in preparation for the academic hurdle of tenure review, I spent nearly every day throughout the 1970s and the 1980s at the Library of Congress (LC), first in the Main Reading Room and later at one of the assigned study desks in the stacks of the Jefferson Building. There I met Pulitzer Prize–winning scholars and writers and developed friendships with people from around the globe (my deskmate was from Australia) as I churned out articles and conference papers, edited volumes, and prepared class lectures. At the time, there was nothing at Maryland that quite matched the intellectual strength, diversity, and warmth of the scholars who made the LC their intellectual home. Indeed, until Evelyn Brooks Higginbotham joined the AASP faculty at College Park in 1982, there were no full-time female faculty members in the program other than myself, and my male colleagues were mostly Africanists. When Evelyn eventually left to join the Department of History at the University of Pennsylvania, I was once again in a department of male peers until we were fortunately joined by brilliant feminist economist Rhonda M. Williams.

I remember that when Rhonda interviewed for a professorship, one of my male colleagues expressed his concern that she might not *really* be interested in the position because she was "so casually dressed"—that is, she had worn corduroy pants. Such inane logic could only be matched with similar inanity: I countered that, on the contrary, she must be interested because she wore a beautiful, brand-new sweater. Fortunately, Rhonda was hired and eventually tenured, but she passed away from lung cancer before she could become chair of a department that became, and remains, predominantly female and widely known for its productive faculty, grants, and interdisciplinary focus on women, labor, gender, and sexuality—as well as one of the few major African American studies departments with a female chair.

In an academic climate that remained skeptical of women's abilities to contribute to serious scholarship, I was aided during my eight-year march (including a one-year extension) to tenure by several postdoctoral fellowships, including one from the Rockefeller Foundation, one from the Smithsonian Institution's National Museum of American History (where I worked with women's historian Edith Mayo), and one from the American Association of University Women (which I had to turn down). With such support, I wrote and published essays that appeared in pathbreaking volumes, delivered conference papers, gave keynote addresses at several major black women's history conferences, got married, and had a baby.

The publications I was able to complete during that time focused on black women's experiences in the nation's capital and in other parts of the South. Among them was the article "Beyond the Classroom: Organized Lives of Black Female Educators in the District of Columbia, 1880–1930," which was published in the summer 1982 special issue of the *Journal of Negro Education* entitled "The Impact of Black Women in Education." It was edited by historian Bettye Collier-Thomas, who is a close friend and one of my daughter's godmothers. For several years, Bettye and I were among the minority of African American historians who attended the annual AHA meetings that then took place over the Christmas holidays; once we gave a joint paper. Every year, we vowed never to present, chair, or comment at the AHA meetings during the holiday break, but nevertheless, we continued to participate for several years in a row. For the past three or more years, we have continued to talk weekly, usually on Saturday mornings, first about any gossip we might have to share and then about our academic work. Those who know Bettye know I mostly listen: she is as funny and folksy (generous with stories of her life in Millersville, Georgia, and the years spent in New York City and the sage comments of her husband, Charles) as she is smart and hardworking. (Her years of assiduous research have made her the holder of as many primary sources about African Americans as may be counted by some national repositories!)

Along with delivering presentations at the AHA, I also spoke at the annual meetings of other major historical associations and at several major women's history conferences. In 1982, I delivered one of my first major scholarly talks, entitled "Sex, Race, and the Role of Women in the South," at the eighth annual Chancellor's Symposium on Southern History at the University of Mississippi, which was the basis for my essay "Black Women in a Southern City: Washington, D.C., 1890–1920," published by the University Press of Mississippi in an anthology edited by Joanne V. Hawks and Sarah Isom. It was an honor to share a stage with prominent southern women's historian Anne Firor Scott, author of *The Southern Lady: From Pedestal to Politics, 1830–1930* (Chicago: University of Chicago Press, 1970) and, at the time, W. K. Boyd Professor of History and chair of the history department at Duke University. Most of the other participants, like Dolores Janiewski and Anne Goodwyn Jones, were junior scholars like me, although I was the only African American presenter. Dolores and I became friends; while on research trips to D.C. repositories, she stayed with me, and we often reconnected at the triennial Berkshire Conference of Women Historians. I remember the Berks meetings as professional and personable, with my daughter, Ashley T. Kershaw (now a rising senior at Hampton University and an experienced student intern at several hip-hop and popular culture magazines, including *Source, Trace,* and *Giant*), often accompanying me.

Despite the connections and friendships formed at the Ole Miss Chancellor's Symposium, the fact that I was paid more money than I had ever received for a scholarly presentation, and my sense of honor at being asked to contribute, being in Mississippi made me recall the virulent racism and racial violence I associated with the state, which dated to my earliest memory of the psychosis of racism: seeing an image of the mutilated body of Emmett Till on the front cover of the local Washington, D.C., evening newspaper. That and other tales of racial violence came to me as we traveled from the Memphis airport to Mississippi's campus. A sense of profound fear ran through my veins, leading me to wonder how many black women, men, and children and white supporters, friends, and lovers had been hung from the trees that lined the streets and roads to the campus. My focus on radical black women, whether in the black church, school system, or black community life, continues to grow out of profound respect for their enormous courage in the face of constant threat and a corresponding anger at those who obliterated their lives and deaths from the pages of history.

The difficult but necessary confrontations about racism that occasionally occurred at the history conferences I attended also served to cultivate networks of needed support. At the 1987 OAH meeting in Philadelphia, I was scheduled to present my paper, "For the Good of Family and Race: Gender, Work, and Domestic Roles in the Black Community, 1880–1930," but suffered a miscarriage the night before I was to deliver the paper. My friend and conference roommate, historian and Anne Arundel Community College professor Elizabeth Kessel, helped me through that traumatic event and then gave my paper in my stead. As other women have observed, the miscarriage was more distressing than I could have imagined (the sense of loss was nearly as great as it would have been if the baby had been born).

In 1988, a decade after *The Afro-American Woman: Struggles and Images* was published, Rosalyn (now a retired history professor at Morgan State University) and I were joined by Andrea Benton Rushing (now retired from Amherst College from her position as a literature professor) in co-editing *Women in Africa and the African Diaspora* (Washington, D.C.: Howard University, 1987). This new volume included the scholarship of Filomena Chioma Steady and other early scholars whose work concentrated on women in Africa and the Diaspora, which was more Roz's bailiwick than mine. Since my involvement in the project reflected more my collaborations with Roz than any significant work I had previously done in Diaspora studies, I contributed an essay about the importance of joining theory and practice.

In 1990, my essay "For the Good of Family and Race: Gender, Work, and Domestic Roles in the Black Community, 1880–1930," based on my 1987 OAH paper, appeared in the winter issue of *Signs: Journal of Women in Culture and Society*, which remains one of the leading journals about women and gender in the United States. It was subsequently reprinted with other essays from *Signs* in *Black Women in America: Social Science Perspectives* (Chicago: University of Chicago Press, 1990), which was co-edited by Micheline R. Malson, Elisabeth Mudimbe-Boyi, Jean F. O'Barr, and Mary Wyer. In their introduction to the volume, the co-editors declared that the essays helped to illuminate a new direction in black women's scholarship, suggesting, "More important than revising existing concepts and theoretical frameworks is work that frees our imaginations and allows us to conceive new theories, new language, and new questions."[3] Looking back at this collection of essays today, I am amazed to have had my work included among that of scholars who are considered giants in their fields, including Patricia J. Williams, Elsa Barkley Brown, Walter R. Allen, Maxine Baca Zinn, Bonnie Thornton Dill, and Cheryl Townsend Gilkes.

The following year, my essay "When Your Work Is Not Who You Are: The Development of a Working-Class Consciousness among Afro-American Women" was published as part of *Gender, Class, Race, and Reform in the Progressive Era* (Lexington: University Press of Kentucky, 1991), co-edited by well-known historians Noralee Frankel and Nancy S. Dye. Originally presented at the Conference on Women in the Progressive Era that was held in March 1988 at the National Museum of American History and cosponsored by the AHA, it reflected a shift in my scholarship from recovering and situating black women's place in history to applying a more incisive analytical framework to women's labor history. I knew my scholarship had grown and was pleased to be at that particular place in my own intellectual development. I was surprised when a white colleague remarked in a less than positive tone of voice that she was unaware I was doing this kind of work. She seemed disappointed that my work had grown to the point that she might have to acknowledge that it was meaningful and good. And this from a person I called "friend" and had rescued in the middle of the night from a "date gone bad"!

After the birth of my daughter in 1986, the completion and submission of these and other scholarly works involved harrowing experiences in attempting to balance motherhood and my professional life. On more than one occasion with my infant child in tow, I sped to Dulles Airport in northern Virginia to drop off an overdue manuscript by the last FedEx pickup time.

In 1993, I received a random call from a New York City literary agent who said I had been "highly recommended" to write a chronology of African and American history and offered what seemed to me at the time a large advance. Not believing the offer would actually materialize, I informed her that I was not an Africanist and that I could offer only a timetable of African American history, and I told her that the advance was too low. I was surprised when she called back two hours later to say my stipulations had been accepted. *The Timetables of African American History* (New York: Simon and Schuster, 1995) introduced me to the world of trade publishing. Quite naively, I thought I would be paid for appearing at book fairs, television and radio shows, and publicity events; when I discovered that I would not be paid, I attempted unsuccessfully to turn down these opportunities to publicize the book, including appearing on a nationally syndicated television show. The book became Book-of-the-Month and History Month selections, sold out at several book signings, and, in the end, provided a supplement to my associate professor's salary that made it possible for me to live a more comfortable life than many academics and certainly soon-to-be-divorced, single mothers can typically afford.

This personal reflection comes thirteen years after I first published an essay that traced the relationship between my personal beliefs as a feminist and my scholarly research and professional path in a volume entitled *Gender, Families, and Close Relationships: Feminist Research Journeys* (Thousand Oaks, Calif.: Sage Publications, 1994), co-edited by Donna L. Sollie and Leigh A. Leslie. I acknowledged in "Reclaiming Public Voice and the Study of Black Women's Work" that it was difficult for me to think and write about the intersection of the personal and the scholarly because I had been trained to be "objective." I wrote, "In my desire to be considered a serious student of history, I learned to place a veil of silence over my personal feelings and my humanity in most of my intellectual discourse, especially in my written work. In choosing to become personally voiceless in my written discourse, which paradoxically involved giving public voice to the black female past, I adopted the expected intellectual demeanor of most graduate students in the 1970s."[4] At the time, the only person I knew who routinely interlaced her intellectual discourse with her personal voice was my fellow graduate student (and future founder and member of the internationally renowned a cappella group Sweet Honey in the Rock) Bernice Johnson Reagon, who did so in part because she wrote specifically about personal experiences and had always seemed comfortable with not filtering black folks' voices and visions through a distant scholarly lens. Fortunately for me, and undoubtedly for many of the readers of this current volume, personal narratives, memory, and reflections are now viewed as critical and, indeed, inseparable from one's intellectual perspectives and pursuits.

In 1997, Bettye Collier-Thomas, a history professor and then-director of the Center for African American History and Culture at Temple University, and V. P. Franklin sponsored a national conference entitled "African American Women in the Civil Rights–Black Power Movement" at Temple. I served on the conference planning committee with Cornell University professor James Turner, and at the conference, I presented a paper on Gloria Richardson and the Cambridge, Maryland, civil rights movement entitled " 'Chronicle of a Death Foretold': Gloria Richardson, the Cambridge Movement, and the Radical Black

Activist Tradition." A revised version of this paper was published in the book *Sisters in the Struggle: African American Women in the Civil Rights–Black Power Movement* (New York: New York University Press, 2001), co-edited by Collier-Thomas and Franklin. The essay and earlier paper reflect my long-term interest in "radical" African American women and my corresponding interest in their deliberate erasure from historic coverage of movements and events in which they played seminal roles. In Richardson's case, although she was featured on the front page of the local daily newspaper and several major national news-papers for nearly two years, she suffered from the same politics of erasure that too often victimizes the black women I and other women historians write about. So it was gratifying that this essay enabled me in the late 1990s to interview Gloria (especially since I believed like others that she had passed away) in her apartment in New York City and to meet her daughter Donna, the high school activist who inspired her mother to join the movement, at a talk in 2006 at the Reginald F. Lewis Museum of Maryland African American History and Culture in Baltimore.

## The Tenure Process and Unlikely Gatekeepers

By the time the grueling process of tenure review began in the late summer/early fall of 1987, I found myself under extremely stressful—perhaps even more stressful than normal—circumstances. For one thing, the year before my life had changed forever when I became the proud mother of my daughter, Ashley T. Kershaw. I could continue to go most weekdays to the Library of Congress to work but only after the babysitter and housekeeper, Dottie McNeil, arrived. My research days could no longer last until 9:30 P.M. for I had to return home by 5:00 P.M. to relieve Dottie, thus commencing the second part of my workday as a mother.

So I had a young child, a less than perfect marriage, and a chair who, despite having some family ties with an HBCU, seemed to share the opinion of a few other colleagues that a Ph.D. awarded from Howard was not good enough for tenure. I was forced to consider whether or not what I presumed to be racist and elitist undertones about the perceived quality of HBCUs would cause my own department head to oppose my tenure case.

But I understand that several anonymous colleagues in the profession wrote stellar letters in support of my tenure and promotion. (The office secretary later told me, "I'm not sure what the director of the program was thinking; you should see the wonderful things important people had to say about you.") This support, along with my publications, ensured my success in winning tenure at the University of Maryland. Although I was elated by the outcome, I found it was somewhat anticlimactic since I had already put the whole process behind me.

### The Administrative Scholar: Choices and Opportunities

Female academics and academics of color are often pressured to take on administrative roles because of the need to diversify university administration, as well as the need to increase their income, especially if they are single women. Furthermore, the perceived opportunity to make a difference in the campus climate by changing policies and hiring more faculty of color (in addition to replacing troublesome administrators) can prevent them from fully appreciating the enormity of the tasks at hand—that is, until it's too late. Unlike the current generation of scholars, mine had few mentors to advise us about the professional risks and sacrifices of choosing between publishing and administration. At the time, my choice to accept a full-time, potentially permanent administrative position had nothing to do with any personal, vested interest in being a college administrator and everything to do with my desire to leave my tenured academic home because of the personal and professional challenges it presented. Although the chair of the AASP at the time was accomplished at securing grants and helped the program become one of the first in the nation to adopt a public policy concentration, he lacked interpersonal skills and a vision for the program that coincided with that of most of the faculty. He operated under the principle that being nice to faculty and staff made one a far less effective chair.

Surprisingly, despite my lack of considerable administrative experience, I was chosen by a selection committee to assume the position of associate dean of undergraduate studies at the University of Maryland under Dean Kathryn Mohrman. I could not have found a better administrative mentor; she was a visionary—smart, focused, and respectful of all, regardless of title or position. But not only did I learn the mark of a good administrator from Dean Mohrman during my stint as an associate dean; I also became more keenly aware of how few blacks there were at the university—or, rephrased, how *white* the university was at the time. It seemed that a faculty appointment in African American studies had limited my daily exposure to the true racial makeup of a historically white university. All of these lessons I took with me the following year when I left the position to replace the outgoing director of the AASP.

Although I was the mother of a two-year-old and had no intention of giving up my life as a scholar when I assumed the AASP chairship, I added the administrative responsibilities to my workload without the slightest awareness of the enormous impact they would have on other aspects of my life. After all, I was already accustomed to working incredibly hard and I did not want the AASP to be subjected to yet another leader, probably male, in a series of chairs who lacked the open and encouraging leadership style that worked so well for Kathryn Mohrman. So I did not think twice about becoming the director of the AASP; besides, with the extra salary and other benefits I negotiated under the advice of more senior black colleagues, it seemed like a win-win situation. And for the most part, it was and has been, except that I have not yet been able to complete the published monograph needed for promotion to full professor. On more than a few occasions, I have regretted having taken administrative appointments before completing the book and securing promotion to full professor, especially since the bar for most promotions continues to rise in the academy. I admire my female colleagues who have been able to pursue academic life without falling into the administrative trap. However, I understand that my decisions have been my own and that they have provided me a plethora of other rewards.

In any case, I have never allowed my chairship to totally divert me from my scholarship; I continue to publish and apply for postdoctoral fellowships to enable that work. I was the recipient of a highly competitive Woodrow Wilson fellowship for the 2003–4 academic year, which would have been an ideal time to finish my book manuscript except that a search for the new chair of the AASP was taking place at the time, my daughter was in the midst of college applications, and I had continued responsibilities related to my Ford-funded "Work in the Lives of Women of Color" research seminar and our grant from the Rockefeller Foundation to hold an international conference at its Bellagio Conference Center in Italy.

My administrative position and grants have thus all been devoted to increasing opportunities to study women and work. It has been my mission as an administrator and a scholar to create a place for women scholars to share their experiences, offer multidisciplinary perspectives on each other's work, and publish their work, namely, in the edited volume *Sister Circle: Black Women and Work* (New Brunswick, N.J.: Rutgers University Press, 2002). Although my life has not been as radical as it was in my earlier years when I was engaged in frontline grassroots work, I have tried to challenge the traditional academic paradigm that emphasizes working in isolation by creating spaces for women scholars, especially those of color, to discuss their work and their lives as academics on college campuses and in the community at-large.

This mission owes itself in part to my desire to keep strong and intact the black scholarly community that I myself have benefited from, that is, the pioneering black women historians who helped to create and develop the Association of Black Women Historians (ABWH) and national conferences about black women's experiences. These women include Rosalyn Terborg-Penn, Darlene Clark Hine, Nell Irvin Painter, Bettye Collier-Thomas, Mary Frances Berry, Deborah Gray White, Sylvia Jacobs, and many others who also provided intellectual support and personal encouragement. We sought each other out at meetings at the Berks, OAH, and Association for the Study of African American Life and History (ASALH) and made efforts to cultivate inclusive collaboration, such as when, after some tense meetings and less than supportive remarks, we persuaded the ASALH to allow the ABWH to hold its annual meeting and luncheon in conjunction with the former's annual national conference. To this day, I make it a point to attend these meetings in order to reconnect with my fellow black female and male scholars.

### "Sister Circle": Sister Scholars Reflect, Write, and Feel

In 1993, I hosted a potluck dinner at my house for female faculty at College Park. Standing in a circle, we introduced ourselves and discovered that eighteen of the twenty-one women present had an intellectual interest in some aspect of black women's work. Dubbing ourselves "Sister Scholars," we began an eight-year collaborative project that would eventually be funded by Sheila Biddle and Margaret Wilkerson at the Ford Foundation (with the support of Ford consultant and Columbia University professor Robert O'Meally) under the title "Representations and Meanings of Black Women's Work." This multidisciplinary research seminar, codirected by my Maryland colleague Mary Helen Washington and coordinated by Bonnie Thornton Dill, resulted in *Sister Circle*.

My contribution to the volume, " 'Working for Nothing but for a Living': Black Women in the Underground Economy," gave me the opportunity to finally respond to the call of my dissertation adviser, University of Pennsylvania professor Mary Frances Berry, to include information about black women in the underground economy in my dissertation, which I had finished in 1981. In the twenty years between her request and my answer, I had learned that opposition to racist and capitalist patriarchy was the root cause of black women's involvement in the underground economy. Indeed, seeing black women in this light brought me full circle back to the radical perspective that had characterized my early graduate education.

As important as the scholarship of this group has been, a major benefit of this collaboration has been the fellowship and community we have developed together. From the first day of the monthly seminar, we regularly shared the joys and pains of being female scholars at both predominantly white and predominantly black institutions of higher learning. Such discussions led to an initial plan to follow up *Sister Circle* with a collection of personal reflections about our experiences of being racially pigeonholed—as the consummate problem solver, the nurturer, or the token person of color needed to diversify a committee—but ran out of steam and settled instead on adding two-page personal statements at the beginning of our *Sister Circle* essays.

Encouraged by the successes of the "Black Women's Work" research seminar, I embarked on an expanded version of that regional project as part of a collaborative effort with Bonnie Thornton Dill and Deborah Rosenfelt in the women's studies department at College Park. With funding from the Ford Foundation, I wanted to launch a research seminar that would include senior African American, Asian, Caribbean, Latina, and white women scholars whose research focused on the intersections of gender, race, ethnicity, and work. Like the discussions that launched the "Black Women's Work" seminar meetings, we began our biannual meetings (alternately taking place on the West and East Coasts) with talk about the difficulties of being women of color scholars in the predominantly white academy, not the least of which was being mistaken for a member of the cleaning staff. Over the years, I expanded this seminar circle to include "junior" (i.e., untenured) scholars of color, with whom we exchanged ideas and contacts, offering support and mentoring when needed— although it became apparent at the conference that such help was not always welcome. Although we all learned from each other, we also had to confront the fact that a sense of entitlement greatly impacted the role and participation of some younger scholars, who seemed not fully aware of the foundation we had laid to make it possible for them to be scholars less burdened by the task of establishing the legitimacy of women's scholarship or women's place in the academy.

Shortly thereafter, in 2004, Lynn Bolles, a women's studies professor at College Park, and I invited mostly senior women scholars from outside of the United States to join our intellectual cohort at an international forum at the Rockefeller Foundation's Bellagio Conference Center in Italy. Scholars attended from Ghana and Nigeria, as well as from the United States (including Puerto Rico), including Sandra Morgan and Deborah Gray White (who were not initially affiliated with our group but served as commentators). This much-needed collaboration successfully culminated in a collection of essays titled *Women's Labor in the Global Economy: Speaking in Multiple Voices* (New Brunswick, N.J.: Rutgers University Press, 2007).

## "Race Women," Past and Present:
## Reclamations of Black Women's Radical Voice

Ending this piece with my most recent publication seems appropriate since it reveals a return to my initial political and research interests in graduate school, when I was an activist studying radicals in the United States and beyond. "Race Women: Cultural Productions and Radical Labor Politics" focuses on a group of progressive late-nineteenth and early-twentieth-century "race women" who openly and courageously fought against racial violence (especially lynching), capitalism, racism, and sexism in their communities and the larger white society. To be able to write about these and other women who combated social injustice wherever they encountered it—in nightclubs, business offices, churches, organizations, hotels, theaters, and even leftist political rallies—feels like coming full circle. The academy may have relocated my activism, but it has never obliterated my principled stand against all forms of injustice, my respect for the working class, or my desire to attain a better understanding of the root causes of racial and gender oppression throughout the world. Furthermore, it has been the place from which I seek to inspire a new generation of activists, inside and outside the academy. Twenty-plus years of university life have shown me that for all of the efforts of the generation of feminist-minded scholars who, like myself, came of age in the academy in the 1970s, we have yet to eradicate sexism, racism, and inequity on university campuses. Rather, our mission continues to find fuel and direction in the late twentieth and early twenty-first centuries as research universities have increasingly tended to apply their resources toward achieving higher academic rankings (determined by such things as *U.S. News and World Report*) instead of toward fully diversifying their student bodies, faculty, and top leadership or funding antiracist, humanist scholarship. As a result, the academy must continue to be the place from which I consistently critique society and my own choices and, simultaneously, reclaim for the public record the lives and voices of generations of courageous and principled black women and men.

NOTES

1. Sharon Harley and Rosalyn Terborg-Penn, eds., *The Afro-American Woman: Struggles and Images* (Port Washington, N.Y.: Kennikat Press, 1978).

2. It did not dawn on me until many years later how atypical it was for two graduate students to publish a book before graduation. I am pleased to know that the book continues to be referenced by scholars and that, due to continued interest, it was reissued nearly twenty years later. As the co-editor, however, I felt some regret about the new edi-

tion because the introduction failed to fully address the tremendous growth and new direction of scholarship in black women's history, which had, by that time, produced several impressive books and articles in the institutionalized field of black women's history.

3. Micheline R. Malson, Elisabeth Mudimbe-Boyi, Jean F. O'Barr, and Mary Wyer, eds., *Black Women in America: Social Science Perspectives* (Chicago: University of Chicago Press, 1990), 5.

4. Sharon Harley, "Reclaiming Public Voice and the Study of Black Women's Work," in *Gender, Families, and Close Relationships: Feminist Research Journeys*, edited by Donna L. Sollie and Leigh A. Leslie (Thousand Oaks, Calif.: Sage Publications, 1994), 190.

Nell Irvin Painter (left) and Nellie McKay at Nell's camp in the foothills of the White Mountains in western Maine, 1985.

*Left to right:* An undergraduate; Atlanta mayor Maynard Jackson; Darlene Clark Hine, assistant professor and coordinator of black studies at South Carolina State College; and president of the college, Maceo Nance, in Orangeburg, South Carolina, in 1973.

Merline Pitre in first grade at Plaisance Elementary in Plaisance, Louisiana, in 1950.

Rosalyn Terborg-Penn (in center with large hat) instructs undergraduate history students in the "yard" at Morgan State University in Baltimore, Maryland, in 1977.

Deborah Gray accepts a check from a New York Bank for Savings representative for a four-year Clifford Alexander Scholarship to Harpur College of Binghamton University in 1967. To her left is Clifford Alexander Sr.

Sharon Harley with her daughter, Ashley T. Kershaw, on Ashley's first day
at Hampton University in Hampton, Virginia, August 2004.

"This is a historic photograph," quipped Pennsylvania State University historian Nan Woodruff as she persuaded characteristically camera-averse historians to pose for a group snapshot at the 1995 meeting of the American Historical Association in Chicago, Illinois, in the process removing herself from the camera's eye. *Back row, left to right:* Thavolia Glymph (Duke University), Tera W. Hunter (Carnegie Mellon University), Stephanie Shaw (Ohio State University), and Linda Reed (University of Houston); *front row, left to right:* Elsa Barkley Brown (University of Maryland), Julie Saville (University of Chicago), and Gwendolyn Keita Robinson (DuSable Museum of African American History).

Before her parents died, Wanda Hendricks remembers happy times. Here in a favorite sweater, she poses for her elementary school picture in Charlotte, North Carolina, around 1962.

Brenda Stevenson and her daughter, Emma Carrie Cones, in 2005.

Ula Taylor at age four in 1968.

Mia Bay and her mother, Juanita Bay, at St. Mary's College in South Bend, Indiana, where Juanita was honored as the college's first black graduate on April 27, 2007.

On December 26, 2003, Chana Kai Lee sits in what her friends
designated "the queen's chair" at a surprise gathering honoring
her progress one year after her stroke.

In addition to photographs and cartoons that illuminated the African American organizational and political scene, Elsa Barkley Brown's father's images captured everyday life in black Louisville, Kentucky. Here Elsa and her brother are the subject, playing in his workplace, Nat Brown Studio, in the 1950s.

Jennifer Morgan and her mother, Claudia Burghardt Morgan (behind Jennifer); her grandmother, Ethel Carter (to Jennifer's right); and her great-grandmother, Mamie Spaulding (to Jennifer's left), in New York City in 1980.

In her fire engine–sized red coat,
Barbara Ransby (center) poses for a
picture at the 1994 MIT conference,
"Black Women in the Academy:
Defending Our Name, 1894–1994."
The other women in the photo
are, *left to right*, Cathy J. Cohen,
Pamela Brown-Peterside, Premilla
Nadasen, Prudence Carter, Tracye
Matthews, Latrice Dixon, and
Melina Pappademos.

Leslie Brown at age seven in 1961.

Nell Irvin Painter and Crystal Feimster at Princeton
during Christmas celebrations in 1994.

# Julie Saville

## HISTORY WITHOUT ILLUSION

"O but Julie, tell me, did I stay free [inaudible] the community [in-audible]?" In the eight months since her stroke, my mother's voice sometimes seems to me to behave like a written document. I hear just enough to know that what she has said is critical, and then her words become indistinct. Her spoken meanings emerge in fragments, never entirely escaping the blank, obscuring invisibility that always threatens written texts. I heard enough from her one September morning in 2006 to understand that she had given me a provocative theme for this quasi-autobiographical reflection on how I came to the study, writing, and teaching of history. Her words might have drawn in part on a frequently aired television commercial for motorized wheelchairs, which por-trays their purchase as a means to "get your freedom back." But what she said also called me to reflect on the changing terms of interaction that I have experienced in my travels between various social and academic communities. Such an approach seems well suited to reckoning with my notion of self as relational and contradictory, defined more by historical processes of interaction and encounter than by actualization of preformulated, individual tendencies.[1] So thanks again to you, my "sweet, adorable, always dear, and now known to be my dearest mother" Betty,[2] for boosting me over narrative obstacles posed by what has become a fairly circumspect temperament during an awkward profes-sional moment. As a child, my mother had rekindled her passion for sports after she found that the plaster body cast that she was advised to wear for nearly a decade freed her from the fear of falling down. As a mother of three who had been advised not to have children, she has known for a long time how to negotiate proscribed limits.

My early impression, growing up in southern cities in the 1950s, was that history had little to do with my life. With the significant exception of a chil-dren's biography of Harriet Tubman, which was on a shelf of about twenty books that my fifth-grade teacher kept in our classroom for us to read if we completed assignments early, I certainly don't remember reading anything ex-plicitly historical in nature. Six weeks' study of "Alabama history," which my seventh-grade social studies teacher initiated by stapling a poster bearing the name of the newly elected governor, George Wallace, to a corner of the class bulletin board, did nothing to enhance my appreciation of the subject. Wallace, I knew, had had something to do with the nasty phone calls made to my house with unusual intensity several months before. The ringing of the phone had taken on more than its usual significance for me during what must have been the gubernatorial election campaign. Could I reach the phone first ahead of my parents or grandparents? How best to outwit the caller and hang up before he or she could speak? Would it be better to slam down the receiver or quickly depress the buttons? Maybe I'd even get to exchange words with the caller, and all the better if I got out a few off-color ones. I invented my own "contests" in response to the extra-electoral pressuring of a political campaign whose meanings no adult ever intentionally discussed with me. No matter. I surmised enough to feel defeated and somewhat betrayed when, even in a school whose newness contrasted so favorably with the cramped, moldy quarters of the elementary school that I had left behind only months before, the roster of the new state officers went up.

Geography and space were probably the first areas of study that claimed my interest in those years. My elementary school principal, Miss Maude Whatley, habitually rewarded students' various accomplishments at the end of the school year—perfect attendance, spelling bee triumphs, athletic excellence, quality report cards—with gift certificates at what was probably Tuscaloosa's only serious bookstore. (Decades later, she remarked to former students of Central Elementary School who attended a ceremony honoring her distinguished service: "You are a distinguished group of lawyers, doctors, educators, business owners, and scientists and I am not any of those things." "But," she chuckled, "I can say that I of course taught you all.") One of my first purchases with her Lustig's (I think) Book Store gift certificate was a book about the "red planet," Mars. Later the bookstore made the local news broadcast since it also stocked a book about a wedding between a white rabbit and a brown rabbit. A sales clerk had pointed the book out to my mother and me, but I thought animal stories a bit juvenile. The story of a prince who traveled the world on a carpet (years later I was amazed to discover that he was purple) and the adventures of detectives Nancy Drew and Cherry Ames were added to my library with these awards. Another year I chose Alaska as the subject of a social studies report, taking special pride in a map that I made using crushed, brightly dyed blue egg shells to outline the silhouette of our newest state. I must have liked topics that put distance between me and Tuscaloosa. My brother, sister, and I ridiculed the city's name. "If man has a loose tooth-a," we quipped, "elephant has a tuska-loosa."

In the end, it was police harassment and my father's near-assault that contributed to our parents' decision to leave Alabama. Entranced by the Mickey Mouse Club, my brother, sister, and I lobbied hard for a move to California. But after a year's sojourn in Little Rock, Arkansas, where both maternal and paternal grandparents and aunts, uncles, and cousins helped us finalize our move and where my sister, brother, and I spent the school year, my family settled down in Memphis, Tennessee. A sign near the Arkansas/Tennessee border at the Mississippi River bridge welcomed visitors, pronouncing the city the "Capital of the Mid-South." Geography told me things were looking up—the "Mid" portended improvement.

Decades later, as I juxtapose these early experiences with the themes of my study of ex-slave workers' political mobilization in South Carolina (*The Work of Reconstruction*)—something that I have never done until I tackled this essay—I am surprised by the thematic parallels: the genesis of political concerns outside the arena of formal politics, the engagement of the unenfranchised with electoral politics, the deliberately clandestine nature of political organization under a repressive regime, the unexpected if fleeting dynamics of cross-racial quasi-political education, and relationships between people, that is, the making of community, as essential circuits of social engagement. Never at any time in working on the dissertation or the book had I stopped to consider how living under Jim Crow might have shaped my ideas about slavery and struggles to make new terms of collective existence after emancipation. I wonder why a commitment to uncovering the historical experiences of others did not encourage me to think critically about my own experiences. Truth be told, what I initially enjoyed about studying history was my view—probably illusory—that I was getting outside my own notions.

My first history teacher was my Louisiana-born maternal grandmother, Mrs. Julia Jase. Mama Julia's stories explicitly introduced me to slave-born kin and to a life history that underscored the distortions of Jim Crow's racial regime. Born in 1899 or 1900 in a lumber camp in southwestern Louisiana, my blue-eyed, black-haired grandmother was the granddaughter of former slaves and the daughter of a central Louisiana domestic worker and an Irish timber worker.[3] Her droll reminiscences of a father who took her for a Sunday outing on a railroad flatcar and of a foster mother who insisted that a prized calf be penned securely before anyone could go out to socialize with friends enhanced my juvenile appreciation of modern conveniences. Her chronicles had little in common with tales of plaçage and quadroon balls that at one time threatened to overwhelm approaches to female racial identities in Louisiana. While my parents shielded me from racial violence and insult, Mama Julia's stories were provocative in ways that neither she nor I intended. Not until the night that a searchlight from a circling police car flooded repeatedly onto our front porch in Tuscaloosa, while inside my mother and grandparents waited with a family friend for word of my father's whereabouts, had I begun to glimpse the brittle path my father must have walked as a new resident physician extended medical privileges at the hitherto segregated Druid City Hospital. My grandmother, however, routinely recounted the making of Jim Crow as part of her coming-of-age. One of her cousins survived military service in a world war only to be shot dead when he returned home to Alexandria, Louisiana, and was opening a schoolhouse; she knew a girl who had been pulled from the Jim Crow railcar by drunken white men primed to beat one of those "white niggers." Other stories schooled me in the distinction between racial identity and racial identification.[4] I delighted in her accounts of the confusion and upset that ensued on occasions when she corrected white people—store clerks, railroad conductors, trolley car drivers, a short-term female employer—about her own racial identity. Depending on the context, the corrections ranged from a "No thank you, I'm just fine where I am" to a questioning, perhaps wistful, "Well you really don't like the Negro people, do you?" to a blistering diagnosis of her interlocutor's canine maternity and his or her immediate consignment to a destination in hell.

Her retelling entrusted to the unpredictable archives of my memory a view of history as the lived experiences of kin and their communities. Oblivious to some of the sorrow, I relished her fierceness. Harriet Tubman had reminded me a bit of Mama Julia, and I know that Mama would have liked the association. To her counsel I give much credit for shaping the terms of my first encounter with an externally racialized self in elementary school. Sometime during the first week of first or second grade, when classrooms were still being set up and students were still being assigned to different classrooms, my teacher sent me to share a seat with a little boy because there were more students than chairs. My hair, pressed, oiled, and curled in ringlets, might have made for certain intolerable ambiguities. "Little girl," the boy whispered, "are you white?" No one had ever posed such a question to me before. I wondered where he came from that he could even conceive of such a notion. "No, I doubt it," I answered. Relieved, we both waited for the real mysteries of education to take shape.

I am still a little surprised by the matter-of-factness with which I came to attend college in Massachusetts. I had hardly ever traveled outside the South or apart from family, with the exception of a failed three- or four-day experiment in interracial living at a camp in eastern Tennessee sponsored by an interfaith religious group and a more successful experience in a summer vacation Bible school at the church of family friends in Birmingham. Resistance to the arbitrary authority of a high school guidance counselor in Memphis helped send me on my way. Perhaps because counseling students about applications to college at a time when only a small proportion of the graduates of the city's eight black high schools pursued postsecondary studies required less than minimal time, the guidance office at Hamilton High School often served as a central node in Memphis's dense network of black social and fraternal organizations. Paeans to a black community's solidarity during eras of racial segregation are selective and can seem more than a little rosy in their claims. When the counselor's office made the monitoring and production of social acceptability an essential component of secondary school instruction, it opened a gate (perhaps inadvertently—I speak in a personal not a historical voice) for intraracial color discrimination, favoritism in the assignment of ceremonial school duties, and other disreputable elements of the politics of social respectability to enter the high school curriculum.[5] By the time I was in twelfth grade, the guidance office disapproved of my conduct. There had been no student council president the year that my slate (the "Red ticket") withdrew rather than participate in a second election, ordered after parties had questioned how votes tallied from voting machines loaned for the occasion had been counted. Even though my grandmother overrode my wish not to purchase a class ring after the color of the stone was changed from blue to white, I was wrongly accused of attempting to undermine the graduation program. Grounds for the accusation deepened after I declined the honor of serving as class salutatorian. (I said I would accept it only if the valedictory was not denied to a student, brilliant in mathematics, whose family responsibilities had contributed to her having to graduate in five years rather than four.) These were the charges that the chief guidance counselor considered when she pronounced me a troublemaker, not "Spelman material," and announced that she just could not write me a letter of recommendation. Of course I was worried. But by this time, using the "List of American Colleges and Universities" in our household's copy of *Webster's Dictionary* to write for college catalogs since we had none in the guidance office, I had made other applications. Her dismissal was more defensive than decisive. Indeed, an unusually large number of Hamilton High School's graduates had been making unconventional applications to colleges such as Southern Illinois University, Albion College, Brandeis University, Yale University, and Valparaiso University for a few years. Rather than interest or curiosity, a somewhat different kind of valedictory from the guidance office traveled along the school grapevine. "Just who do they think they are going off to all those places," a counselor reportedly expostulated. "Well, when they all fail and are sent home, I am going to be right down there at the train station to laugh in their faces." More solicitous counsel smoothed my path, to be sure. But the counselor's conduct remains in my memory a basis on which to question even the faintest suggestion that Jim Crow fostered meaningful cross-class, intraracial community among black southerners.[6]

It was college study in Massachusetts in the late 1960s that helped me begin to appreciate the power of the historical imagination at work in my grandmother's accounts. Having never heard of the Whigs, I probably misunderstood the first sentence in C. Vann Woodward's *Origins of the New South*: "An honest genealogy of the ruling families of southern democracy would reveal a strain of mixed blood."[7] Even though the genealogical broadside must surely have unsettled a few post–World War II southern Democrats, Woodward's allusion to miscegenation as a metaphor for the conservative realignment of post-Reconstruction southern Democrats took my breath away. I abandoned my weekend plans in order to read *Origins* without interruption. Wedged snugly into a corner on the floor behind my bed, the book's pages lit faintly by a small desk lamp, and supplied with food smuggled out of the dining hall by a supportive suitemate, I glimpsed a southern past that I had never imagined.

To read in 1969 that segregation had been produced was portentous. Until then, virtually nothing in my undergraduate experiences seemed to have warranted my parents' faith that college would teach me how to make a better future. My father had been characteristically practical when, during one of the stream of phone calls that flowed on reversed charges from my dormitory room at Brandeis University to Memphis in the early years, I tried unsuccessfully to explain why I felt such utter isolation. "You are at Brandeis to prepare yourself for life, Julie," he later wrote me, "not to prepare yourself for life at Brandeis." Ahead of me, he had understood that the negotiation of distance is ongoing; it has remained a component of terms of belonging in my experiences of both home and academic communities. Some differences between home and university were immediately satisfying. Serious study required me to abandon habits of complaisance that I had mastered inadvertently (if unsatisfactorily, to some) under Jim Crow. Now, in the wake of political murders, *Origins* drew the contours of the seemingly eternal into the frame of time.

Of course, that time has proved long, even to what is now my more historically informed sensibility. This earlier moment, when I decided to study history, is still relatively easy to describe. It probably represents a point when personal experiences, the ties of family, the bonds of friendship, and making the world a better place seemed part of the same effort. Graduate study and teaching have not always sustained that illusion. Having made a commitment to read, write, and teach history during a moment of significant political change that rested on unprecedented grassroots mobilization, I find myself continuing these efforts under the weight of a different political moment. Still in search of stable ground on which to stand, I accept the importance of keeping faith with at times irreconcilable commitments. What follows is of necessity a different kind of account.

Reading against the grain, which I think discontinuities of my early life prepared me to do, is far less burdensome than living against the grain. The further removed I am from graduate study, academic life has increasingly required an insistence on an individualized identity that I find not only intellectually false but personally unpleasant and socially unfortunate. The result can at times be a somewhat commodified form of public personhood. I am taken aback when relations between people assume the discursive forms of website biographies or blurbs on dust jackets. My heart sank when a first meeting with a colleague with whom I was to share committee responsibilities began as follows: I knock lightly on an open office door. Looking up from the computer screen, my colleague says, "Hello, I'm Z." "Hello, I'm Julie. I hope that I'm not disturbing you." "Oh no, I'm sitting here working on my second book." Some of us are more comfortable than others with the proposition that the "Compleat Professor" is an item of display.

Somehow the notion that independence of mind and judgment, which I regard as essential to critical scholarly authority, is most fully manifested through the pursuit of separable and distinct areas of scholarly inquiry or expertise has been very difficult for me to grasp. My own understanding is that learning (not to mention teaching) is most often collaborative and always unfinished—a process, not a product. At the same time, I also realize that scholarship is conventionally understood as a singular and individual accomplishment. Tensions between these two models require continuous balancing. When I manage to describe some aspect of my work as singular (which doesn't happen nearly often enough as far as many are concerned), I feel fraudulent or boastful. When others cannot see any particular thing that I have contributed to the discussion of a problem, I find my invisibility irritating and disturbing. I remember feeling very conflicted some time ago when, at concluding exercises of an international scholarly colloquium, a colleague incorporated my brief previous comments into her own remarks with the attribution "as Julie just said," but the final videotaped version edited out my remarks and my colleague's prefatory acknowledgment. The film showed her speaking the sentence that at the time she had attributed to me. Rather than spend time wondering about why my own words were deemed most suitable when spoken by someone else, I obligingly paid for a copy of the videotape and then immediately threw it away.

Although the university still seems to me a good place from which to sustain a critical perspective on the world, it is also in principle if not always in practice a frankly hierarchical institution. I sometimes think that perceptions of my social location have made me especially useful as a testing ground on occasions when the seeming boundaries of the academy's ranked orders begin to chafe. I laughed at the e-mail message from a freshman who was requesting an appointment outside of my scheduled office hours in order to talk about an upcoming paper: "Hey Julie (Say, is it allright [*sic*] if I call you that?)." Even though my seasoning began before e-mail, I was glad that we were not then face-to-face. After making the appointment, I added a postscript: "Oh, and as for names—by all means use my first name if this is easiest. I don't want you to feel that you have to address me any differently than you do your other instructors."

Sometimes silent observation is the only feasible response. "Hello, Julie, I have talked with Professor X and Professor Y, and I was wondering . . ." began a conversation with a graduate student. "Hello, Julie," from a middle-aged security guard; "How are you, Professor," to the gentleman immediately behind me. Certainly, members of an academic community have a special obligation to ensure that our interactions are not held hostage by institutional hierarchies. At the same time, it can be tiresome to be perceived as the weakest link in a hierarchical chain. I recall with real affection the patina of informality in the University of California system, where no one—including students, faculty, and administrators—had last names.

Rather than challenge the premises of such behavior, it can be more interesting to look for patterns and try to infer the contexts in which people might have previously encountered other black women. On occasion, the limited gendered vocabulary for expressing admiration of female authority has resulted in oddly combined forms. An African American undergraduate provided what is now (for me) a classic illustration: "Excuse me, Ms. Saville. But I was wondering—do you ever, like, go out on dates?," he asked. I replied: "Why? Does your father want to know?" Laughter all around.

With cultivated detachment but less amusement, I sat quietly through a classroom outburst in which a white student chafed at the interim deadlines that I had established for the preparation of research papers. The tone with which the student dismissed the usefulness of intermediate stages for preparation of the essay (problem statement, annotated bibliography, prospectus, revised prospectus, first draft with group discussion, second draft with short conference) and the anger that laced the outburst "I don't do drafts!" fascinated me. It required my best sense of a nursemaid's rehearsed patience to keep the discussion focused on the mechanics of research and writing. Those few occasions when the behavior of sophisticated, articulate, self-possessed students metamorphosed into juvenile tantrums still seem odd, triggered by differences of opinion or by a recommendation for course action that departed from their preferred alternative. Sometimes I wonder whether some falsely maternal analogy has rendered me a suitable object of such a tirade. On other occasions, the analogy seems closer to relations between a dissatisfied employer and a household employee. African American women's historic association with domestic employment prefigures terms of interaction that do not mesh easily with frankness and civil terms of disagreement. A colleague disdained to discuss a conflict in teaching schedules with narrowed eyes and the curt dismissal, "I just don't teach in the fall." It was as though cook had asked boss to make supper.

Given black women's rarity in the university, I am not surprised when non-academics press to know the precise nature of my professional responsibilities or my exact connections with the history department at the University of Chicago. "So what kind of students do you teach?," came the awkwardly phrased inquiry of a cordial but skeptical white businessman in an Amtrak dining car. I was less understanding when a senior colleague in another department asked, "So, do you also teach graduate students?" I was very appreciative when a member of the office staff went out of her way to intercept a young man who seemed intent on getting me to take a message that he wanted to leave for a faculty member.

The university is also a cultural system, and I do not expect to be unaffected by the social plight and historic denigration of black women in the United States. Scholarship requires long bouts of work in solitude. The infrequency of obligatory interactions can allow abstract commitment to tolerance to exceed concrete experiences of diversity within the university community. The everydayness of the interactions that I have characterized, their seeming pettiness, and their inseparability from my own perceptions might easily be used to argue for their insignificance and/or nonexistence. I have become pretty good at not seeing them, mostly for my own peace of mind.

It began differently. To see clearly and state precisely became during my college years a precious, hard-fought privilege that I enjoyed because of the struggles being waged by others. I never had the illusion that force of intellect alone had gained me access. For the longest time, I felt especially obligated to teach only in public institutions. I still feel a keen sense of obligation to help build bridges between my home university and the black communities that surround it. I participate in an adult education program in the humanities for low-income residents of neighborhoods close to my university campus. This involvement is far different from feeling that I am a spokesperson for those who cannot represent themselves. (Certainly these older students represent their opinions freely and without coaxing.) Indeed, I distrust autobiographical narratives that use the author's dramatic change in social position as the basis for claims of authority. Does a secretary of state and former National Security Council executive offer something other than a state-sponsored claim to define the meaning of freedom because she once knew the four young black girls blown into eternity by a bomb set off in a Birmingham, Alabama, church? To belong to incommensurable, perhaps disparate constituencies rarely seems to provide a basis for speaking for any single one of them in isolation. It is more similar to speaking only bits of several languages, no one of which is adequate for communication.

Staring at the once blank wall by my office elevator last winter, I wondered whether my persistent "not seeing" had made me dangerously proficient in disavowing my inescapable alterity in the university. Shocked by penciled lines that suddenly became legible, I read: "Julie Saville is a stupid liberal bitch. And she is ugly too. I hate Julie Saville." I left the comments there as a reminder of the fault lines in our university community that my liminal presence can still provoke to open expression. I am grateful for the anonymous kindness that inked through the lines before the wall was painted last summer.

When she looked over an early draft of this essay, a good friend told me that I still needed to explain more about what has made me wish to remain an academic historian. I don't actually think that making a long-term commitment is the best way to think about this outcome. More important have been those reasons that we can re-create and re-invent with friends and colleagues on a daily basis. In this regard, there has been a close correlation between my academic interests in the ramifications of the everyday and my personal experiences. One way for me to think about how to respond to her question takes as a given that there are broad continuities in the work that race does in the university and in other domains of life. What is bad here could probably be easily reproduced in other environments. But what is good here I can reproduce nowhere else.

"Human freedom is a complex, difficult—and private—thing. If we can liken life, for a moment, to a furnace, then freedom is the fire which burns away illusion."[8]

NOTES

1. The idea that personal identities emerge in the circuits of women's relationships is developed in techniques of narrative analysis employed in Toni Morrison, *Beloved* (1987), and Nell Irvin Painter, *Sojourner Truth: A Life, a Symbol* (1996). Encounter with a racialized self as a key event in black autobiographies is considered in Thomas C. Holt, "The

Political Uses of Alienation: W. E. B. Du Bois on Politics, Race, and Culture," *American Quarterly* 42, no. 2 (1990): 301–23, and in Elizabeth Fox-Genovese, "My Statue, My Self: Autobiographical Writings of Afro-American Women," in *The Private Self: Theory and Practice of Women's Autobiographical Writings*, edited by Shari Benstock (Chapel Hill: University of North Carolina Press, 1988), 63–89. Elizabeth Fox-Genovese's *Feminism without Illusions: A Critique of Individualism* (Chapel Hill: University of North Carolina Press, 1991) inspired the essay's title; her friendship inspired much more.

2. The phrasing reproduces patterns of address that my mother began to use during the summer of 2006 when talking to family members.

3. The color of her eyes did not figure prominently in my grandmother's self-description. She was an adult, so she told me, when a comment of a suitor (who subsequently became my grandfather) about her "beautiful blue eyes" so startled her that she ran to find a looking glass to see them. Her mother had quit the camp and my grandmother's father after a few years in search of a healthier and better life in New Orleans, where she became a loyal Garveyite.

4. The distinction is emphasized in Barbara J. Fields, "Of Rogues and Geldings," *American Historical Review* 108, no. 5 (2003): 1397–1405, and Earl Lewis, "To Turn as on a Pivot: Writing African Americans into a History of Overlapping Diasporas," *American Historical Review* 100, no. 3 (1995): 765–87.

5. Evelyn Brooks Higginbotham, *Righteous Discontent: The Women's Movement in the Black Baptist Church, 1880–1920* (Cambridge, Mass.: Harvard University Press, 1993); Victoria W. Wolcott, *Remaking Respectability: African American Women in Interwar Detroit* (Chapel Hill: University of North Carolina Press, 2001).

6. Insistence on the centrality of organized activist projects to the making of community-grounded solidarity is an enduring contribution of David Montgomery, *The Fall of the House of Labor: The Workplace, the State, and American Labor Activism, 1865–1925* (Cambridge: Cambridge University Press, 1987).

7. C. Vann Woodward, *Origins of the New South, 1877–1913* (Baton Rouge: Louisiana State University Press, 1971).

8. James Baldwin, *Nobody Knows My Name*, in James Baldwin, *Collected Essays*, edited by Toni Morrison (New York: Library of America, 1998), 208.

# Wanda A. Hendricks

## ON THE MARGINS

### CREATING A SPACE AND PLACE
### IN THE ACADEMY

My place in the academy has been defined as much by personal transformations as by race and gender. Orphaned as a teenager and unsure of my place in the world, I struggled to find the resources to attend college. The need to fulfill a personal and professional dream drove me to teaching. A combination of frustration with teaching in public schools and the support of a college professor led me to the academy.

My background does not fit easily or neatly into the traditional characterization of faculty in the ivory tower. I began the academic journey as an outsider and in many ways remain so. College was an abstract concept that had little meaning for my family. I had a general elementary understanding of American history throughout my youth, knew little about the broader African American experience until high school, and only acquired the knowledge and ability to articulate the historical challenges of black womanhood in graduate school. My family was black, poor, and southern. Born in rural Union County, North Carolina, my mother graduated from high school but lacked the financial resources and probably the aspiration to explore other options besides marriage and work. Raised in the small town of Kings Mountain, North Carolina, my father did not graduate from high school. My maternal grandmother only had an elementary education. Little is known about my maternal grandfather or my paternal grandparents, but they had few if any opportunities beyond rudimentary education. I became the first and only member of my immediate family to attend and graduate from a four-year institution. I am the only one to obtain a Ph.D.

Born in 1954, I grew up in an all-black segregated neighborhood in downtown Charlotte, North Carolina. The paradoxical nature of the insulation created opportunity to form community while simultaneously stifling equal access. With the exception of a few teachers and social workers, most of the people in my neighborhood had barely graduated from high school. They worked hard, yet few owned their homes. Like my mother and father, most were tied to menial jobs. My mother worked as a maid, cleaning the houses of whites on a daily basis. My father was employed as a janitor at the local newspaper. It was also a community steeped in family and tradition. There were churches, schools, movie theaters, stores, and libraries. The all-black elementary and high schools educated children. A source of pride, these institutions and the teachers and administrators who governed them fostered hope for the next generation. Black children learned to read, write, and count from people who worshipped in the same churches they attended and shopped in the same stores they patronized.

Two tragedies shaped my youth and in many ways determined my future. The first occurred when I was nine and my father died. The transition to life without him was not a smooth one. The parenting shifted solely to my mother, and the lost income devastated our family. My mother could not afford to pay the rent on our house on her meager wages and, I suspect, could no longer bear to remain in the environment she had shared with my father. So we moved about a mile to a black area surrounded by a predominantly white middle- and upper-class community. White children played within a few blocks of our rented duplex. Due to the school system's adherence to federally mandated integration in the wake of the *Brown* decision nearly a decade before, those children also became my classmates. After I was plunged into an overwhelmingly white neighborhood school where white teachers and administrators governed my day, my educational experience was transformed. My mother's refusal to be intimidated or cower in the face of what had to be the most difficult time of her life supplied support and fortitude. Fiercely protective, she held me and my teachers jointly accountable for my success. She insisted that I do well, and she made appointments with teachers to ensure that I was treated fairly. By the time I reached junior high school, I accepted life's travails and engaged in a bifurcated race and class environment.

My mother died in 1968. I was thirteen. Limited resources and the physical and psychological strain of parenting five young children alone, coupled with a long-term debilitating illness, weighed heavily on her mind and body. Her death shattered our security and altered our lives. My four siblings and I, unsure of our place, sought support and strength from our family. Fortunately, my maternal grandmother made the bold decision to ensure that we remained a family unit. In spite of her advanced age, lack of economic resources, and rusty parenting skills, she welcomed us into her home. Always frugal, she clothed, fed, and housed us. More important, she continued the process of teaching us how to face life's challenges.

By the time I entered one of the premier high schools in the city, the black power movement had waned and busing was used to achieve public school integration. In conceptualizing a framework to defuse criticism and address the history of discrimination, administrators constructed a plan to transform the racial dynamics of the school system. But because the best-equipped schools remained in residentially segregated white neighborhoods, the only means to create racial balance was to physically move black children from their communities. Consequently, the children of maids and janitors waited on corners to board buses that transported them from their stable environments across the racial divide to commingle with the children of doctors, lawyers, and business owners. The fissures in what was expected to be a successful experiment in racial cooperation, however, quickly appeared. The smoldering resentment of deferred dreams and the long-term effects of poverty and discrimination ensured that long-festering bitterness and anger would erupt. Administrators failed to comprehend the cohesive nature of black neighborhoods, the centrality of the schools in our communities, and the volatility of racial and class strife. Though deficient in necessary resources, our schools played a dynamic role in the development, sustenance, and maintenance of our community, and black parents did not want their children removed from the security of their surroundings. So when one of the two black high schools closed as a result of reorganization and integration, black citizens, angry at the betrayal, vigorously campaigned to reopen it. Stunned by black reaction but steadfast in their vision, white administrators insisted that they were acting in the best interests of blacks. But the burden of integration weighed most heavily on our community. The majority of kids being bused were black kids from poor communities who only interacted with white students and their families as subordinates.

Class, race, and place of residence complicated my relationships with black classmates and illuminated the complexity and paradox of my situation. The fluidity of class boundaries in our community allowed my grandmother, who worked as a maid, to own a home located at the border of a working-class black neighborhood and one of the most prestigious inner-city white communities. While home ownership and location could not transcend the rigidly defined racial boundaries, they did prove to be advantageous. The location determined my school assignment, which allowed for daily interaction with both blacks and whites. The setting also underscored the flexibility of race and class distinctions through the shared public spaces at the nearby mall where we all shopped for groceries and clothes. My ability to navigate the black and white worlds offered access that many of my fellow black classmates did not have. Succeeding academically and actively engaging in campus life allowed me to develop strong ties to teachers and establish a mixture of black and white friends and acquaintances. I volunteered at a local hospital and was inducted into one of the all-female, predominantly white service organizations. Success in academics broadened my relationships, enhanced my skills, and tied me to some of the most academically gifted students in the school. Unlike most black students, who operated under a system of limitations rather than possibilities, these students expected to attend college, become professionals, own businesses, and travel. My association with them increased the distance between me and many of the other black students.

Meanwhile, integration did not go smoothly. Although 30 percent of the 2,400 students in my school were African American, my classes rarely included more than one or two black students at a time. The one exception was an African American literature class. The overwhelmingly black class read Ralph Ellison's *Invisible Man*, which introduced me to the concept of racism. Still, I, like my white classmates, teachers, and administrators, was surprised when race riots erupted and angry black students spilled into the hallways and parking lots denouncing injustice and calling for equal opportunity. For nearly a year, fights and rioting erupted and police patrolled our corridors, mocking the persistent argument that integration provided equality regardless of color.

Motivated by friends who boasted of their plans to attend college and by the expectation of teachers, counselors, and administrators, I, despite my grandmother's wishes that I go to work, made plans to enroll in college. A small liberal arts institution in South Carolina welcomed me. It was in many ways similar to my high school, predominantly white and situated in an all-white middle- to upper-class neighborhood. There were no black professors or, for that matter, black administrators. The maids and cafeteria workers were all black. The small residential black student body shared common backgrounds. Most came from southern working-class families struggling to meet the financial needs of their lives. We created the Black Student Union primarily as a social group. It allowed us to congregate and enjoy each other's company. Because no specific classes on African Americans were offered, one winter term I enrolled in an independent study on the the centrality of the church to the black community. Good grades and campus activism generated accolades but did not invite encouragement to pursue graduate work. I graduated in 1976 and fulfilled my dream of teaching in the Charlotte-Mecklenburg school system.

But the lack of creativity of administrators, the anti-intellectual climate, and the enforcement of a homogenized curriculum coupled with the politics and racial polarization among faculty, administration, staff, students, and parents proved too frustrating. Race, busing, and testing undermined most of my attempts to teach students. I found tracking to be a pedagogical method of determining life status and employment opportunities. Many black students enrolled in remedial classes were socially promoted, whereas successful black students found themselves isolated from their peers. Black parents struggled to find common ground. Fearful of losing the battle to educate their children and mistrustful of school administrators, they demanded that their children be treated fairly. White parents, emboldened by their privilege and their desire to enroll their children in the best colleges and universities, demanded that their kids be placed in the most advanced classes. Racial divisions in classrooms spilled over into every aspect of school life. There was little social interaction outside the classroom. Lunchrooms and activity areas like basketball courts remained segregated. After six years, the challenges proved insurmountable. I burned out.

I continued to teach during the day but sought intellectual solace in the master's program in history at the local university. Evening seminars enhanced my understanding of the centrality of race in the American South and South Africa. I struggled to understand racism and discrimination as a global phenomenon and grappled with the gendered context of both. But my program, too fragmented for serious study, failed to provide answers. Additionally, my constant criticism of the school system and denouncement of the inequities led one of my professors to suggest that I consider alternative employment opportunities. During one of our general discussions, I rather flippantly told him that I would like to become a professor like him. Of course I really had no idea what it took to be a college professor and, for that matter, did not know what professors really did other than teach and counsel students. The professor encouraged me to take a leave of absence from teaching and pursue graduate school full-time. The gracious offer of free room and board from my great-aunt, a retired elementary school teacher who had traveled to New York each summer to attend classes in the teacher education program at Columbia University during the height of Jim Crow segregation, alleviated some of my financial concerns. With some lingering trepidation, I took a leave without pay and moved to Winston-Salem to attend a private university.

Despite the transformative intellectual experience provided by the university, I often felt the weight of being "the" black representative. During my tenure, there were no black students in my classes or black faculty in the department. Still, my committee offered no objection to a thesis on a historically significant black church. My major professor's genuine concern about my educational aspirations led me to apply to Ph.D. programs. By the time I returned to my junior high school classroom the following year, I had sent applications to several colleges and universities. By the end of the school term, I had been accepted into a Ph.D. program in the Midwest.

Actively seeking to diversify the student body, the history department drew in a substantial percentage of minorities and women. There were at least three African American students, an African student, and several women. Most striking, my graduate classes often had more than one black student and one woman. Many of us were older, having had professional careers and employment experience outside the university. Some had families and were used to multitasking. The diversity of the student body, however, did not translate into a diverse faculty. The full-time white male majority was joined by two white females and two black females, although one of the latter remained on extended leave and eventually terminated her employment. Over the years, more white women joined the faculty, but the number of blacks did not change.

Still, I benefited from the struggles of early pioneers. African American history courses appeared on the curriculum each semester, and several of the faculty, regardless of race, had been trained in some aspect of African American or women's history. Two of those professors graciously nourished my interest in black women's history. Moreover, my major professor was one of the leading black female scholars in the field. She successfully built an infrastructure designed to institutionalize the history of black women and African Americans. Her presence on the faculty and as an administrator sent as positive a message as the class she taught on African Americans. To highlight the glaring inadequacies in the intellectual treatment of the black experience, she produced a major conference at the university and launched a project collecting and housing materials on black women. And as one of the university's top-ranking administrators, she controlled the financial resources to ensure that her students could network at conferences. As a result, my work on black women in graduate courses was never questioned, ridiculed, or rejected, even after she moved to another university.

The department strongly encouraged professional development and social interaction. Helpful faculty supported students and assisted with conference presentations and fellowship applications. Stimulated by the warm reception and financial assistance from the chair, a couple of us created a newsletter, held receptions and picnics, and invited prominent speakers to campus. Those years probably generated the most activity the department had seen up to that time.

There was, however, a negative undercurrent. One white male student who attributed the increase in the number of black students to affirmative action seemed especially agitated. He reveled in his status as a senior student, often pontificating on the difference between my status as a teaching assistant and his as an instructor. He took delight in noting that only a few graduate students were instructors and that instructors taught their own classes, earned better pay, and were highly competent. He never acknowledged that departmental needs as well as departmental politics often determined the type of position graduate students acquired or that his own place in the department was tenuous. Dire warnings from the administration to my classmates and me about limited funding and the expectation of completing the degree in a timely manner had not convinced him to satisfy his own requirements any sooner. His prolonged stay of nearly a decade stemmed from his fear of seeking a job in a tight market in a subject specialty where the scarcity of employment opportunities severely limited his tenure-track prospects. Out of sympathy to his plight, he had been encouraged to remain in the nebulous world of "all but dissertation." Nevertheless, before he was finally forced out, he insisted on "helping" me understand my career options. For the first time, I came to understand the clear distinction between the perception and the reality of professional opportunities for black female academics. He was convinced that affirmative action privileged me over him and insisted that, unlike him, I did not have to search for a job because colleges and universities were actively seeking to meet their quotas for blacks and women. The sharp contrast in our views spoke to the polarizing reaction to affirmative action. Ironically, what he determined as privilege, I viewed as compensation for successful navigation and hard work. What he attributed to the disadvantages of whiteness, I understood as an attempt to level the field. Unlike him, I had consistently worked two jobs while keeping office hours and grading. I had presented conference papers and won fellowships. I had enhanced my understanding of the academy by serving on faculty as well as dean search committees in the department and the university. More important, my research interest blended three areas of study: U.S. history, African American history, and the evolving field of black women's history. Yet to him, my race and gender superseded all of those accomplishments. Ultimately, he questioned the intellectual legitimacy of African American and black women's history as fields of academic inquiry. He ghettoized my work, devalued my experiences, and reinforced negative stereotypes.

Variations of this incident would be repeated throughout my career. In one instance, a senior colleague, in an attempt to assist with my transition from graduate student to faculty, began periodically visiting my office to unearth issues unique to my situation as the first full-time tenure-track African American in the department. Rather than discussing the department and my place in it, he utilized the time to lecture me on the peculiarities of race. He noted his sympathy with the plight of blacks and highlighted his role in civil rights rallies of the sixties. By the time the sessions ended several months later, he had reminded me of my privilege, devalued his own, and schooled me on my role as a black female academic. Opportunities for him as a white male were limited, he opined, while those for me had expanded. More important, he insisted, my minority status in two categories meant that I had responsibilities to the department, the university, the students, particularly African American students, and black people in general. The impossibility of satisfying everyone eluded him, as did the discriminatory implications of his demands. He didn't ask any junior white faculty to meet these criteria, nor did he engage in similar discussions.

Through the years, I have noticed that most vocal objections to affirmative action have shifted from specific individual categorizations to those that speak to the broader limitations of race and ethnic diversification among faculty. Complaints seem to have increased in direct proportion to the decrease in departmental hires and the tightening of budgets. While the overwhelming majority of the faculty remained white in every institution where I have been employed, the uneasiness of many faculty with the notion of diversity continues. Dissent, however, has become more sophisticated. Rather than challenge a particular minority candidate, white faculty challenge the hiring *process*, even after the criteria for hiring has already been determined. Or faculty question the teaching and research of the potential candidate whose qualifications exceed the criteria. The debate in some cases has been so acrimonious that the entire process has been compromised.

The difficulties that define junior faculty existence also determined mine during those first six years. I wrote lectures, juggled classes, interacted with colleagues, served on committees, and squeezed in time to research and write. Added to these universally exhausting difficulties were the caretaker responsibilities I assumed for my sister, who suffered from a chronic and debilitating illness. The pressure was immense.

More often than not, however, my issues were circumscribed by race or gender or both simultaneously. The liabilities of being the first and only black female professor determined my place among faculty, students, and staff. It was often an uncomfortable place. For example, as a member of graduate committees of African American students or students working on African American topics, I have been coerced into becoming the lead reader while the tenured professor received primary credit. On one occasion when the primary professor failed to even read his student's thesis, depriving the student of much-needed assistance, I, as an African Americanist and the only black faculty, was forced to take over. Rank proved to be a defining criteria. In this case, my junior status made it impossible for me to decline, for the professor was not only my senior but white and male, highlighting the race and gender dynamics. I have found that even chairs and colleagues have expectations that are at once exploitive and contradictory. To promote the department's strengths or diverse curriculum, African American history is often used as a draw for graduate students, yet the responsibility for actually teaching undergraduate and graduate courses in African American history falls on the shoulders of one or, if lucky, two faculty. Moreover, as a black faculty member, I have often been asked to entertain visiting black students regardless of their field of inquiry, while my white colleagues were only asked to entertain students in their field of interest. And my experience tells me that most administrators pay only lip service to limiting the amount of service work required of black faculty.

Gender has also complicated my experience. A black male faculty member, for example, challenged the grade I gave a popular black male athlete in one of my courses. Determining that I had been hasty and unreasonable in my requirements and final grade assessment, he dismissed my objections to his interference. In denying this promising athlete his chance to excel, I, in his mind, was a sapphire, an emasculator of black manhood. Student responsibility apparently ceased to have meaning to this professor. The student had rarely attended class and had taken only one of three exams and none of the quizzes. The faculty member's solution was for me to give the student an incomplete and allow him to do the work over the summer. In the end, the collegial relationship suffered and the student failed.

Gender, race, and status have often informed students' reactions to me as well. Survey courses have been especially problematic. While gender played a significant role in the way I was received in the predominantly black male–dominated African American history class in my first tenure-track position, race clouded my reception in the U.S. history course. Young black male students in the African American survey course, mostly self-trained in Afrocentricism, challenged me on several occasions, particularly when I equated black male and female activism. But their reaction paled in comparison to my reception in the predominantly white U.S. history course. Most of the students had rarely been taught by a black woman, and many had never encountered or expected to encounter a black female professor during their entire college careers. One student later confessed that on the first day of class many were wondering when the "real" professor would appear, suggesting that a black female was certainly not the person they expected or desired to teach them "their" history. Some challenged me in overt ways, questioning my authority and my facts, particularly when I attempted to integrate material about the role of African Americans in the social, political, and economic development of the

United States. Their anger, reflected in the final course evaluations, centered on my inclusion of African Americans in American history. Several expressed their distress by noting that they had enrolled in U.S. history and did not want to hear about "n—ger history." Reeling from the criticism, my initial reaction was to question my skills as a teacher. I reviewed my syllabus and re-examined my lectures for any hint of bias. I indeed found an imbalance in the lectures and discussions—the overwhelming percentage of the material highlighted prominent white men and their role in the major economic and political forces of the nation. I had essentially marginalized minorities and women. Even after this discovery, I sought the opinions of my colleagues, who assured me that they saw nothing to support the contention of the students. Outraged at the remarks, they dismissed them as the complaints of a few disgruntled racist students. I, on the other hand, could not dispense with the remarks so easily. By then, I had seen and heard enough to understand that course evaluations impact yearly reviews, tenure files, and pay increases. Moreover, I knew that undergraduate course enrollments played a significant role in course assignments.

Students' general perceptions of black women academics have further complicated my career. I have simply been overwhelmed by the number who considered me to be more of a psychologist than a scholar. Both black and white students, having rarely encountered a black professor, let alone a black female, have visited me during and after office hours to discuss personal issues rather than academic ones. Their topics have fallen into two camps: universal race/racism and their family dynamics. Office hours have evolved into sessions about racism in their everyday lives. For some, my mere presence seemed to encourage them to confess their racism or that of their family. They wanted to discuss the ways racism shaped their ideas. Each of them looked to me for guidance.

Thankfully some things have changed. More than a decade after receiving my Ph.D., many of my students still tend to see me as teacher and therapist, but I have developed better coping strategies. Students show a maturity in their response to me as a black scholar and to race and gender course content. Heightened interest in African American history underscores the transformation. Graduate students develop concentrations in the field, seeking me as their adviser. Undergraduates flock to the courses, and unlike when I first started, African American history attracts an equal number of blacks and whites and, in some instances, more whites than blacks. Although some advisers still think the course lacks academic rigor, many students view it as a central part of their educational development. Education students, particularly those expecting to teach in urban or rural southern communities, find that it enhances their skills.

Male students tolerate or even embrace the discussions about black women and their significant role in the African American community. The U.S. history course is less of a battleground about race, but it continues to prove difficult. My physical presence still evokes some criticism, albeit from a small minority. Southern students today tend to accept discussions about blacks more readily than students in the Southwest, where I started my career and earned tenure. The overwhelming white majority in that area had no sense of shared history with a group that made up less than 5 percent of the population. Still, students in both regions seem to require that a higher percentage of the lecture and discussion focus on a business or political model of development. Few relish the social history that contributed to America's economic and political climates. I attribute much of this to college core requirements and to the increasing number of students majoring or interested in business.

The most significant transformations in the academy during my tenure have been the increased visibility of African Americans and black women, the explosion of monographs and biographies on and about black women, and the increase in integrative studies examining the interracial and parallel lives of black and white women. Much of this can be attributed to the work of black scholars who persistently challenged white and male privilege and the marginalization of black women's history. Black women have been president of several major organizations, including the Organization of American Historians (OAH), the Southern Historical Association (SHA), and the Southern Association of Women Historians (SAWH). They have served on numerous committees and chaired departments and programs. Many of these scholars originated in the first wave of black female scholars whose early historiography shaped the evolution of black women's history and opened doors for me. The organizational infrastructure of the Association of Black Women Historians (ABWH) and the Association for the Study of African American Life and History (ASALH) probably played a central role in their success. For me, both organizations proved essential for networking and resources.

Through the ABWH, ASALH, OAH, SHA, and SAWH, I have begun to understand how far we have come in the contextualization and theoretical development of the history of blacks and women. By the 1990s, sessions on these subjects had increased substantially, and they now dominate many of the conferences. In the twenty years since I began my graduate work, the maturation of the field and my own evolution can be credited to the fortitude of the early pioneers. The publication of my book and articles and my election to the presidency of the ABWH in 2004 symbolized a completion of the circle. Moreover, in 2008 the OAH will institutionalize black women's history by creating an award for the best book on African American women and gender.

Yet I remain only cautiously optimistic. While my position in the academy affords me opportunities that my parents and grandmother could not even have imagined, I still must struggle to maintain a central rather than marginal role in determining the internal policies of my department and the academy as a whole. Overburdened, I often find myself wrestling with the demands of committee work and weighing the consequences of what I must do to succeed against what I must do to be a productive scholar. The demands in and outside the classroom require inordinate amounts of time. Departments, organizations, academic communities, administrators, and students constantly vie for my productive energy. Race always seems to complicate things, and even cooperation along gender lines presents challenges. For example, when some of my colleagues decided to develop a concentration in women and gender, I should not have had to remind them to include my course on African American women on their list of courses. Tenure and promotion also remain problematic. I have been employed at three major universities and seen a number of black faculty struggle unsuccessfully to earn tenure. Black female full professors are still rare in all disciplines. I have never been in a department with one. It has only been in the last decade that I have been in a department where I was not the lone black female. Though but a small change, I hope it reflects a new pattern for black women in the academy.

# Brenda Elaine Stevenson

## HISTORY LESSONS

I actually never liked history very much as a child. Or at least I didn't think I liked it. I grew up in segregated Virginia. My hometown was the typical small southern town with a huge Confederate memorial in the middle of downtown. Blacks and whites there were as separate as "the five fingers" of the hand. I attended public schools—at that time, some of the worst in the nation. I remember that in the fifth grade, we did not have a library, laboratory, musical instruments, or art supplies. We did, however, have marvelous black teachers who really cared about our education. Thankfully, our schools were not among the many that closed in Virginia to prevent mandatory integration.

I did not attend an integrated school until the ninth grade, not that integration made much of a difference in the spin on history that the teachers taught. About all I can remember from Virginia history in junior high school was the "red-letter year" of 1619. Three important historical events, we were told, took place that year: 100 English women arrived to marry English settlers, general land distribution occurred, and the first slaves arrived in Jamestown. World history excluded Africa altogether. American history in the tenth grade pretty much boiled down to the Civil War. I remember well my teacher's stern declaration that we had to remember only one thing about the Civil War—it absolutely was not fought over slavery. Teachers rarely mentioned women—white, black, or blue for that matter. Not a very auspicious beginning for a future historian of African Americans, and African American women in particular.

But that was not really my "beginning" in history. My mother's stories were. She was a great oral historian. She taught me all about life in the South from the era of slavery through Jim Crow. I learned about growing and picking tobacco, breaking sugarcane, "geechee" culture, the importance of "riceee" in the pot, the lynching of black men *and* women, segregated one-room schools, the poll tax, black disfranchisement, and the depression-era realities for black famers, all before I was ten. Mother also had an affinity for "Negro history." She knew all about Booker T. Washington, George Washington Carver, Harriet Tubman, and many others whom she had learned about in her one-room schoolhouse.

She provided me with a wonderful education, teaching me so much more about history than I have been able to teach my daughter.

My mother, Emma Gerald Stevenson, was born and raised in Mullins, South Carolina. Her father, Edmund Gerald, owned two farms on land that he had inherited from his father and that his father had bought from his father long after the Civil War was over. My great-grandfather must have relished buying this land, land on which he had been enslaved and that had belonged to the man who had owned and raped his mother. My great-great-grandmother, so the family stories go, was an African girl sold from Virginia to South Carolina. She first was sold to someone on Sullivan's Island, probably to work in the rice fields. Later, she was bought by a tobacco farmer on the coastal mainland. It was this man who forced her into physical and sexual slavery. She bore two children by him, according to her son. My great-grandfather would tell my grandfather that his "father" used to beat his mother until her back was bloody. The other slaves would wash her down with saltwater. His "father" would do this, my great-grandfather explained, because even after bearing him two children, she still refused to have sex with him. He beat her when she refused.

That was my beginning as a historian of enslaved women in the American South. Those stories took root in me. My two sisters do not remember them. There were so many stories, they remark. But I could not forget them. I loved my mother's stories, but that was not my only incentive to remember. My mother, as the youngest female child of her parents' fifteen children, had inherited many of the family's personal items. Among them was a painting of my grandparents on their wedding day (which I thankfully inherited as my wedding gift from my mother) and a photograph of my mother's two grandfathers. One was Albert Williams, a handsome man with dark wavy hair and dark eyes. He was part black, part Creek, and part white, and his family were free people of color. The other was Henry Gerald, a former slave with sandy hair and light-colored eyes. That picture haunted me as a child. The eyes of the two men seemed to follow me around the room. I asked my mother about her father's father, and she told me the stories of his mother. The combination of these stories and my great-grandfather's anguished, pale face indelibly marked me. He was, my mother recalled, a very mean man. She had asked her mother why "granpappy" was so mean. My grandmother told my mother that he said he could never be happy after what he had witnessed as a child slave, after he saw his father whipping his mother. He would never get over it. He hated his blue eyes, his father's eyes, which were passed down to so many of my uncles and cousins. That was my beginning.

College provided a wonderful formal education. It was true that I had managed to graduate from high school, as class valedictorian no less, without learning very much history. My interests at the time were firmly in math and science. I went off to the University of Virginia with a DuPont regional scholarship that paid all of my expenses. This was quite a relief to my longshoreman father, who already was paying my sister's full tuition at another college. I also was an Echols Scholar at Virginia, which meant that I had the privilege of taking whatever classes at the university I fancied, whenever I wanted to do so. It was enormous intellectual freedom that meant that I started as a pre-med student but graduated as an African American studies major. I began taking history and literature classes—lots of them—and I loved them. I was particularly excited about my courses in African, African American, southern, and Caribbean history taught by Paul Gaston, Barry Gaspar, and Joseph Miller. Truthfully, however, I was equally excited by courses in literature and poetry taught by Arnold Rampersad and Ray Nelson. I fell absolutely in love with Richard Wright, Jean Toomer, and Langston Hughes. My southern roots, my mother's stories, and my many trips to the Carolinas had ignited a great passion for all things black and southern. Wright's *Uncle Tom's Children* and Toomer's *Cane* burned fervently in my imagination. Professor Vivian Gordon introduced me to fieldwork in the black community of Scottsboro, on the outskirts of Charlottesville. Charles Purdue's course on black folklore led me to the WPA slave narratives. Courses on francophone literature connected the black South with the African Diaspora. I was having the time of my life.

My parents, however, were not pleased. What in the world was I going to do with a degree in African American studies? They had not gone to college, but they knew this was not a traditional major that would guarantee me a "good job." They were right. No one in my small southern hometown was interested in hiring a black female college graduate with a degree in African American studies. I had decided to take a year off before going to graduate or professional school, and I could not find work for months. A family friend finally took pity on me and hired me as a waitress. I cried when I had to buy that white uniform. My mother and father were bitterly disappointed. They said nothing, but I knew they were at their wits' end. I had been my high school class valedictorian, I had gone off to the big university and graduated with honors, but I was going to end up as a waitress? I tried to reassure them that I was going off to law school soon and would get a much better job upon completion. They were skeptical. I eventually landed a job at the local welfare agency, helping old high school acquaintances who had not gone to college apply for food stamps. Well, at least I didn't need food stamps.

My supervisor, Dorothy Redford, had fought to hire me. She told me later that her supervisors had not wanted me to have the job because I would be the only person in the office who had finished college. I had a B.A. from the University of Virginia and was overqualified for the position. But, she noted, she had a daughter in high school who wanted to go to UVA. She would be horrified if, after graduation from UVA, her child could not find a job. Thank you (thank God), I told her. A few years after I had gone off to graduate school, Dorothy Redford launched the Somerset history project, a family history project that identified and then united the descendants of blacks enslaved on the antebellum Somerset Plantation in North Carolina. My interest in African American history, she once told me, had inspired her interest. Wonderfully, we black female historians sometimes find soul mates and solace in the least likely of places.

The notion of law school continued to pull at my ambitions. Like my parents, I was not at all convinced that I could make a career studying black people's history. Certainly my experiences trying to find a job after college did not instill confidence. We knew doctors and lawyers; we didn't know any Ph.D.'s. Education was extremely important in my family, but education in pursuit of a career that would guarantee financial security, not education just for the sake of education. I took the LSAT. I also took the GRE. In the end, I only applied to graduate schools. While I was admitted to several Ph.D. programs in history, I decided instead to pursue the M.A. in the African American studies department at Yale.

Why the M.A.? And why Yale? The M.A. was a compromise between myself and my parents. I would, I assured everyone, enjoy African American studies just a little while longer and then go to law school. Yale? Well, there really was no other choice for me. When I was a third-year student at Virginia, Barry Gaspar had insisted that I go to a talk by a Yale professor who had written a book that was revolutionizing slavery studies—John Blassingame. I never forgot his talk. I was riveted. If I was going to "indulge" myself in African American studies, then I was determined to go for it. He was the one person I absolutely wanted to mentor me.

The M.A. program at Yale was all I could have wanted it to be, if not more. The faculty was magnificent. I had the privilege of studying with John Blassingame, Robert Steptoe, Gerald Jaynes, Charles Davis, V. P. Franklin, Sylvia Boone, Robert F. Thompson, and Henry Louis Gates Jr., among others. I also benefited mightily from conversation and collaboration with other M.A. students who would go off to have wonderful academic or artistic careers of their own: Marcellus Blount, Gordon Thompson, Herman Beavers, Rae Linda

Brown, Roger Smith, and Vera Kutzinski, to name a few. Yale is a superb university, and I felt enormous intellectual freedom and power there. The interdisciplinary aspect of the master's program and the marvelous support of faculty and peers helped to create and sustain these feelings.

My seminar papers centered on, not surprisingly, the American South. Research papers under the direction of Professor Blassingame included a study of black slavery among the five "civilized" Native American "tribes" of the antebellum era and an analysis of the work of missionary aid societies in the Civil War and Reconstruction-era South. Both won awards from the National Council of Black Studies. The latter inspired me to annotate the diary of Charlotte Forten as my thesis project.

Blassingame was immensely supportive of my work on this free black woman and allowed me to draw on his resources at the Frederick Douglass Papers to help with the annotation. He also directed the secretarial staff at the African American studies department, which he then chaired, to type my draft manuscripts—including the lengthy diaries. An individualized reading course on black education in the post–Civil War South, under the purview of V. P. Franklin, lent itself to my first academic publication—a review essay, which Vincent arranged. Skip Gates was kind enough to include my Charlotte Forten diary in his groundbreaking Schomburg series of primary source material on black women. A course with Sylvia Boone, the first black woman to receive tenure at Yale, began my long-lasting interest in African cultural retention. I am finally publishing my first article on that topic this spring. I was so blessed to be among this brilliant, kind, and supportive faculty cohort. It was a very special time for me and had a great impact on the kind of career I eventually would have.

Professor Blassingame encouraged me to apply for the Ph.D. program in American history, and I did. Every year when I was there, Yale admitted one black student to the nation's top-ranked program. That year, it was me. My admission came with a full fellowship, courtesy of the Graduate Fellowship Opportunity Program. Thanks to my work at Virginia and in the master's program, I was ready. I devoured courses by Edmund Morgan, Nancy Cott, David Brion Davis, Sydney Ahlstrom, and, of course, John Blassingame. Most of my research now was on southern women and family from the colonial through the antebellum eras. A paper in Sydney Ahlstrom's class on antebellum America landed me a third prize from the National Council of Black Studies. I was told by conference organizers that I would not be allowed to apply again for the prize. I grinned proudly.

Nancy Cott took a particular interest in my work. She especially encouraged my developing passion for women's history and invited me to take part in the programs sponsored by the women's studies department, which she then chaired. She hosted my first public paper at Yale, a methodological, historiographical, and theoretical treatise on black women's studies. David Brion Davis and John Blassingame both championed my first research efforts on slaveholding families. Years later, Davis reviewed my book, quite favorably, for the *New York Review of Books*. It was one of the most important stepping-stones of my career.

After two years of Ph.D. coursework, I was ready to decide on a dissertation topic. I wanted to write a social history of slave women (we did not use the word "enslaved" in the 1980s). Blassingame was doubtful. "There is already someone else doing that topic," he responded dryly, "and she's almost finished." That "someone else," of course, was Deborah Gray White. He could not imagine that more than one book on slave women would be marketable.

Two weeks later, he asked me to meet him for coffee at Naples, the notoriously dark Yale hangout where you could always find him behind a cloud of cigarette smoke, drinking coffee, chatting, and laughing with faculty and students as they filtered in and out. I sat down, wondering why I had been summoned. He handed me a slip of paper. "Take it," he gestured. "It's your dissertation topic." I looked down at it and inwardly cringed: it read, "antebellum southern family." "Thank you," I responded dutifully, and I left.

I always have had enormous respect and admiration for Professor Blassingame. Many people found it difficult to work with him, but I never did. He was tough, had extremely high standards, did not suffer fools, and knew who the expert was—he was, not his students. I had no problem with this worldview. I had grown up in a strictly patriarchal southern family, as had he. My father ruled our home with stern but loving efficiency, successfully moving us up the socioeconomic ladder in the newly desegregated South. Blassingame was a cupcake compared to my father. And I trusted him completely. I knew that I was blessed to work with this visionary scholar of African Americans, and I never forgot that. Long after I had completed my Ph.D., I still called him, as I do today, Professor Blassingame. He deserves that respect. He was a magnificent scholar and mentor.

So I put aside my desire to write my dissertation on slave women and began to think about writing one on southern families. It was hard. I spent about a year just trying to wrap my brain, and my interest, around the subject. I had done some work on the subject, but I did not want to base a dissertation on that work. Slowly, however, after a lot of historiographic work and some preliminary primary research, I was able to craft a dissertation proposal that was truly mine. I would write a social history of southern families, but it would be one that focused equally on women and men and would include not only elite southern white families but also yeoman farmers, free blacks, and slaves. I was overwhelmed but pleased—and so was my adviser.

I taught for a year to support myself while I applied for research fellowships. I had not been a teaching assistant, so I had no experience. The year I taught at Wesleyan and UConn (Stamford) was a reality check. I did not like teaching very much. I was in love with the research. It would take some time for the balance between the two to happen. Support for my dissertation did come, and it came from many quarters. I received offers of fellowships from the American Association of University Women, the Carter G. Woodson Institute, the Mellon Foundation, and the Smithsonian Institution. Blassingame, of course, had been right. My topic was one that many people were interested in supporting. In the spring of 1985, I went off to Washington, D.C., and Richmond to begin my research in earnest. I stayed for fifteen months.

Like any inexperienced graduate student in the field—despite how wonderful my classes at Yale had been—I was not prepared initially to do the vast amount of research my topic required. I really did not know what I was doing. I started at the National Archives doing census work. That was boring. I would have to come back to that after I had dug into something juicier. I left for Richmond, rented a room from a local black woman, and began visiting the state archives daily. I was lost. The archives were not particularly user-friendly for the inexperienced, the staff was not very solicitous, and I feared I was wasting time. After about three months, I finally hit pay dirt. I came across a wealth of divorce petitions. But soon I had copied all of those, had completed most of my census work, and was tired of reading microfilm. After repeated attempts to get staff assistance, I was finally told by a woman behind the desk: "You're right, our archives are not that well cataloged. You should go to the historical society. It's private, everything is meticulously cataloged, and it has a wealth of letters and diaries that you can review both in manuscript form or on microfilm."

She was right. The Virginia Historical Society was exactly where I needed to be. An added bonus was that it was literally two blocks away from my new apartment—I had moved because the local woman had soon tired of me. I had been walking the six miles round-trip from my residence to the state library every day in the Richmond heat, and I was ready for some physical relief.

The Virginia Historical Society has wonderful collections, a fine staff, and a comfortable environment. Soon, I was immersed in letters, diaries, slave lists, freedom papers, etc. It did not take long, however, for me to annoy the staff. It seemed that this eager black student from Yale could be very demanding. My privileges began to be whittled away. I was not allowed, for example, to photo-copy everything I wanted to take home with me. One archivist even tore up one day's worth of photocopies in my face. "You can't take all of this," she snapped as she ripped the pages. Then I was not allowed to view all the documents in manuscript form. "You need to read the microfilm instead," I was told. Mechal Sobel had warned me about the society. When she had gone some years before, the staff had been befuddled by her Israeli citizenship. They asked a local rabbi to guarantee that she was an appropriate person to work in their archives. The rabbi was reluctant to do so. He eventually went on vacation, which gave her an opportunity to apply again without his sanction. The staff finally relented. Thankfully, I did not have to withstand that kind of scrutiny. I had brought a "letter of authenticity" of my graduate-student status from Yale, which seemed to satisfy most of their concerns regarding my intentions.

All in all, however, it was a productive experience. I came to appreciate their rules; they came to appreciate my appreciation of their rules. When their new brochure was published a year later, there I was, sitting at a desk reading a document. It seems that since I was the only black person using their facility, I became the token black face that assured the world that the organization wel-comed researchers of color.

After a few months in the archives, I took my first trip back to New Haven to review my findings with Blassingame. It did not go well. We sat down, at Naples, of course, and he began to grill me about what I had found. He listened patiently. I was finished in about ten minutes. He smiled, looked me directly in the eyes, and said pointedly, "Go back. There must be more." Of course, there was more, and I should have known he would know that. So I went back. Months more at the historical society and then at the UVA archives proved enormously beneficial. My research year was running out, but I had landed a two-year fellowship at Rice University. I also had been offered one from the Carter G. Woodson Institute in Charlottesville. I should have taken the Wood-son fellowship, but I left Virginia and a rocky romantic relationship that was much too distracting.

I began writing my dissertation in Houston. I gave up the second year of my fellowship to take a full-time appointment at the University of Texas, Austin—another mistake. The students at UT were not ready for a young black woman, with braids no less, to teach them American history. I was quite proud of my history-survey lectures, brimming with stories and statistics about women, native peoples, blacks, and the poor. The white students were not. A group of them complained to my department chair that I was not teaching the "tradi-tional" history they had learned in high school. I defended myself by noting that this was college, not high school, and that I had chosen the social history route. My chair was unimpressed. I reminded him that we both had been trained at Yale. He was even more unimpressed and unconvinced. I was flabbergasted. He clearly was taking the students' complaints seriously. That year, all the junior faculty had their first-year reviews with a potential for a raise. I was told that although I was the only assistant professor who had a substantial publication in my file (my Forten diary had been published by Oxford that year), I had not yet completed my dissertation so I would not be getting a raise. I had completed a full draft of the dissertation—700 pages. Blassingame thought it was marvelous, but it was still a draft. He wanted me to spend the summer rewriting. He, of course, was right, but that opinion hardly impressed the senior faculty. I began to understand that the enthusiasm that African American women met when universities were trying to recruit a "double minority" barely lasted past the signing of the contract. The letter of the law now was applied particularly heavily. A further complication was that I had a senior black male colleague in the department who already was tenured and was chairing the black studies program. He was kind and generous to me and warned me that I was inheriting some of the hostility that was meant for him. He had come in as a young recruit and had quickly gone up the ladder in status and pay, leaving behind some of his peers. They were going to make certain, he told me, that my experience was different. Thankfully, UCLA came knocking that year. I accepted the offer but was allowed six months to complete my dissertation before I had to arrive in Los Angeles.

In the meanwhile, life happened in spite of all of my studies. I married, happily, the man I had left Virginia to avoid (yes, he had followed me). We spent our honeymoon doing follow-up dissertation research in Leesburg, Middleburg, and Harpers Ferry. My personal happiness, however, was shredded when my mother became ill and we were told she only had six months to live. Thank God she lived another two years but not long enough to see me graduate. A year after the passing of my mother, my first history mentor, I graduated from Yale and settled into life as an assistant professor in southern California.

UCLA has a great history department, ranked in the middle of the top ten. The university seemed happy to have me on board, but I soon discovered that some did not particularly value the kind of work I was doing. I was an African American woman, with braids and a black husband, doing African American history—they saw nothing unique, exotic, or wonderful about that. That year, UCLA had hired another black woman—a Stanford Ph.D. who did English history and had a Jewish husband who had received a spousal appointment. They were "special."

I also soon learned that there was simmering resentment among some of the faculty regarding my hire. One of our most prestigious Americanists had reported to the department chair after my lecture that I was "arrogant" but that she would not oppose my appointment. I was told more than once by this same faculty member and others that the department had been forced to hire a black person to teach black history. The implication, of course, was that it did not want to do so. There had been, I was informed, another perfectly good Ph.D. who had taught the survey courses in African American history for the past few years, and the students had adored him—but he was white and could not be offered the job. Hmmm. Others, supposedly well meaning, warned me that I would never be tenured. Department members were so awful to Margaret Washington, my predecessor, I was told. "You won't last." Someone placed an advertisement for a job in Virginia in my faculty mailbox. Subtle, right? But others offered friendship and support. I was in no mood to give in to this pressure. I had left one tenure-track position because of racism and sexism. I was not going to leave another.

I worked really hard. I had learned from my adviser that we could "make it" in the professional world of academia only by working harder than everyone else and expanding our exposure by networking. I had begun presenting at conferences when I was still at Yale. The "black history faculty network" was extremely welcoming and instructive. Darlene Clark Hine, in particular, and Barry Gaspar, V. P. Franklin, Rosalyn Terborg-Penn, and Evelyn Higginbotham were, and are, great role models. Moreover, they extended themselves tremendously to aid the careers of my generation of African American historians. Important slavery scholars began to hear of my work, and soon I was invited to give talks at seminal conferences.

One of those conferences was held at Clemson University and convened by Carol Bleser. I was the only black female historian invited to participate, and I felt especially proud to be among such illustrious southern historians as Eugene Genovese, Elizabeth Fox-Genovese, Drew Faust, Catherine Clinton, and Bertram Wyatt-Brown. I was still a graduate student but had been recommended by Elizabeth Fox-Genovese, who, along with Darlene Clark Hine, had favorably critiqued a paper I had given on child slaves at an Organization of American Historians conference. Sheldon Meyer, the legendary Oxford University Press editor, was also invited. I knew this would be a good opportunity to try to interest him in publishing my book, once completed. I was really looking forward to the conference, but a funny thing happened on the way from the airport.

Carol Bleser picked a number of us up that morning. I asked her about accommodations since I had not received any prior information. "Oh," she noted, "you all will really enjoy the place. I've arranged for some of you to stay at a local bed and breakfast," circa 1840. This was fine with me since I had lived, when first married, in Petersburg, Virginia, in the 1840 home of the surgeon general of the Confederacy. But then Carol said something quite curious. "I have chosen the rooms," she added, "to suit your personalities." Well, I thought, this will be interesting since she does not know me. When the innkeeper handed me my key, he said with special care, "Now, I want to be clear that this is not your room. Your room is occupied until tomorrow at noon, and then you will be moved." Okay. The room I had that first night was great and quite similar to our bedroom in Petersburg. Wow, I thought, how did Carol know? The next afternoon, a note at the front desk informed me that my new room was available. My things were moved, but to a decidedly different part of the house—the domestic slave quarters at the back of the house. I did have a view—I could look out of my window down on the slave kitchen. What could I say? Nothing. I was, after all, a graduate student, the only one invited to speak. I kept my mouth shut. I delivered my paper. It was well received and chosen for inclusion in the published conference proceedings. Sheldon was impressed and promised to look carefully at my manuscript when completed. Oxford subsequently published my book.

Another important conference for me occurred at Johns Hopkins. It too brought together important scholars, but they were all slavery scholars, not "southern historians," and there were a few more African Americans. These Johns Hopkins conferences can be intense, and I was very nervous. I had submitted the fifth chapter of my book manuscript for the group to read. The day before, I had witnessed papers being torn to shreds. Good grief, I thought. Finally, my time came. No one said very much, and I was quite surprised. Finally, Lorena Walsh, whose work I had read since I was a student and whom I admired greatly, raised her hand. "This is one of the best chapters on slavery I have read," she commented, "and I agree wholeheartedly with her conclusions." People all around me nodded likewise. I was as happy as I could be. I had submitted part of this chapter to the *Journal of Southern History* the year before, and the journal had rejected it. I felt sweet vindication.

Slowly but surely, my reputation in the larger world of the academy began to filter its way back to the history department at UCLA. A two-year postdoctoral fellowship at Berkeley, working with Leon Litwack and Mary Ryan, was very useful. Mary, in particular, helped me to think about framing the larger issues in my book and was very encouraging. I was mostly finished with my rewrites by then and was on to another topic—one that took me out of the South for the first time and into the twentieth century. Still, it was about women.

Junior faculty in my department are put through a series of reviews every two years; the fourth-year review is supposed to predict your chances for tenure. My fourth-year review, I was told by the chair, was a triumph. The external review reports of my manuscript from Oxford were particularly laudatory, as were the external review letters the department had solicited. Good, I thought, now maybe I can relax enough to try to have a baby.

After two miscarriages, our daughter Emma was born, a month after I received tenure. I had been offered jobs at Stanford and Berkeley but had decided to stay put during my pregnancy and the months following it. My galley proofs arrived the week Emma was born. Back to work.

Having a child did make a difference. I wanted it to make a difference. I loved being a mother, which, believe me, definitely marked an evolution in my feelings. All through my years in graduate school, I had been convinced that I did not want to be a mother. Still, I knew when I married my husband that he really wanted children. By the time Emma was born, I was more than ready to have her and to slow down or at least to shift professional gears.

I turned from research to administration. My research archives are primarily located in the South, and I was not willing to leave my child to conduct research. After an outside offer from Virginia, the department chair at UCLA asked if I would consider being a vice chair for undergraduate studies. Sure—it would satisfy my service requirement, get me an annual course release, and pay a salary. What's not to like? A year later, an offer of a full professorship came from the African American studies department and the history department at Yale. This, I knew, was what I had been waiting to achieve. This was my dream come true.

The way back to Yale was clearer after my book received David Brion Davis's wonderful review in the *New York Review of Books*. I was one of the first black historians to be reviewed in the journal—Davis even noted my race in his review. But I must add that Nancy Cott, in particular, as well as faculty in African American studies, championed my offer. In the end, after much soul and house searching, I did not take it. Maybe it was a mistake. I certainly have sometimes regretted it. Still, Yale is notorious for not taking care of faculty spouses, and when I was a student, I had watched too many couples disintegrate over this issue. My husband is a clinical psychologist who had sidetracked his career when he left the army to join me in California. We had not asked for a spousal hire at UCLA when he first arrived because he had landed a job at UC

Irvine, some fifty miles away. The commute was difficult, but he had grown used to it. Going back to New Haven would mean that he would have to commute from New Haven to New York. My daughter was barely three years old. I did not want that kind of family life. I had hoped that he eventually would get a job at UCLA. I did not realize then how difficult it is for a black female faculty member, even one of high status, to get a spousal appointment for her husband when he too is black.

That summer, I was asked to become acting chair of the history department, and I accepted the position. I should not have. By late fall, the dean asked me to become chair. Again, I accepted. This was an even bigger mistake. I was now chair of the largest history department in the country—with the largest and one of the most distinguished faculty, the largest number of undergraduate majors, and the largest number of graduate students. The department produces from thirty-five to forty Ph.D.'s a year. It was an extremely difficult job not only because of its magnitude but also because I had a small child, I had relatively little administrative experience, and I was young (relatively), black, and female. I was only one of three black female full professors in the Division of the Social Sciences at UCLA. None of the others had been department chair. Now I, the youngest of the three, was chair of the largest department not only in our division but also in all of UCLA's colleges.

I did have lots of help. My vice chairs were magnificent, and we have remained close friends. I inherited a great manager of our staff, and my black female assistant saved my life more than once. Our faculty members generally are good about teaching and service, with the occasional slacker in either or both. The dean was very solicitous and generous. The department grew even larger and more distinguished when I was chair. We also were able to offer more substantial aid packages to our graduate students, and we successfully refurbished our honors thesis program. I am particularly proud, however, of the reduction of teaching load from five classes per year to four for all ladder faculty and a successful proposal that I put forward that allows faculty to teach in only two, rather than three, quarters.

I had tremendous highs in that job but also some lows. There always was a group of faculty, mostly women but a few men, who had little confidence in my ability and were envious. Even some of my African American peers, at both UCLA and universities around the country, found my new position hard to accept. I remember, for example, going to a Southern Historical Association conference while I was chair and being approached by a black male peer from another university. "You must be tenured by now," he smiled. "Actually, I'm a full professor and department chair," I remarked. "Oh, so you're running the joint," he snapped and walked away. He was not the only one to respond in that manner. After four years, I had had enough. I count that experience as one that reminded me of the joys of research and professional solitude.

Returning to professional life after being department chair can be a little difficult. After being off of the research/writing path for a few years, it is hard to reinsert/assert oneself again. I am doing that now, but not just that. I have just completed a second draft of a book, have had three research articles published, have convened a major conference, have been a distinguished lecturer for the OAH, have served on profession-wide committees, and have finished the second cut of my first documentary.

I have stayed active in UCLA's history department, despite the subtle hostility of some who are still angry that I was chosen as chair before them. My time is spoken of as "the other regime," and few seem to remember that I reduced their teaching load by 20 percent and guaranteed them a research quarter every year. When I completed my four years, my dear friends gave me a nice party that they funded. When my successor ended his three years, he was given a megaparty out of departmental funds that virtually everyone, except me, attended. He also received money for a vacation, a fellowship in his honor, and an enormous raise (and I do mean enormous!). He's a very nice man and we are friends, but I think you will understand why I raise these comparisons. We had an eight-year review last year, mandated by the university. Although I had been chair for four of those eight years, no one asked me to participate in or contribute to the review.

I now chair the Interdepartmental Program in Afro-American Studies. It is severely underfunded and understaffed and has no real physical space—we borrow three offices from a research entity. Still, we have a marvelous faculty and wonderful students—the few that UCLA admits. It reminds me a little of my segregated elementary school without the library, laboratory, musical instruments, and arts equipment. Go figure. This time, however, we have great history lessons. I remain inspired and thankful for my life, my family, and, of course, my work.

## THE DEATH OF DRY TEARS

Have you ever cried dry tears? I learned to weep without visible evidence in my departmental office after the passing of my two senior colleagues, pioneering literary critic Barbara Christian (1943–2000) and renowned poet and activist June Jordan (1936–2002). The loss of these two colleagues and the mounting pressures of a workplace where I felt their absence daily sent me into a tailspin of sadness and worry. The loss of my father and sister followed within the next two years. In the wake of their deaths, however, I discovered two unexpected sources of healing: wet tears and intellectual work. This essay is the story of learning a different way to cry and a different way to work.

I missed both Barbara and June deeply, although I was not especially close to either one. It's too often assumed that black women who work in close quarters should somehow instantly become the best of friends, leaping over the time and steps it takes to cultivate a meaningful professional relationship. I mourned for Barbara and June because I was in awe of their passionate commitment to their scholarly work as well as to their teaching. They were the departmental "stars," and their classes were always packed with students who also followed them around campus and cluttered the hallways outside their offices like groupies backstage at a rock concert.[1]

I felt both proud and humbled to be an assistant professor at the same university that had employed these intellectual heavyweights. Unlike many who teach at top-ranked institutions, I lack an Ivy League degree, and my working-class background placed me outside the inner workings of the academy. Moreover, I am severely challenged in the area of advancing my career via cocktail parties. In fact, I tend to avoid work-related social events (occasions that can allow scholars to flex their knowledge and get the attention of influential people) because of my uneasiness in social circles. It meant a great deal to me to think that I had been hired to work at the University of California, Berkeley, because my senior colleagues in the Department of African American Studies recognized my intellectual potential (of course, I will never really know and my fragile ego has to hold on to the positive).

Although we didn't share an academic discipline, I felt connected to and supported by Barbara and June in several important ways. First, I am also passionate about my work. I know it may sound trite, but I actually love the challenge of finding my own analytical voice in the midst of archival evidence and secondary readings. The process of researching the experiences of black women, particularly those who sought empowerment via comradeship with other black people (black nationalists and Pan-Africanists), helps me to understand the complexity of race, gender, class, and culture in America. What is at stake in this endeavor is not only the importance of black women as historical subjects who have produced transformative knowledge but also our value and worth in a contemporary world that too often devalues us and renders us worthless by linking us to social ills.[2] Second, although Barbara and June were not historians in the traditional sense, their work and teaching reflected keen historical sensibilities and an understanding of the importance of embracing, and at times tussling with, black women subjects. Moreover, both of them had lived in the United States during the era of Jim Crow and had participated in political struggles against racism and sexism.[3] My historical work helped to connect our disparate generations, and I took comfort in knowing that they were always progressive allies during periods of crisis at the university and in political debates and actions in the world beyond the campus.[4] Everything changed, however, with Barbara's diagnosis of cancer in the fall of 1999, four months after I had earned tenure.

When I was told that Barbara was sick with breast cancer, I sincerely believed that she would undergo chemotherapy and radiation treatments and live. After all, June, who had been treated for breast cancer in the early 1990s, was doing fine. Given my optimism, combined with my daily prayers, I was upbeat every time I saw her. In hindsight, I was in a fog of denial; I didn't see that her already-small frame was quickly giving way to the illness. During our visits, my words were few and usually related to her questions regarding the happenings on campus. Sickness did not stop Barbara from being gracious and concerned about others; she always asked how I was doing and advised me to pace myself in the face of increasing departmental demands.

One day following a visit with Barbara, I received a phone call from a massage therapist to schedule an in-home massage. I told the caller that she must have the wrong number, but she quickly explained that the massage was a gift from Barbara Christian. After I got over the shock, I set a date and immediately called Barbara, who informed me (in that strong voice of hers that always sounded to me like Miss Ella Baker's) that I needed to have a massage. I had never had a professional massage before, and with each stroke of the masseuse's hands on my oiled, bare body, I cried wet tears.

Barbara's untimely death on June 25, 2000, occurred during the summer I was serving as acting departmental chair. Although the department planned to hold a large memorial during the fall semester, I felt that those of us who had known and worked with her needed an immediate space to mourn and share, especially since Barbara's home-going service was going to be private. We arranged for a time and space on campus, and when the day came, the room was packed with students and faculty members who took turns acknowledging Barbara's contributions and her impact on their lives. Toward the end of the two hours, I looked up and saw June standing in the back of the room. With a slight dragging of one of her legs, June walked up to the podium, handed me a poem that she had written for her dear friend, and asked me to read it out loud. Not surprisingly, the poem was beautiful, and I did my best to read it slowly as I blinked back tears. Afterward, in an effort to bring closure to the somber occasion, I stated that Barbara was now one of our ancestors—an ancestor, I quickly added, "that we actually knew." Although my "add-on" was more a reflection of my social discomfort than a display of wit, it brought a wide smile and lovely laughter from June, which put me at ease as I wiped away my tears.

The transformation of my wet tears into dry ones began when I was asked to chair the departmental search not to "replace Barbara" (that would have been an impossible task) but to hire a person with a specialization in African American literature. As the hundreds of applications, writing samples, and letters of recommendation filled my office, I felt the weight of the search and the finality of Barbara's death. There were times when I thought I heard her speaking to me from the hallway, telling me everything was going to work out. More often, however, she simply said, "Hello, Ula."

As the committee identified its short list of candidates, the spirit of collective mourning over Barbara's passing turned into a minefield of competing opinions that, as chair, I was left to navigate. My grief was now combined with a load of stress and anxiety. I would sit at my cluttered desk, look at the boxes of files that covered the floor, and silently cry. Those dry tears reached an all-time high when several graduate students approached the search committee and demanded to know why a particular candidate had not received an interview. Showing no respect and styling themselves as the "graduate-student collective," they behaved more like playground bullies than like concerned members of a community. The presence of a graduate representative on the search committee was not enough to satisfy the small swaggering posse, who submitted a letter demanding that the committee make all applicant files available to them for review. For me, the already-taxing search now became a saga of sadness.[5]

I seldom saw June during this time. With a departmental office located near the back elevator, she easily slipped in and out and our paths rarely crossed. I was instantly intimidated, however, when she arrived at the decision-making departmental meeting regarding the candidates' ranking. I had heard that the graduate students were seeking her support, and I didn't have a clue about her position regarding the search. After I gave the report, one of my colleagues stated that we needed to talk about the graduate students' letter that critiqued the process. Before I could reply, June spoke up: "Ula, never respond to a document that people don't have the courage to sign their name to." Praising my efforts, June went on to encourage the faculty to vote in support of the committee's decision. Even though I knew the committee had done nothing wrong, I felt vindicated by June's words of support. This was the last faculty meeting that I can remember June attending. Audaciously opinionated but always friendly toward me, June succumbed to cancer on June 14, 2002.

After June's death and the department's public memorial, I did my best to shake off my sadness, but it loomed over my spirit. Moreover, my departmental and university duties had magnified now that Barbara and June were no longer there as buffers. It seemed as though I now had to be on campus every day for one meeting or another, and I had no energy for my own research. Fortunately, I had already earned tenure; still, something had to change—my sanity and happiness depended on it. Then, instead of getting better, circumstances got worse: my father was diagnosed with inoperable lung cancer in October 2002.

Historians are taught to identify "change over time," but my formal education had not prepared me for the difficulty of living through such rapid transitions heavily laced with confusion. My dry tears continually flowed in my office, taking their toll on my inner self. I was wilting away. The reclamation of my spirit began with a phone call from Professor George Sanchez encouraging me to apply for a position at the University of Southern California. Unsure about whether or not I should submit an application, I sent a courtesy e-mail to my departmental chair indicating that I might apply for a job at USC. His reply, that "faculty are free to go as they please," sealed my desire to leave.

In retrospect, giving a job talk based on a newly formulated project was probably not the best idea. The room at USC was filled with faculty from both the history department and the Program of American Studies and Ethnicity. Although I had timed my presentation, my pacing was off (I spoke too quickly), and it appeared that the audience was only halfheartedly listening. Fortunately, the question-and-answer period, which lasted longer than the talk itself, was a success. Providing thoughtful responses to even the most convoluted questions, I felt that I had redeemed myself. Not long after that, I received a call from the chair of the history department at USC offering me a tenured appointment.

Seizing the opportunity, I took an unpaid leave of absence from Berkeley for the following year (fall 2003–spring 2004) and addressed two major concerns with one move: fleeing the location of my dry tears and moving home to Pasadena (only thirty minutes from USC) so that I could care for my ailing father, William.

Although my new colleagues knew that my father was ill and lived locally, I told only a few people when my younger sister, Yolanda, developed stomach cancer at the beginning of the spring semester of 2004. It happened so fast: she entered the hospital complaining of stomach pains and left it on a hospice program. I took care of my father and sister at home, with the assistance of other family members and hospice workers, while doing my best to fulfill my teaching duties at USC. No longer crying dry tears, I now had a continual headache from weeping drenching wet ones. Living in the midst of my dying loved ones was overwhelmingly painful. My priorities were clear—family first—but I also knew that I had to somehow separate or else I would come apart.[6] Searching my soul for life was what brought me back to my work.

Resuscitating the commitment to my own research projects under the most distressing emotional circumstances required a close examination of my professional patterns. My propensity over the years had been to work hard; now I needed to learn to work smart. For example, administrative duties were gobbling up my time, and given my somewhat antisocial demeanor, I was feeling weary and resentful about attending meetings. (I am convinced that heated departmental meetings shorten the life span of faculty.) Working smarter meant that I had to figure out how to do enough to be considered a good departmental citizen while saving the better part of my intellectual focus for my own research and writing. Evaluating every administrative request as if it were a piece of archival evidence, I began to reject anything that had unclear expectations in terms of the workload. Already behind on several projects, I did not know where to begin to direct my energies—only that I had to begin somewhere. A phone call from Professor Rosalyn Terborg-Penn gave me the directional nudge that I desperately needed.

Professor Terborg-Penn called because I had agreed to write a short essay on black feminism for a book she was co-editing: the second edition of *Black Women in America*. I told her about my family situation and that I had no time to comb the library for new work on black feminism. She listened carefully and gently encouraged me by mapping out how I could build a piece from my previously published work on the subject. After hanging up the phone, I took my laptop into my father's bedroom, sat down in his faded peach-colored chair, and started to open files. The clicking from my dated keyboard jolted my father out of his sleep. As I whispered that I was sorry for waking him, he asked me, "What are you doing?" I told him I was working, and he replied, "That's a good thing for you." As usual, he was right.

I always find it unsettling to reread my published work. It's nerve-wracking to find errors (whether my own or an editor's) or to confront ideas that no longer exactly match my thinking. So you can imagine my hesitation over merging several published articles. Tweaking my old essays, however, revived my spirit in the midst of my dying family. Every time I figured out a new way to think about and categorize black feminism, I would snatch some library time to flesh out my half-baked ideas. With both my father and my sister by my side, I tinkered, sliced, deleted, and ultimately wrote a new piece on black feminism. Frankly, it's not a ground-shaking, knee-slapping, high-fiving essay, but it rejuvenated my intellectual senses, and I was thrilled to finish it and send it to the editor.[7] Days later, on May 13, 2004, my sister passed away at 7:00 A.M., and my father followed at 3:00 P.M. Yes, on the same day. The floodgates opened once again. I thought I would never stop crying.

All of my colleagues from both USC and UC Berkeley showered me with love and kindness. I was surprised to see some of them in attendance at the funeral service. Over the years, I have witnessed how death can bring people together who otherwise would never share the same space. Perhaps it's the fear of dying that allows us to let down our defenses and quit sweating the small stuff. The untimely passing of Barbara, June, my father, William, and especially my thirty-five-year-old sister, Yolanda, affectionately nicknamed Toolie, underscored what we all know but try not to think about—that no one is promised their next breath of life.

Over the next few months, every time I heard an ambulance siren or a particular song on the radio, the tears began to flow again, but the time had come to make some critical professional decisions. USC wanted me to resign from Berkeley (where I was still officially employed), and Berkeley wanted me to return.[8] Both institutional deans were sympathetic, but they also needed to do their job and they needed my answer. Feeling that I could not handle the stress of teaching at this point (I am extremely nervous no matter how much I prepare), I decided not to go back into the classroom at either institution. I had just become reacquainted with the fulfillment I could find in research and writing about black women, and I knew that this was the work I needed to devote myself to in the wake of my father's and sister's deaths. My savings and nonlavish lifestyle would allow me to spend at least one semester doing what I wanted and needed to do: catch up on my work projects and learn how to grieve in a healthy way.

Hospice programs provide support groups that I should have attended. Opting instead to receive counseling over the phone, I found myself quickly ending the conversations; eventually, the volunteers stopped calling. I am not exactly sure why I cut short this potentially helpful communication other than anger at God for taking away my loved ones. The summer months crept by as I planted the ferns and flowers that had been sent by caring friends to my father's home during the month of May. I also created a gaudy scrapbook with photos and encouraging sympathy cards. Keeping busy, however, did not keep pain away from my racing mind. I would read fiction to keep my thoughts occupied, but the last page of every book brought the loss of my family and colleagues rushing back.

Reading a packet of literature from the hospice program (no longer calling, they now sent me pamphlets) helped me to begin beneficial mourning. With the help of certain coping strategies (recognizing that my anger at God underscored the knowledge that a relationship actually existed) and suggestions on how to move forward (allowing myself to experience the cleansing renewal of wet tears), I slowly began to embrace memories and seek out new experiences. At the age of forty-two, I learned to swim after enrolling in a course at the local junior college. Physical movement in the water raised my spirits so much that I easily ignored the laughter of my nineteen-year-old classmates as I awkwardly attempted to learn the different strokes. The class provided exercise (another helpful suggestion from hospice), but more important, it also completely altered my relationship to water—and ultimately to wet tears. Mastering the backstroke allowed me to pray while looking at the sky, tears usually rolling down my cheeks, bringing comfort to my soul. I have since vowed the death of dry tears because wet ones remind me that I am alive.

The sense of spiritual renewal spilled over into my work. Waking up in the wee hours of the morning, I felt a sense of urgency and excitement peppering my commitment to catch up on overdue projects. Driven by a new intellectual freedom, I began to find new meaning in the wonderful interdisciplinary conversations I had had or had overheard in the African American studies department at Berkeley. I would spend days following the trail of interesting endnotes and reading academic books across the disciplines. Taken aback by the legions of new texts on African American women's history, I realized I had been in a time warp. The field had blossomed tremendously since my graduate-school days in the late 1980s. Privileged to be a part of the first generation of scholars to be trained in the history of African American women, I took pride in the sturdy foundation my colleagues had built. Now more than ever, however, my research was first and foremost for me.

Embracing my historical imagination as never before, I had fun chipping away at projects. An anthology on Harlem gave me the opportunity to revisit familiar territory with my newly dilated interdisciplinary eye.[9] After reading the work of dance theorists, for example, I began to consider basic bodily movement in new ways. Incorporating the language of stylized movement with my analysis of organic intellectuals, I began to reconsider the image of women walking the streets of Harlem gathering information. Naming these women "street-strolling scholars" put a fresh spin on a familiar activity; strolling became a way of knowing, further complicating our understanding of activists in an urban space.[10] Exhilarated by these new paths, I tinkered with the street-strolling concept further and developed a set of protocols describing the structured movement. For example, one has to make contact with others, position one's body to hear, and be able to quickly calculate the value of the information one is encountering. Being prepared for a shift in ground tactics (heated arguments) demands a focused lens and a willingness to restrategize an idea. Crowded, dynamic streets engender a certain quickness of mind; thus, street strollers had to master the intellectual skill of thinking on their feet. Personally, thinking creatively about ideas that I could shape freed me from obsessing about ideas linked to my father's and sister's deaths.

Writing the final version of this essay coincided with the end of my self-imposed sabbatical. It was now time to make my decision about where I would return to teach. Feeling blessed to have a choice, I weighed the pros and cons of usc and uc Berkeley. Keenly aware that my quality of life depended on my ability to conduct research, I replayed my experiences at each university and factored in the treatment of other faculty of color.

My brief stint at usc had unfortunately included the passing of Mauricio Mazon, a passionate Chicano historian and one of the few people in the history department who had sincerely befriended me.[11] Separated by one office door, Mauricio had been a wonderful colleague who gave me insight on the hiring practices of the university and the history of faculty of color there. Appreciated and loved by all who really knew him, Mauricio had served as the vice provost for minority affairs and twice as the departmental chair of history, and he was also instrumental in the creation of the Program of American Studies and Ethnicity.[12] I was shocked at his untimely death and embarrassed to learn that after twenty-five years of service, the university had not promoted him to a full professor. Moreover, all of the women associate professors of color that I knew at usc were laden with administrative work.

usc was certainly not an exception in this regard. At most research universities, faculty of color are put in a no-win situation, knowing that publications are the premium tickets to promotion but saddled with burdensome administrative demands that too often keep us from doing our own work. I would be facing that challenge at Berkeley, too, I knew. But I remembered the example of Barbara and June, both of whom had done more than their share of administrative duties over the years but had somehow managed to publish outstanding scholarship, earning them the title of full professor. My hiatus from teaching and committee assignments had affirmed the centrality of scholarly work to my happiness. Moreover, aware that interdisciplinary conversations had nurtured my thinking, I concluded that the African American studies department at UC Berkeley was the better option for me. Envisioning working smart so that I would manage to protect more of my time for my own work, I packed for my return North.

When I got back to the old Berkeley office, it looked bigger than I had remembered it. As I removed books and papers from boxes, the weight of my personal and professional losses lightened. The memory of those losses still occasionally makes me cry, but the tears are not the dry tears of depression anymore; they are tangible wet ones, loaded with energy propelling my life and scholarly work forward.

NOTES

1. I would also add Professor VeVe Clark to this group of senior scholars.

2. See the insightful work of Regina Austin, "Sapphire Bound!," *Wisconsin Law Review* 539 (May/June 1989), which details how single black mothers are often linked to social ills.

3. June Jordan's activism included working with Fannie Lou Hamer, and Barbara Christian's activism against apartheid in South Africa helped push the University of California to divest.

4. John McWhorter, a former member of the Department of African American Studies at UC Berkeley, authored an extremely conservative text, *Losing the Race: Self-Sabotage in Black America* (New York: Free Press, 2000), which linked low academic achievement to black culture. June Jordan correctly dismantled McWhorter's highly reactionary argument. Also, Barbara Christian was active in the student-led protest that culminated in UC Berkeley establishing the Center for Race and Gender.

5. Professor VeVe Clark and Professor Saidiya Hartman provided me unconditional support during this time. After the first search failed to yield an appointment, I served as the chair of the second search committee the following year. Unfortunately, once again, the top applicant declined the offer.

6. My partner, Javane Strong, was extremely supportive and encouraging during this period.

7. Unfortunately, I never received the page proofs for the essay and a major error was

not corrected. The outstanding black feminist work of Professor Joy James was initially cited within the text of the essay but in the published version was removed to an endnote. I was extremely upset by this change and sent a letter of apology to Professor James. See Ula Taylor, "Feminism," in *Black Women in America*, 2d ed., edited by Darlene Clark Hine (New York: Oxford University Press, 2005), 435–43.

8. I am aware that I have been blessed with choices that many people are equally deserving of.

9. The core of my book, *The Veiled Garvey: The Life and Times of Amy Jacques Garvey* (Chapel Hill: University of North Carolina Press, 2002), highlights Garvey's experiences in Harlem.

10. See Ula Taylor, "Street Strolling: Grounding the Theory of Black Women Intellectuals," *Afro-Americans in New York Life and History* 30, no. 2 (July 2006): 153–71.

11. Professor Tom Cox was also a wonderful new colleague who extended himself to me during my USC tenure.

12. Professor Mauricio Mazon authored *The Zoot-Suit Riots: The Psychology of Symbolic Annihilation* (Austin: University of Texas Press, 1984).

# LOOKING BACKWARD IN ORDER TO GO FORWARD

## BLACK WOMEN HISTORIANS AND
## BLACK WOMEN'S HISTORY

One of the reasons why it is hard for me to explain how I came to be a historian of African American history is that I did not grow up in the United States. My family moved to Canada when I was five years old, and I lived there, and at times in Northern Europe, until I was twenty-five and returned to the United States to pursue a Ph.D. in history at Yale University. My years in junior high school, high school, and college (known in Canada as university) took place in the polyglot multiethnic world of Toronto, where neither African Americans nor African American history had much meaning. Moreover, from the age of five onward, I spent more time in my Norwegian father's faraway homeland than I ever did in the United States. African American history is in certain ways not my history. Yet it called me all the same.

A refugee from the Nazis during the Second World War, my father had exciting stories of skiing to freedom in Sweden after the Nazi forces occupying Norway threatened to arrest the law school students at the University of Oslo who protested the occupation. But World War II was long over by the 1960s and 1970s when I grew up. The Allies had won, the Nazis were no more, Norway was free—and I could never pass as a Norwegian in any case. Moreover, my father had abandoned Norway. The war had reshaped his life, leaving him with enduring questions about freedom, fascism, and democracy that led him to become a political scientist—a career that he ended up pursuing in the United States and Canada. If I had any history anywhere around me, it lay in the African American history that shaped my mother's past and was still inexplicable and unfinished in my own life.

In Edmonton, Alberta, and Oslo, Norway, where I spent the second five years of my life, African American history did not exist, so our black and white family was an anomaly that virtually defied explanation. The Ukrainian cleaning woman who commanded our household after my mother enrolled at the University of Alberta to pursue a postgraduate degree warned me to be on the lookout for Orthodox Jews with earlocks—they sounded scary but did not live in Edmonton, as far as I could tell. She had a still more mysterious relationship with the racial irregularities in my own home. "Mrs. Nimko is prejudiced against Jewish people," my mother explained, attempting to assuage my fears that earlocked men with a taste for human flesh posed a threat to the whole family. But her explanation was lost on me: I had no acquaintance with either the idea of prejudice or the existence of Orthodox Jews, who continued to strike me as a terrifying danger that my mother was unaccountably unwilling to acknowledge. "Well she doesn't really like black people either," my mother said, expanding on the concept of prejudice. "She actually doesn't much like me." All of a sudden, I knew what she was talking about without having ever thought about it before. And so race and some vague notion of African American identity surfaced in my life, around the edges, as a mystery. Maybe it is no surprise that I became a historian.

### My Mother's History

I am still startled, looking back, that my mother is the first person who comes to my mind when I think about how I became a historian. All my life, she's been a reluctant historian even of her own life. In recent years, she has taken to writing in an effort to overcome her inhibitions about laying out the facts of her own past. Her African American history was not a history I grew up with. On the contrary, when was I growing up, the facts of her life came out in only the most piecemeal fashion, adding up to a fractured and incomplete story that did not strike me as odd only because I got used to it at such a young age. Most black women learn their family histories from their grandmothers, a friend told me the other day. Not me. My mother was estranged from her mother, far away from her family, and not at all inclined to discuss the past. Indeed, I only learned her mother's name—at age twenty or thereabouts—from my father, who commented one day on the coincidence that both his mother and my mother's mother were named Ruth. Likewise, I found out that my mother was born in Mount Kisco, New York, from either my birth certificate or hers—I can't remember—but it puzzled me because I was under the impression that she was from Virginia, which is more or less true. But every once in a great while, my mother would tell stories about her past, often when she had a point to make.

I did not appreciate some of her stories, especially the ones that revolved around housecleaning and how black women such as her grandmother—whose teaching credentials were of no use to her once she married—had had to master the art of cleaning to the point where a white lady with a white glove who tested their dusting would find no dust. My cleaning skills never passed that test, and I resented the idea that I too might someday have to clean for a living. But I was more humbled and instructed by a story she told me about persevering with schoolwork even when you are feeling discouraged that illustrated the opportunities of my historical moment as well as the challenges of hers and, in the long run, helped me understand that each generation must live up to its opportunities and challenges.

Like all of my mother's stories about her past, this one was unexpected. My mother was inspired to share one of her rare sustained reminiscences late one night during the first semester of my freshman year in college. Popping her head into my room on the way to bed, she found me, the overanxious freshwoman, in tears over my unsuccessful attempt to produce a coherent paper about the nature of tragedy in Shakespeare's *Romeo and Juliet*. First, she tried words of comfort and encouragement, and then she offered to make me tea. But nothing she said or did could break the agonizing writer's block brought on by my inability to say anything interesting about Shakespeare's most famous play. So, at length, her thoughts turned back to her freshman year in college. Did I know, she asked me, that news of her graduation from college was published in the *New York Times*? No, I replied dully, thinking, why is she telling me this?—*I'll* never graduate. But I soon forgot all about my troubles as my mother recounted the story of her college experience.

Her graduation was noteworthy, she said, because she was the first Negro to graduate from St. Mary's College in Indiana. The sister school of Notre Dame, St. Mary's is a Catholic college that recruited my mother when it made its first move to desegregate in 1947. That year, the college admitted four black girls in its freshman class, one of whom was my mother. For my mother, and her grandmother who raised her, St. Mary's early effort at desegregation was nothing less than a Godsend that proved the Lord works in mysterious ways.

Too poor to have much hope of attending college without the scholarship that St. Mary's offered her, my mother accepted the scholarship as a blessing that was as unlikely as it was unexpected. Not only did she not apply for it; she was not even from a Catholic family. Rather, she had converted to Catholicism as an adolescent after attending a Catholic after-school program while living with Louisiana cousins in California. When she got back to Virginia, she reentered the Protestant world in which she had grown up and might have easily drifted back out of the Catholic Church, especially since nobody expressed any great enthusiasm over her conversion to Catholicism. Her grandmother, who was a Baptist, told her she was free to continue to be Catholic as long as she ate fish on Friday. Knowing my mother, it is not hard to see what my great-grandmother was up to: my mother hates fish. But the ruse did not work; she tolerated the fish and remained devout all through high school. A hard worker, she got excellent grades at Armstrong High, the all-black school she attended. But unlike many of her peers, she had no plan for college since nobody could pay for it, until one day in her senior year a teacher at her school informed her that she had won a full scholarship to attend St. Mary's College in Indiana. To this day, my mother has no idea how she came to receive this scholarship. She had not even heard of St. Mary's, let alone applied for a scholarship there. But the award launched her on a long strange journey that is not over yet.

Traveling north from 1940s Richmond, Virginia, where there were plenty of black spaces, as well as signs that said, "No colored allowed," my mother got her first inkling that she was going someplace different when the Pullman porter pulled her aside as she prepared to get off the train in South Bend, Indiana. "Girl, are you sure you know where you are going?," he asked her with concern in his eyes. "Don't no colored ever get off here." And, indeed, my mother and the three other black girls who arrived that year were the only blacks in South Bend, as far as she could tell. Whiter than any place she had ever been, it also seemed to be a town without rules when it came to race. After dutifully observing Virginia's segregation laws her entire life, in South Bend my mother had her first experience of being kicked out of segregated space when she made the mistake of trying to shop at Woolworth's. You could buy but not eat at the Woolworth's in Richmond; you could do neither at the Woolworth's in South Bend.

Indiana was cold, and the nuns' desegregation project had little support among the student body, which included many southerners. So by Christmas, my poor mother was the only black student of the original four who remained. Moreover, she lacked not only black companionship but also white. All through college, she was the only girl at St. Mary's with her own room, as the college did not want to offend any of its students' parents by asking a white girl to room with her. She was set apart from her fellow students in other ways as well. She was a charity case in an affluent student body. Unlike other students, she worked. Moreover, being the only black girl meant being entirely left out of certain college experiences. One day, she noticed that all the girls were getting ready for a big event. After watching the other girls air out their fanciest dresses and do their hair, she finally asked what was going on. "There's a class prom this evening," one of them told her. "I'm sorry, we didn't invite you. . . . It's just that we knew there was no colored boy to be your date."

My mother did not talk about why she stayed on after the others left, but it seemed clear enough. It was her opportunity to go to college. No one in her family even knew where St. Mary's was or had ever traveled to Indiana, but everyone was proud to see her enrolled there and fully expected her to finish. "South Bend Takes Negroes" (in stride), ran the story (which was actually published during my mother's sophomore year) when she was at last joined by two more black women. Glossing over this history, the *New York Times* reported, "Authorities at St. Mary's say that the 'girls are well received now, and all opposition has broken down in clubs and dormitory life, and, of course our classes.' "[1]

## My History

My mother's story did not help me finish my paper, but it stayed with me all the same. My mother's history is not mine, but it has framed my history and my understanding of history. Even growing up outside of the States—as the United States is called in Canada—I never felt very far removed from the history of exclusion and racial discrimination encapsulated in my mother's college experience. My curiosity about that history drove me to explore American history as an undergraduate at the University of Toronto and also forestalled any nostalgia about the past in my collegiate mind. Whereas my fellow students could fantasize romantic pasts for themselves in the mists of North America's Anglo-European history, I could not get past the fact that interracial marriage was illegal in many parts of the United States prior to the Supreme Court's *Loving v. Virginia* ruling in 1967. Indeed, my father's study contained issues of *Progressive Magazine* dating back to when my parents became engaged in the late 1950s that had articles that made clear that most of my parents' white contemporaries would have regarded their marriage as ill-advised. *Progressive*'s left-leaning writers supported interracial marriages on principle but fretted over the tragic children often produced by such unions—at that time, mixed-race children were evidently considered to be at high risk for criminality and mental instability. I couldn't help being relieved that I was born after the 1950s and that my parents had produced a family despite these perceived dangers.

Moreover, such issues were further complicated whenever my family traveled back to the United States and especially when I returned there to go to graduate school in the late 1980s. In the United States, I could not help but be aware of a racial regime quite different from any I had encountered in Norway or Canada. When we were with my mother's family, most of whom had migrated to California by my teens, we visited black people, who were scarce in my experiences above the forty-ninth parallel. And while black people were wholly familiar to me, when I returned to the United States from elsewhere, I noticed that African Americans were preoccupied with another group that was rarely discussed in racial terms in Canada or Norway: white people.

Black discussions of white people would become the subject of both my dissertation and my first book, *The White Image in the Black Mind* (2000), and they defined the distinct world of American race relations for me long before that—historians are never very far removed from their topics, I guess. While there were plenty of white people in Canada and Norway, no one ever talked about them as white people per se. In Norway, where virtually everyone is white, people were first and foremost Norwegian or not. Torontonians tended to group people along the lines of religion or nationality. WASP versus Catholic was an important distinction among Canadian nationals, and beyond that, Toronto housed immigrants of every conceivable nationality and color. But only among African Americans were white people routinely discussed as a singular marked entity.

My African American relatives could not get through any story without identifying any white people involved not by name but as a generic: "this white woman did that," "only white people put sugar on their grits," "only white people shop there." My relatives varied greatly when it came to skin color, so much so that the sharp distinctions they made between themselves and white people could sometimes fold into comedy. But even the comedy seemed to reify the race distinctions. When I was visiting my great-aunt Irma in Oakland one day, for example, one such comedy unfolded as one of my cousins was regaling us with an amusing account of the frustrations of her day. Nothing had gone right, she told us. "I really finally lost it when I was driving back from the supermarket and got stuck behind this old white lady who was driving ten miles an hour. She was just poking along, and I was cursing her out, talking about these old white ladies who hold up traffic as if they own the whole damn world," my cousin said, beginning to chuckle. Grabbing my aunt's hand, she was laughing in earnest as she went on to explain: "And then, just as I got really mad at the white lady, I realized that she was you, Aunt Irma! That old white lady was you." A light-skinned woman with wavy hair, Irma could easily be taken for white by anyone driving behind her (and she drove none too quickly, for that matter). But the mistake was somehow uproarious all the same and cracked my great-aunt up as well.

Such moments seemed to suggest that the color line wasn't exactly about color, for blacks or for whites. Rather, the question of whether a person was white or black transcended what could be seen by the naked eye. In college, these conjectures would get me thinking about the black side of racial thought.

While discussions of the ways in which white people believed that color transcended the naked eye were well documented in the texts I read in my history course on race relations, the same could not be said of black ideas on the same subject. Among whites, an endless array of depressing racist theories, which changed over time but never quite went away, had long held that black people were different and inferior to white people by virtue of rationales that included religious inferiority (black people were under the curse of Ham), biological inferiority (black people were descended from a separate creation, closer to apes than whites), and intellectual inferiority (black people had lower IQs and SATs). But such theories were never popular among African Americans, so what were they talking about when they described white people in racial terms?

My interest in the history of racial thought took me to graduate school and back to the United States. Indeed, getting to know the United States as an adult produced new questions. When I headed off to New Haven in 1987 to study nineteenth-century African American and American history at Yale University, my knowledge of the modern United States was sketchy at best. My only image of Connecticut came from old Hollywood movies featuring pretty New England towns—films that, come to think of it, may not have even been set in Connecticut. Nonetheless, they allowed me to envision my new home as a peaceful and bucolic place, complete with rustic houses separated by white picket fences, until I talked to my mother, who had actually visited New Haven at some point in her life. "No sweetie," she told me, "it's more like a ghetto—unless it's changed."

She wasn't far wrong. In decline since the 1950s, New Haven was hit hard by the waves of suburbanization and deindustrialization that shrank American cities during the post–World War II era. Hardest hit were the city's African Americans, who arrived during the wartime boom years when work was plentiful and who predominated among those left behind as the city declined. When I moved there in the late 1980s, New Haven was one of the poorest cities in America. Poverty there was concentrated in the city's black neighborhoods, along with attendant evils such as crime and crack. In many ways, it was a terrible place to live. But, especially in its odd symbiosis with the world of privilege at Yale, it gave me a crash course in American race relations—something I did not even know I needed to learn.

Most striking to me in New Haven was the racial segregation, which I hesitate even now to call by that name since no one else ever did. Newcomers were constantly besieged with instructions about all of the places in New Haven no one should ever go—which turned out to be pretty much all of New Haven's black and/or Puerto Rican neighborhoods. Such neighborhoods figured prominently in the crime map handed out by the Yale police, which marked the locations of recent crimes in the city with little black dots. On the map, the black neighborhoods to the east and west of campus were covered by clusters of dots so dense and overlapping that you couldn't even make out the streets. I would soon learn that the information was not wrong—Yalies foolhardy enough to settle in such areas often became crime victims. But nothing in my previous experience had prepared me for New Haven's grim realities or their racial axis. I moved there from Toronto, where my family had ultimately settled. A racially and ethnically diverse city far larger than New Haven, Toronto had no places where anyone could not go and few places where I had not been.

I ended up being not quite sure what to do with this advice. Much of it came from graduate students with cars who lived in the suburbs and drove to campus, avoiding New Haven entirely except as a place to park. But my only form of transportation other than walking remained my bike; I couldn't make it to the suburbs or avoid the city. Moreover, the very idea of avoiding New Haven confused me. Many white people seemed to be trained to not enter black neighborhoods, even during the day, while black students, as well as some of the more adventurous Yalies, gave more measured advice. The rules were frustrating and not all that clear. Surely I could walk down Whalley Avenue in broad daylight? How else would I be able to go to the health food store? Over time, I developed answers to these questions that had more to do with conditions in New Haven than with my relationship to the color line. Trial and error taught me that New Haven buses could be ridden, as needed, despite the fact that their ridership was almost exclusively black—so much so that some riders referred to the bus that crisscrossed New Haven as "the slave ship." But the southern-born mothers, grandmothers, children, and assorted others who traveled to New Haven's suburban malls and grocery stores on these buses posed no threat to anyone. However, the same could not be said of the inhabitants of some of the city's roughest neighborhoods, where poverty, drugs, and town-gown tensions made for some genuinely dangerous streets.

"Why don't you just ask your parents to buy you a car?," one of my white classmates asked with real curiosity after listening to me worry out loud about whether the dangers of bike riding after dark in New Haven outweighed those posed by riding the Yale shuttle. Her question underscored another way in which Americans were different from Canadians that I found almost as striking as the racial divide that split New Haven streets: namely, the affluence of many of my white classmates, as well as much of Yale's undergraduate population. Prior to that moment, I had never met anyone who assumed that all students' parents would have no trouble buying them a car. In the Toronto neighborhoods where I grew up, Canadians were generally comfortable without being wealthy, and they expected their adult children to fend for themselves. And in Scandinavia, where I had lived after I finished high school, prosperity was the norm, but wealth was rare and subject to high taxes that limited lavish spending even among the well-to-do. In urban areas, few young people owned cars. Although not untouched by distinctions of class, postsecondary education in both Canada and Northern Europe was public, affordable, and accessible. Places like Yale, where the children of the middle class, the affluent, and the truly wealthy seemed to congregate—alongside a smattering of others—did not exist.

Indeed, when it came to class as well as race, it soon became clear to me that the only Yalies whose backgrounds I understood tended to be African Americans. My strongest connection to the United States, once we left it, involved my mother's family. As a result, although many of the people I met in the United States came from backgrounds that seemed utterly unfamiliar to me, black Americans were an exception. The black students I met at Yale were from all over but tended, like most African Americans, to have southern roots if you went back far enough. And we had certain things in common as a result. Southern-inflected food, manners, and idioms were points of connection for many of us, whatever the specifics of our backgrounds. And while our class backgrounds were more diverse, very few of us came from any kind of real money or the desperate poverty that surrounded us in New Haven's black neighborhoods. Old money, Ivy League traditions, and any sense that Yale was a place where people like us would inevitably end up were rarer still. We were all strangers in a strange land and formed strong ties as a consequence.

Unlike my mother, we had all entered American higher education well after the early years of desegregation and had little isolation to complain about. I was the only person of African American descent in my Yale history cohort. But other students entered the program during years immediately preceding and following my arrival at Yale—probably one or two a year. Bracketed by this steady flow, I met black students from the years before I came and took classes, studied, and traded dissertation chapters with students who arrived after me. Moreover, within the close confines of New Haven, African American students from across the disciplines all knew each other, and many had ties to other minority-group students through campus connections and programs that brought together students of color. For instance, I got to know many Latino students when I took a job teaching writing in a summertime enrichment program Yale offered to minority freshmen.

To my inexperienced eye, exactly how issues of class, color, and gender would shape the academic lives of black Ph.D.'s of my generation was by no means clear. How could it be clear? Those of us in the field of history came into a profession far more diverse with regard to both race and gender than it had been even a decade earlier, but the change was too recent to have completed even one generational cycle. We met many African American students but few African American faculty, almost none of whom were women. And although white women faculty were more numerous, when it came to gender, it was impossible not to notice the extent to which large numbers of women were a recent addition to the Yale community. If nothing else, women's restrooms were hard to find, and many of them still had urinals.

Despite such practical realities, however, I remained largely oblivious to issues of gender while I was in graduate school, perhaps because male-dominated academic institutions were not new to me. As an undergraduate, I had attended the University of Stockholm and the University of Toronto, where my father taught. I had worked with mentors who were almost exclusively male, women faculty being rare at both institutions. Not unaware of sexism or of the fact that I had encountered no female intellectual role models at the University of Toronto, I relished the sheer size of the school. Classes there were usually large, making most students utterly anonymous to their professors. I felt that I could establish my academic credentials by writing excellent essays and exams and chose to bypass the gender politics of closer encounters whenever possible. Merit, I assured myself with a naïveté that now seems almost unaccountable, would take me wherever I needed to go.

Given my particular experience and convictions, it is perhaps not surprising that I remained largely unaware of the field of African American women's history while I was in graduate school. As a history graduate student in the late 1980s, I was following in the footsteps of African American female pioneers who were barely a decade or two ahead of me, but I did not know it, nor did I know much about their contributions to my field.

Like my mother, these pioneers were often the first African American women to enter their institutions. Trained in isolation and subject to challenges from black men as well as whites of both sexes, my role models came of professional age in the 1980s and 1990s and were acutely conscious of gender as well as race—in part because of the double burden they posed. Black women historians such as Deborah Gray White, Darlene Clark Hine, Evelyn Brooks Higginbotham, Elsa Barkley Brown, and Nell Irvin Painter not only carved out a new place for black women in their profession but also created a new historical subject: black women. Their pioneering works were transforming African American history just as I entered the academy in ways that still have yet to be fully recognized and appreciated by the profession at large.

Indeed, any appreciation was slow in coming. In the quiet groves of intellectual history where I toiled during my years at Yale, Deborah Gray White's *Ar'n't I a Woman: Female Slaves in the Plantation South* (1985) did not trouble our classroom debates over Eugene Genovese's much-discussed class analysis of slavery in *Roll, Jordan, Roll: The World the Slaves Made* (1976). Usually at issue in the debates over that book, as well as other contemporaneous scholarly controversies over slavery, was the masculinity of the slaves and by implication the maleness of black men, although these categories went wholly unmarked in our discussions of whether Genovese's Marxist analysis captured the true dynamics of the slave-master relationship. Indeed, I read Elizabeth Fox-Genovese's spin-off project, *Within the Plantation Household: Black and White Women in the Old South* (1988), which told an oddly entwined history of black and white plantation women from within the confines of her husband's class analysis, well before I ever came across White's analysis of slavery as a gender system built on black women's reproductive labor.

By the time I finished graduate school in 1993, however, even Yale faculty had begun to notice black women's insistence that the study of African American history embrace both genders. Pioneering black feminist texts such as *All the Women Are White, All the Blacks Are Men, but Some of Us Are Brave: Black Women's Studies* (1982) stated the problem quite plainly: the history of black women was synonymous with neither women's history, which focused largely on chronicling the activities of white women, nor African American history, which was male-centered. Moreover, historians such as Evelyn Brooks Higginbotham complicated the issue by suggesting that not just black women but the relationship between social constructions of race and gender required more attention in both these fields of scholarship. Her influential 1992 article, "African-American Women's History and the Metalanguage of Race," called for a more complex historical understanding of the interplay between race and gender in studies of societies where "racial demarcation is endemic to the social fabric and heritage."[2] Adding a new dimension to white feminist Joan Scott's forceful 1986 call for the study of gender as a useful category of historical analysis, Higginbotham noted that in many societies "gender identity is inextricably linked to and even defined by racial identity." She noted by way of example: "In the Jim Crow South, prior to the 1960s, and in South Africa until very recently, for instance, little black girls learned at an early age to place themselves in the bathroom for 'black women,' and not that for 'white ladies.' As such a distinction suggests, in these societies the representation of both gender and class is colored by race."[3]

Clearly, black women academics had brought new questions into the academy, questions that I began to wrestle with once I left Yale. I had the good fortune to get a job at Rutgers, a women's history and women's studies powerhouse, and for the first time, I had to answer to female colleagues—both black and white. They had questions that made me rethink not only my own work but, in time, much of American and African American history. Like most young scholars, I spent the first years of my professional life expanding and revising my dissertation into a book, so the gender questions began there. When I discussed my work on *The White Image in the Black Mind* at Rutgers, my female colleagues almost always asked me: "Why did so few black women write about race in the nineteenth century?" It was a question I had not encountered at Yale and had never encountered among intellectual historians, whose work focused almost exclusively on men. The intersection between race and gender was an unmarked corner in my historical training.

So for me, works such as Evelyn Higginbotham's article on the metalanguage of race were nothing short of revolutionary. Her work, along with that of other sister academics such as my new colleague at Rutgers, Deborah Gray White, helped me grasp gender's central but unrecognized place in the history of racial thought. Their ideas pushed me toward a new way of discussing the social construction of race as largely made up of racialized gender ideals and insufficiencies, many of which were embraced by thinkers on both sides of the color line. Accordingly, as my dissertation became a book, it ended up underscoring that the domestic ideology of true womanhood that prevailed for much of the century made race and racism particularly difficult subjects for black women to address directly. Not just a gender ideal, womanhood was a racial ideal even more narrowly circumscribed than the racial manhood black men sought to claim. The elusive privileges of true womanhood were accorded only to women who maintained a "ladylike" decorum in an era in which it was considered unseemly for women to enter the public sphere. Little wonder, my book maintained, that nineteenth-century black women were for so long, as Anna Julia Cooper would comment in 1892, "mute and voiceless."[4]

From the vantage point of the 1990s at least, the pioneering work of black women historians such as Higginbotham and White promised to steer the historical profession toward a more sustained engagement with the political, social, and intellectual history of black women, as well as toward a greater appreciation of the many intersections between race and gender. Important works on the history of black women's activism by Elsa Barkley Brown, Nell

Irvin Painter, Darlene Clark Hine, Tera Hunter, and others suggested that attention to black women as both subjects and actors in the public sphere would transform our understandings of topics such as black leadership during Reconstruction, race and representation in the abolitionist movement, the gendered character of the Great Migration, and Progressive Era urban history.

All blacks are not men, and scholars of African American women's history demonstrated that careful attention to the activities of black women could greatly enlarge our understanding of the history of the black community as a whole. They also showed that subjects that have been particularly hard to get at as a result of the long exclusion of black men from traditional forms of male political participation, such as voting and labor unions, open up when black women's political activities and labor struggles are considered. The history of black women's activism points us to the many more informal venues that have long sustained black communities and engaged the political energies of both black men and black women. Such sites include men's and women's clubs, African American churches of all denominations, black student movements, and African American kinship networks and remind us that racial oppression has structured gender relations inside the black community as well as outside, giving both black women and black men distinctive histories that cannot be represented by studies of African American history that privilege male leadership and activism.

### The Evidence of Things Not Seen: The Invisible History of Invisible Women

If black women's scholarship and scholarly status have progressed by leaps and bounds since my mother's college days, in recent years I have begun to wonder how far we have come and to think about how far we have to go. Black women's history is still largely neglected outside the fields of African American and women's history. Intellectual history, my own field, remains largely dominated by white male scholars studying white men. Moreover, even works on the intellectual history of American women, such as Linda Kerber's *Towards an Intellectual History of Women* (1997) and Elaine Showalter's *Inventing Herself: Claiming a Feminist Heritage* (2001), largely ignore black women. Oprah Winfrey is the major African American player in Showalter's book, and black women authors are featured on only two pages of Kerber's book. Black feminist scholars such as Elsa Barkley Brown have documented distinct intellectual traditions, such as "womanism," among African American women, and students of black women's literature have chronicled prescient and pioneering work on the intersection of race and gender among black women novelists and journalists during the Women's Era, as the late-nineteenth-century renaissance in American women's leadership and literature is known. But black women are still so rarely represented as thinkers that Farah Jasmine Griffin and I dedicated the better part of two successive fall semesters to a fruitless attempt to secure NEH funding for a collaborative research project entitled "Towards an Intellectual History of Black Women," which would have brought together a collective of scholars in this field to carve out new historiographic territory. Alas, both of our collaborative-research grant applications were turned down, and during years in which the major African American–themed project that the NEH funded centered on black mortuary traditions—even dead people rated higher than black women thinkers. One NEH committee member questioned whether black women's intellectual activities merited study and why history featured so prominently in our proposal, while another complained that the subject had already been addressed—dismissing our distinguished roster of subjects and participants.

Moreover, in recent years, I've found that intellectual history is difficult to combine with black women's history—with or without the support of the NEH. Current historical perspectives on Sally Hemings are a case in point that I've discovered since beginning work on an ever-expanding project on antebellum black views of Thomas Jefferson. This subject has proved to be a minefield with many danger zones, not the least of which is Hemings. Journal referees have had a host of problems with my subject. One dubious reader suggested that I needed to avoid any suggestion that Jefferson was a hypocrite—a difficult charge given that the antebellum-era black thinkers whose thought I discuss often say as much. While no one has written about African American views of Thomas Jefferson, several others maintained, nobody needs to: black critiques of Jefferson sound "familiar." And one particularly nefarious reader at the *Journal of American History* twice insisted that my subject needed to be "centered in a substantial context dealing with the post 1975 work on Sociobiology"—evidently so I could better consider the possibility that Jefferson's outrageous comments about black biological inferiority were correct. He kindly included a bibliography of modern-day sociobiologists (who insist that nature is more important than nurture) whom I should consult before revisiting my subject. The authors he suggested, to name only the most well known, included R. J. Herrnstein and Charles Murray, who wrote *The Bell Curve* (1994), and J. Phillipe Rushton, the author of *Race, Evolution, and Behavior* (1999), a modern-day manifesto for scientific racism with more supporters among white supremacists than among fellow scientists.

Still more egregious elements of this project, however, have been published discussions of Sally Hemings that I've had to follow to keep up-to-date on my subject. A testament to the ways in which the sparsely documented history of African American women is often configured in fantastical terms, many recent discussions of Hemings are so ahistorical that they raise alarming questions about the extent to which scholarship on African American women's history has crossed the color line or successfully challenged the master narrative.

Sally Hemings was long viewed by mainstream historians as little more than an ignominious rumor trailing the father of American democracy.[5] Only in 1998 did she become a historical figure. That year, DNA tests performed on her descendants and members of the Jefferson family at long last documented blood ties between the two families, revising more than a century of Jefferson scholarship. Of course, her relationship with Jefferson was never in dispute among the antebellum black thinkers I've long studied. And the possibility of a Jefferson-Hemings liaison, likewise, has posed no contradictions to any understanding of slavery illuminated by the historiography on black women. Relationships between slave owners and slave women, while rarely talked about by white southerners, were both common and inherently coercive, as scholars of female slavery such as Deborah Gray White maintain. The product of a power structure that made the question of "whether or not slave women desired relationships with white men immaterial," they underscore that for black women slavery involved sexual as well as racial exploitation.

Yet this is a history that many Jefferson scholars have felt alarmingly and unaccountably free to ignore as they have revisited the Jefferson-Hemings relationship in the post-DNA era. For example, eminent Jefferson biographer Joseph Ellis, who long considered Jefferson too fine a man to consort with his slave maid, now celebrates Jefferson as a man made all the more human by his flaws. Published in 1997, his Pulitzer Prize–winning work, *American Sphinx: The Character of Thomas Jefferson*, maintained that Jefferson, who was widowed in his thirties, remained celibate thereafter, all those rumors about Sally Hemings notwithstanding: "Jefferson consummated his relations with women at a more rarefied level, where the palpable realities of physical intimacy were routinely sublimed to safer and more sentimental regions. He made a point of insulating himself from direct exposure to the unmitigated meaning of both sex and slavery." Just a year later, however, Ellis assimilated the DNA evidence into his Jefferson hagiography without missing a beat. Writing in the *New York Times*, he maintained that the DNA evidence of a Jefferson-Hemings liaison would only enhance the founding father's stature: "Our heroes—and especially Presidents—are not gods or saints, but flesh-and-blood humans. . . . Within the larger world the dominant response will be Jefferson is more human, to regard this as evidence of his frailties, frailties that seem more like us. The urge to regard him as an American icon will overwhelm any desire to take him off his pedestal."[6]

Evidently no amount of exposure to "the unmitigated meaning of both sex and slavery" could compromise Jefferson's reputation in some quarters. Instead, in recent years, I've watched with surprise as historians have abruptly reframed the liaison as a romance. We learn, for example, from eminent historian of the Virginia gentry Rhys Isaac that "Sally Hemings bore Thomas Jefferson's children and *his* children *only*. She loved him and probably he her." Moreover, Isaac goes on to suggest that Jefferson and Hemings's long and monogamous union made them akin to a married couple. Like "most married partners throughout the ages," they shared "a kind of love and affection within a framework of profound inequalities as to power and freedom."[7] And likewise, Jefferson biographer Christopher Hitchens is confident that "Jefferson and Hemings did not have a 'master-slave relationship' in the usual vile sense that it is normally understood. . . . In status, Sally Hemings was barely a slave."[8]

Moreover, these ideas seem to have taken hold even outside the realm of Jefferson scholarship. When, at a conference last year, I made the seemingly uncontroversial argument that Hemings's relationship with Jefferson could not be discussed without reference to the slave system that framed it, a furious commentator accused me of "ruling out love" in my discussion of Hemings and Jefferson. Like Isaac and Hitchens, this preeminent historian insisted on placing Sally Hemings outside historiography of women under slavery. Nowhere in the work on female slavery by scholars such as Deborah Gray White, Brenda Stevenson, and Stephanie Camp do we find the history of black women who were slaves in name only and all but married to their loving owners.

I am not sure how love, if we could find it, would change the vastly unequal power relations that framed such relationships. But I do know that everything we know about both the history of women under slavery and the basic facts of Sally Hemings's life testifies against casting her relationship with Jefferson as a romance, which makes the post-DNA history of Sally Hemings ever more distressing. Described by her son, Madison, as Jefferson's "concubine," Hemings remained enslaved all her life, receiving only the "gift of her time" after Jefferson's death—such gifts were an informal form of freedom that evaded the difficulties and expense of actually manumitting a slave. And likewise, the four children that Hemings had with Jefferson who survived to adulthood did not benefit from any real filial largesse. Jefferson allowed the older two, Beverly and Harriet, to "escape" after age twenty-one and made provisions in his will to free

Hemings's two youngest children, Madison and Eston, at the same age. Gradually emancipated by their father, all four Hemings children probably served as slaves long enough to pay for their keep by the logic of gradual-emancipation plans used to free slaves in the post-Revolutionary era. Under these plans, slave children worked well into adulthood in order to compensate their owners for property losses involved in setting them free. Moreover, neither Sally nor her children received anything more than freedom from Jefferson, whose will directed that his entire estate be auctioned off to support his white daughter, Martha. Sold alongside domestic animals and farm equipment were 130 slaves, many of whom were relatives of Sally and her children.

### Back to the Future: Scholarship, History, and Hope

"Mama's Baby, Papa's Maybe" is how the black feminist critic Hortense Spillers describes the reproductive burdens of black women, and her words certainly seem to apply to Sally Hemings's experience.[9] They also underscore that the history of slave women defies romanticization and is told without the aid of sentimental fiction in works of black women scholars. So, too, is the history of black women more generally. But as the latest excesses in the Hemings saga suggest, both black women scholars and black women's history still lie outside the mainstream scholarship that often predominates in both the academy and the public sphere. Carrying the double burden of race and gender in the academy, as elsewhere, black women historians are frequently bearers of unpleasant and unpopular news. Many Americans are unwilling to consider the possibility that the gracious, scholarly Thomas Jefferson was a typical slave owner and Sally Hemings a typical slave—as I've found every time I've spoken on this subject. Moreover, the more we know about the history of black women, the more unpleasantness we seem to uncover. Recent historical work by young black historians such as Crystal Feimster and Leslie Brown suggests that black women were subject to more violence, sexual abuse, and economic exploitation than has been previously acknowledged.

However, black women historians both illuminate and exemplify one equally important countervailing force—the relentless resistance with which African American women have met racial and sexual discrimination and exploitation that for so long excluded them from the best of what American society has to offer. Schooled in hard work and raised by determined mothers like my own, many black women scholars bring a multigenerational commitment to the efficacy of effort into their academic careers. We walk in the footsteps of the women who have gone ahead of us, not in the least because so many of us were raised to believe that black women have to work twice as hard as anyone else to get anywhere. I know I was, as much as I hate to admit that my mother was right on that subject. I suspect she still is.

African American women historians have yet to establish a truly secure place in the academy or to topple the fictions that make African American history anything other than central to the story of American history and black women anything other than prime movers in both histories. So as historians, then, perhaps what African American women still need to teach their students and their public is that we must keep looking back in order to go forward. By studying and honoring the strong and determined women who preceded us, maybe we can learn how they found the courage, persistence, and optimism to overcome obstacles far bigger than the daunting ones we still face today. And better yet, maybe we can acquire and pass on the strength that allowed them to do so.

This April, I'll return to St. Mary's College with my mother to see her honored as the college's first black graduate, more than fifty years after the fact. We'll celebrate one step in the right direction.

NOTES

1. *New York Times*, February 7, 1949.

2. Evelyn Brooks Higginbotham, "African-American Women's History and the Metalanguage of Race," *Signs* 17, no. 2 (Winter 1992): 254.

3. Ibid.

4. Anna Julia Cooper, *A Voice from the South* (New York: Oxford University Press, 1988), I.

5. Writing in 1995, Joseph Ellis described the Sally Hemings story as "a tin can tied to Jefferson's reputation by James Callendar in 1802 that has rattled through the ages and the pages of the history books ever since" ("Money and the Man from Monticello," *Reviews in American History* 23, no. 4 [1995]: 588).

6. "DNA Evidence Finds Jefferson Fathered Slave Child," *New York Times*, November 1, 1998; Joseph Ellis, *American Sphinx: The Character of Thomas Jefferson* (New York: Alfred Knopf, 1997), 306–7. This quotation appears only in the first edition. Ellis removed this statement in his more recent edition.

7. Rhys Isaac, "Monticello Stories Old and New," in *Sally Hemings and Thomas Jefferson: History, Memory, and Civil Culture*, edited by Jan Lewis and Peter S. Onuf (Charlottesville: University of Virginia Press, 1999), 119.

8. Christopher Hitchens, *Thomas Jefferson* (New York: HarperCollins, 2005), 61.

9. Hortense Spillers, "Mama's Baby, Papa's Maybe: An American Grammar Book," *Diacritics: A Review of Contemporary Criticism* 17 (1987): 65–81.

# Chana Kai Lee

## JOURNEY TOWARD A DIFFERENT SELF

### THE DEFINING POWER OF ILLNESS, RACE, AND GENDER

The Rock of Gibraltar myth be damned. The life of a black woman academic can be just as eventful and fragile as the lives of others. Over the past four years, I have learned some very tough lessons about my body, my character, and my professional community. When I pull back from the agonizing intricate details of every lived moment, I get some helpful perspective. From a distance, I can see that my experiences have been about choices, some that I have been fully aware of and others that I came to realize only through the process of living and looking back. But this philosophical way of seeing goes only so far in capturing what I have endured.

Truth be told in the language of the heart and psyche, life has brought me to my knees in recent years, and I have been reeling and doing my best to put the pieces back together, one day at a time. I have cycled through a range of consuming emotions, mostly unbearable anger. If the prevailing wisdom is correct, then anger really does hold a core of sadness. In my case, it has been an unremitting sadness about my body's betrayal and an exhausting frustration with Western medicine's inability to make me better, despite considerable time and expense.

Ambivalence and slight shame have come with some of this territory as well. I find it hard to present an imperfect, diseased self to a world often unready to receive me in a reasonable and humane way. This seems especially true in the workplace, where some of my more insensitive colleagues shocked and disappointed me in my weakest hour. I have arrived at a deeper awareness of just how limited the academic world can be in understanding black women, illness, and our relationship to our work. The revelations have been staggering and dispiriting. But at some point in this journey, I also have come to appreciate the tremendous care and generosity of those still in touch with their own humanity—especially my small, precious circle of African American women friends within the academy. Their loving support has anchored me at critical junctures, and my body, mind, and spirit have continued to move along in the face of all that has been so unpleasant.

I am still here.

On Friday, September 6, 2002, I heard the dreaded word for the first time in relation to my own body: STROKE. During a visit with my rheumatologist, I casually mentioned some strange but fleeting experiences I had while lecturing to my large women's studies class. On those occasions, my tongue did not go where I intended as I spoke. My words came out in a bizarre staccato cadence, as if my brain were short-circuiting. Dr. Kate[1] recalled some recent lab work that revealed the presence of antibodies that cause blood clotting. The condition occurs in many individuals with systemic lupus erythematosus (or "lupus"), an autoimmune disease that affects African American women disproportionately. Doctors had diagnosed my condition back in 1991. I had lived with the disease past the all-important ten-year mark, when my survival chances jumped to 90 percent. For the most part, my disease course had been relatively mild and uneventful.

When Dr. Kate mentioned the lab results, I was not too concerned. I had made considerable progress in addressing what I had always considered my main risk factor for stroke—obesity. In August 2001, I made a radical shift in lifestyle. I began exercising regularly and eating differently. I worked with a wonderful nutritionist and a relentless personal trainer for a little less than a year and lost seventy-six pounds. I felt great. I had more energy as I learned to be in my body in new and healthy ways. New activities gave me boundless pleasure: running, weight lifting, hiking, boating, fishing, camping, and gardening. I turned forty years old and felt incredibly fortunate to reach this milestone. After seven miserable years in Indiana, I was creating a "new life" now in Georgia and loving the adventure. I seemed to be coping quite well with a serious chronic illness. My life was not severely limited.

Like most caring physicians, Dr. Kate applauded these changes and affirmed my optimistic attitude. I expected to go into remission at any time. However, in my case, lupus posed its own stroke risk. She suggested that I begin taking an anticoagulant in the meantime. We agreed that I would check into the hospital for outpatient testing the following week. She told me to call her cell phone if something came up over the weekend.

I awoke Sunday morning feeling strange. I was weak and a bit disoriented. Something was not quite right. I remembered the anticoagulant prescription that I had placed in my book bag as I left my doctor's office. I sent my partner Alicia to get it filled. When she returned, I took the medicine and decided to begin my Sunday routine, which included preparing a PowerPoint lecture for my Tuesday-Thursday class. Trying to ignore the discomfort, I alternated between sitting at the computer and lying in bed. Nothing was bringing me much relief. My head was still spinning, and Alicia observed that I appeared listless.

Monday, I woke up unable to feel my right arm, and my headache persisted. Finally, I called Dr. Kate, and she directed me to meet her right away at Piedmont Hospital, where a nurse and technician rushed me to radiology for a CAT scan. I ended up in a hospital room on the "neuro" floor, where a team of nurses started an IV and administered the blood-thinner Heparin. (Over the next three months, I would learn more than I cared to know about strokes and stroke treatment.)

As the Heparin coursed through my veins, I began to stabilize. Slightly more lucid, I was fatigued beyond words and still had little feeling on my right side. A comical-looking father-and-son team of neurologists visited me and told me what we suspected. They diagnosed a cerebral vascular accident (CVA) or stroke and told me that I was lucky. Their prognosis was simple, straightforward, and good. Barring any complications, I would make a complete recovery without any significant deficits. They emphasized that my young age was in my favor and noted that the sooner I began physical therapy the better. Dr. Kate soon entered the room fumbling through film, the radiologist's reports, and my medical file. She added some details about what happened, including a description of a blood clot on my brain. As I learned to do throughout most of this ordeal, I checked out and went to some place deep inside of me. I felt lucky but very sad. I needed to reflect. I could not believe that this was happening to me.

On Tuesday afternoon, I spoke with the chairs of the history and women's studies programs at my university. I thanked them for their phone calls and flowers. (Alicia had sent them an e-mail on late Monday.) I was groggy and still in a detached space, although my mood was lifting a bit. Both conversations were rather awkward. After getting through the polite "How are you doing" and "Boy, what a surprise" from them, they addressed my absence from work. My history chair asked, "So how long are they saying that you will be in the hospital?" He interrupted himself before I could answer, perhaps feeling as if he was starting to sound too much like the pushy boss: "Well, we know that you will probably be out for the rest of this week. That's to be expected." This was typical Rick. He was always interrupting and talking over me. We had a very uneasy relationship. Some of it was personality and personal style.

Political differences also accounted for our somewhat strained relationship. He had just come on board as the chair of the department, and his selection had been slightly contentious, although there was consensus around his candidacy because senior professors valued his national reputation. For the bean counters in the department, he was the model senior professor with quite a record of productivity. He also did not have a known history of conflict with any particular constituency in the department, although the younger, smarter professors in the department seemed unimpressed with him as an intellectual. He seemed to have a decent relationship with the other four African American professors in the department, but I did not trust him. I had served on an important twentieth-century U.S. history faculty search committee with him the previous semester, and throughout the search, he had repeated comments about candidates who did "certain kinds of history." He rarely read the candidates' files and often skipped committee meetings. (He usually weighed in via e-mail to the committee or conveyed his sentiments to Oliver, the chair of the committee and a white male associate professor.) When Oliver asked Rick what he thought about our final list of candidates, Rick indicated that he wanted to know the ideas and concerns of Harry (another committee member and white male associate professor). Rick added that Harry's opinion mattered most to him because he was "thoughtful and reasonable." It mattered less that Harry was a colonialist who whined constantly about not knowing as much about candidates as the twentieth-century U.S. historians on the committee (Oliver, Rick, and I). Still, Rick had made his point. So this was our history. I did not matter much to Rick, and he did not matter much to me. I dealt with him because he was the department's chair. This is how I regarded his person and his phone call.

As Rick rambled on that Tuesday afternoon, I responded politely. Soon I made it clear that I was anxious to get off the phone, but he continued to ask about my return to the classroom. Gradually, I grew pissed, but I just did not have the energy to engage him in a defensive way. I added, "Rick, it looks as if I will be out for at least a week. I will let you know for sure when the doctors discharge me. I'm . . ." He started to interrupt me again. I said to myself, "Enough of this shit." I started talking over him and ended with ". . . so I'll call you when I know how much longer I will be out." He mumbled something, and, as my mother likes to put it, I excused myself from the conversation. I was not in the mood to deal with him. I was busy processing information about something far more important—my health!

Soon after I spoke with Rick, the women's studies director called. Marcia was much more efficient in her approach: she wanted to know how I was feeling and what she should do about my lecture course. I told her the same thing I told Rick: I would be out at least a week. She indicated that the teaching assistant would take over temporarily. She then requested that I send her my reading notes and lectures. A little puzzled, I paused. What part of being in the hospital did she not understand? I said that I was hooked up to an iv and a heart monitor, and I could barely use one arm. I reminded her, "The class is one of our introductory classes. Everyone has tried the course at least once. Surely someone else has notes for this class." I found it telling that she did not offer to travel seventy miles to retrieve my class presentations. She expected me to e-mail her the notes from the hospital once I had the materials delivered to my room. (I still had a minor stress headache from my conversation with Rick. Talking to Marcia was making it worse.) It occurred to me that this had to be white-people-just-don't-get-it day. The direct, clear approach was getting me nowhere. Annoyed and impatient, I responded with pointed sarcasm: "Look, Marcia. We are still at the very beginning of the course. I am still defining really difficult concepts like, you know, 'gender' and 'race,' 'sexism' and 'racism.'" She snickered and sighed.

There was a larger context, a history, behind my first hospital exchange with Marcia. Our women's studies program offered two versions of an introductory course. After I joined the faculty, I pointed out that this made little sense, intellectually or politically. The first version was "Introduction to Women's Studies," and it covered "all women," meaning white women plus others. I taught the other introductory course called "Multicultural Women in the United States," which focused on Native American, Asian American, Latina, and African American women. This course met the state's "diversity requirement." Most of our faculty considered it far more difficult to teach because it required much more preparation across several women's histories and other disciplines. I had worked my butt off to develop the course. My training is in the contemporary and historical experiences of African American women, but this did not make me refuse to prepare a course that included other women. I was curious and felt a professional responsibility to learn what I did not know in order to teach the course. Hell, I had taught the "white women's intro course" a couple of times, too, and I had to prepare for that as well. I noticed that, with two exceptions, the white women in the program tended to shy away from the "multicultural course." What angered me more than anything was the lame, racist excuse a couple used for their laziness: "I just do not know much about those other experiences." This seems contrary to the knowledge-seeking mission of any college or university. Were they not the least bit curious about women who were not white? It was clear that Marcia did not want me to ask her to teach the course, and even though she was the director, she was not prepared to do it and had no interest in doing it. She also knew that my teaching assistant was not prepared to teach the course on her own.

It occurred to me that Rick, Marcia, and I had a different understanding of hierarchy and responsibility within the academy. When they learned that one of their faculty had had a stroke and would not be returning right away, instead of offering practical support in line with their responsibility as administrators, they could only nag me about what would happen in my classes. After the frustrating conversation with Marcia, I knew that I would not be talking to either one of them for a while. To do so would prolong my recovery.

Soon I learned just how much rehabilitation work I needed, even after a mild stroke. I had not been out of bed and on my feet since late Monday afternoon. While Drs. Kate and Holt (the father neurologist) gave me extensive neurological exams that measured for weakness, diminished sensation, poor reflexes, and other stroke consequences, I did not have a clear sense of what my body could do until physical therapy began.

On my first day of physical therapy, Rachel (the therapist) began by asking me to lift my left leg. Fine. She asked me to do the same with the right. I could not lift it. She looked at my face and said, "Do not worry. You will get better. I promise you." She then asked me to attempt getting out of bed. The result was the same: I moved my left leg with no problem, but I needed to lift my right leg with my hand and arm. With her help, I stood up and held on tightly as she tried to move away. She needed to check for balance, but I knew that we were one disastrous fall away from giving her the information she needed. Still holding on to her like a toddler learning how to walk, I gradually came to stand on my own, but I told her not to pull away too far. I laughed a bit as I stood there by myself. Rachel said, "See. Told ya. When coming back from a CVA, you have to be patient and try everything slowly." I then quickly grew very tired while standing.

The first mornings with Rachel were emotional. My progress happened in stages. Once I regained enough strength to stand up and keep my balance, we turned to walking. Initially, I could walk only with the use of a walker. All sorts of panicky thoughts came up. I was surprisingly vain about using a walker. My own political and moral contradictions surfaced. While I respected and valued the elderly (even championed their causes), I remembered thinking how much I did not want to *look* slow, helpless, and old. The actual truth seemed to matter less to me: indeed, I was slow and in need of much help. When Rachel walked me, we took trips around the entire "neuro" floor. I was elated to be out of my room and not on my way to radiology. I took note of everything around me, including other stroke patients undergoing rehabilitation. We were our own community cheering each other on. When I passed the nurses' station for the first time, my wonderful nurses applauded and cracked jokes. When I passed my floormates, they all seemed to utter some variation of the same observation: "But you are so young. How did you end up here?" I usually gave a genuine but vague response without going through my entire medical history. Although Rachel counseled against setting my expectations too high, I promised myself (and told no one else) that I was not leaving the hospital with a walker. When I graduated from the walker and moved to a quad cane, I made a new silent promise: "I will not be leaving here using a quad cane either." I needed to stay task- and goal-oriented to keep from falling deeper into paralyzing depression and self-pity. This was certainly not like graduate school. It was harder and scarier.

After Rachel left each morning, Terri, the occupational therapist, came in. She was there to help me reacquire the strength and skill to perform essential self-care duties, including brushing my teeth, combing my hair, and washing my body. I could brush my teeth with my good hand and arm, but I could not wash my own body or style my locks. Of particular concern to me were my impaired fine motor skills, which took the longest to return.

After a little over a week of rest in the hospital and later at home, I expected to be back at work by September 19. However, on Monday, September 16, I suffered a major setback. I had been emotionally upset the entire weekend. I was very impatient and wanted to go home. I also had a nagging chest pain, which I figured was from lying in bed for long stretches. Dr. Kate was not quite ready to release me: "Chana, I am uncomfortable releasing you without a chest X-ray and EKG."

Something happened during my trip to and from radiology. (I had been off the Heparin for twenty-four hours and had just started Coumadin, a blood thinner taken orally.) I returned from radiology very nauseated and dizzy. While retching violently, I collapsed in my hospital bathroom. I pulled the emergency plug, and a number of hospital staff came to my aid, but I could not communicate what was going on. I could make sounds, but I could not form words, much less sentences. Whatever I tried to utter as the staff worked on me, it came out slurred and heavy. Few understood me. One side of my face would not move. I felt as if I were choking to death. My heart was racing. I remember thinking, "Oh, no. This must be the big one that kills stroke patients." I had sat through a week of watching educational videos for stroke patients, and I had done my best to complete the reading material left by my medical social worker. I had learned that it is not uncommon for a second stroke to follow soon after the first. As nurses worked on me, the on-call physician reached the neurologists and Dr. Kate by phone; all of them were in their offices seeing patients. I received an injection, and I saw my nurses bring an oxygen bag and other equipment into my room. I kept removing the oxygen mask from my face. The choking sensation frightened me.

Dr. Kate ordered more scans of my brain to rule out hemorrhaging. She ordered the same for my chest and spinal column. Because I could not move my mouth, I could not eat solid food for several days. I remember the almost childlike way that I tried to eat at the head nurse's request. She said, "We have to make sure that you will not choke." She fed me a small piece of bread, which I could not chew. I moved it around in my mouth for several exaggerated turns, and I was dismayed to see the bread come out barely chewed. My body was not listening to my brain. I could not make myself do things that I had once taken for granted and to which I had never given much consideration. I was scared. I did not want to lose my independence. I did not want anyone else taking care of me.

Dr. Kate broke the latest news: "Well, it will certainly be a while before you leave here now. I need to start pulse therapy right away. We have not tried this with you. It is a kind of chemotherapy using high doses of steroids. I am concerned that we are not addressing the underlying cause of your blood clotting problems." She added, "Meanwhile, we need to see if we can get you walking again, although you will always be weaker on one side." I mumbled in a loud voice (loud for my condition, at least): "Walking? I need to be able to talk. I talk for a living, remember?" She stared back at me with a sad and bemused look on her face.

I spent the next period of my stay undergoing intensive rehabilitation therapies—physical, occupational, and now speech therapy. It all seemed so elemental and yet necessary. Doctors and nurses reiterated their upbeat prognosis when they diagnosed the first, milder CVA: you are young and you will recover, but you need to begin rehabilitation right away. Now I would need to take this advice more seriously. Clotting and inflammation were affecting my central nervous system in ways that left me more disabled than before.

Embarrassed by extremely slurred speech, I asked someone else to call or e-mail my employer about the latest turn of events. My situation overwhelmed me. I had more on my plate than I could handle. The following day, Rick and Marcia called again. Both seemed genuinely stunned by my new condition, and it was hard for them to understand my speech. Without bringing up my class, Rick got off the phone quickly. Just as she was about to hang up, however, Marcia asked about receiving my lectures again. I was so weary that I had little energy to get angry or offended this time. She seemed so out of touch. I mumbled that I would ask another colleague to come retrieve the disks I used to save my lecture notes.

Eleven days later, Dr. Kate discharged me at my request. My meticulous medical social worker had arranged all of my rehabilitation care at an outpatient facility. My physical therapist and physician would not clear me to drive until I passed a driving test again. Local friends organized their own shuttle service to help. For the next six weeks, I rehabbed four days each week. On Tuesdays and Thursdays, I attended physical and occupational therapy. On Mondays and Wednesdays, I did the most difficult work of all in speech therapy. I had to relearn very basic elements of speech. The process fascinated me. I began first with consonant clusters. Of course, I remembered what they were and how they sounded, so to "learn" them was to practice making the sounds in a slow and deliberate way without slurring. I read aloud very simple sentences while Donna, my brilliant outpatient speech therapist, took notes and recorded my sounds. I relearned how to breathe as I spoke. I relearned how to form words by listening and repeating words as I looked in the mirror. It was a humbling experience.

For each aspect of rehabilitation, my therapists helped me identify small and large goals. In physical therapy, I wanted to strengthen both legs and my stroke-affected arm and hand. This proved to be the simplest, most straightforward work. Each day, I got on a very slow-moving treadmill. Then I stretched and did some strength training that was boring as hell and not at all similar to the strength and cardiovascular training I did to lose weight. This was another reminder of just how different things were for me now. The deep sadness that overcame me in the hospital lingered during my rehabilitation when I thought about my life in before-and-after terms.

I stayed in touch with my employer as I rehabilitated. Gradually, Rick and Marcia came to accept that I would be absent for weeks. However, to my surprise, they both expected me back before the end of the semester. I explained my demanding rehabilitation schedule. I had very little stamina after leaving the hospital. Walking from the bed to the bathroom made me tired, as did walking from the front door to a waiting vehicle. I stayed dizzy and out of breath. Each day after rehabilitation, I slept for hours, often not waking to eat full meals. I ate just enough to take my evening medicine. I began the process all over again the next morning. It took me twice as long to bathe and dress. I simplified my wardrobe until my fine motor skills returned—no blouses or dresses with buttons, no shoes with laces. I asked others to button my sweater or jacket. After family members left and Alicia returned to work, I ate very simple breakfasts that required little preparation, which usually meant cold cereal. Several times, I burned myself as I tried to cook. I had lost sensation and did not know when I touched hot objects. The same was true for using knives. More than once, I cut myself while preparing fresh vegetables and was not aware of the cut until I washed my hands in the sink and noticed bloody water.

This was my life for several weeks. It was more demanding than any teaching schedule. It was even more grueling than writing a dissertation. Speech therapy alone required a level of intense concentration that surpassed any energy output for academic papers or a book. I tried to convey this to my employer, especially when I learned that my sick leave would soon expire. Obviously, I needed additional time from work for rehab and recovery. Soon Rick and Marcia expected another update about my plans for the remaining weeks. Initially, the associate dean informed them that I had two options: leave without pay or long-term disability (which, for income purposes, could only begin after a ninety-day "elimination period" without pay from any source). Neither was an option for me. I had hefty copayments due on nearly $100,000 in hospital and rehabilitation costs.

Rick grew increasingly impatient and annoyed with the entire matter. When I inquired repeatedly about other options, he snapped, "Look, just come back and grade the papers in the final week. That's all I'll ask of you. Your teaching assistant will cover any remaining class meetings." In women's studies, unnecessary drama unfolded around my sick leave. The teaching assistant assigned to the course stayed disgruntled and in a tizzy. She finally acquired all of my lecture notes, reading notes, PowerPoint presentations, and assignments (including essay test questions and sample answers). Understandably, she pressured Marcia daily because she remained so overwhelmed. Marcia needed me to return as soon as possible.

Frustrations reached a boiling point a week before my hours expired. I complained to Joe (the associate dean) about needing the support of my employer during a difficult recovery period. I even shared with him my rehabilitation schedule. I also indicated to him that I was disturbed to learn that one of our colleagues had taken leave to take care of his dying father and that the history department had covered his course without any problem. I needed a senior professor to advocate for me, and I foolishly expected it to be one of my unit heads. I conveyed this information to Joe first by e-mail and then by phone. He said, "Let me speak with both chairs again. I will see what they say. I am sure that they can work something out. I will call you back."

The next day, Rick copied me (and Marcia) on an angry e-mail he sent to Joe. He felt it necessary to address "Professor's Chana Kai Lee's perception that our department is treating her unfairly when it comes to leave." He wanted to assure the associate dean that this was absolutely not the case. In closing, he noted that the other professor in question was a "distinguished full professor who holds one of our prestigious chairs" and that the department had offered him support accordingly. Insulted and outraged, I fired back that, on matters of sick leave, university rules and custom should apply to both of us, irrespective of rank or distinction. At the end of the day, we were both state employees. From my reading of published materials on policies and procedures, I already knew that unit heads have some discretion over faculty sick leave. This includes tracking sick leave and assigning other duties when a professor is unable to return to classroom duties.

I thought I could reason with Marcia. I asked her what the problem seemed to be. Why was it such a big deal for unit heads to replace ill faculty? She replied that she expected faculty to find their own replacement. I inquired if the university had a shared-leave program. (At that time, it did not. It does now.) I then asked if I could take a course overload in the spring when I expected to be better. She said she would have to ask Joe. Joe replied that I would have needed to have made this request during the previous academic year. It was all becoming clear to me that neither the associate dean nor my unit heads were going to use their discretion to accommodate me. Tired and dispirited, I felt myself about to cry. I told Marcia that I would call her back. She asked me to do so quickly since she needed to make some decision about my course. I asked her for twenty-four hours.

I cried and cursed as I told my small professional and personal circle about my situation. My academic friends seemed amazed and disgusted. Two shared their experiences when they had faced similar situations. In both cases, their departments had arranged immediate coverage for their classes and encouraged them to take time to get well. I sat and thought. This was all unbelievable to me. I then made a decision that proved to be a mistake from the standpoint of my health. I called Marcia back and told her I would be in class the following Tuesday. She seemed quite relieved, happy even.

I went to speech therapy the next morning and told Donna that she needed to prepare me for returning to class sooner. She looked at me and shook her head in disgust. "That's interesting," she commented. Her look said it all. I said, "I need you to be my class of students. I need to lecture and see if you understand me. Let's do as we usually do. Tape me." She added, "Okay, let me find a room that approximates the size and sound of a lecture hall. I need to check your breathing and ability to project." We found a room. I gave two lectures (without notes), one on the origins of the civil rights movement and one on the end of the Civil War and the beginning of Reconstruction.

The civil rights lecture proved to be the most difficult, and not just because of my impaired speech. I had tremendous anxiety about my memory loss, short and long term. I had discussions with Dr. Kate and both speech therapists about cognitive deficits following a stroke. I knew what was different for me. Comprehending what I read took much longer. I had to stop and recall what individual words meant, and I had to read a sentence, then look up and repeat it to comprehend its meaning. In addition, I found myself looking directly at the mouths of those who spoke. My relationship to language, spoken and written, had changed in noticeable ways. I was afraid that if I delivered a lecture in my field of specialization and could not remember basic information, I would be overwhelmed with emotion too heavy to bear. Donna coached me to focus on articulation and not factual accuracy. I did and decided I was ready.

On the following Tuesday, I was incredibly nervous as I walked the short distance to the classroom. When I entered, I looked over a sea of faces and recognized no one, not even my teaching assistant. I took a breath and tried what frightened me the most—speaking: "As you all know, I have been ill. Thank you so much for your wonderful messages. They helped me quite a bit." There was then silence. I could not go on. I heard my own voice. I had tried out my badly slurred speech in front of students, and it had taken so long to say so few words. I was horrified. I broke down and cried. I could not finish. In tears, I dismissed the class by telling them that we would discuss how to resume the course. (We had about six weeks left in the semester.) I noticed some students crying as they left the classroom. I felt so vulnerable, so weak and embarrassed. I hate crying in front of anybody, even my own mother. That I cried in front of students was deeply disturbing to me. My embarrassment soon turned to rage.

I returned to my office and called Marcia immediately. I was still sobbing. For a moment, she took off her administrator's hat and asked, "Chana, what's going on? What happened?" Through my sobs, slurred speech and all, I told her that I could not do this. I was not ready to return. She replied, "Well, what do you want me to do?" I heard the administrator coming back. I exhaled and asked her to help me understand how the university was regarding my case. Why was the university responding to my situation in such a way? She sighed hard and offered, "What is it that you want?" I told her I wanted the dean to excuse me for the remainder of the semester. She continued, "And what will you do?" What would I do? Was she really asking me what I would do? I took another breath and calmly replied, "I will finish my recovery, Marcia." It took all I had not to blow a fuse at that moment. She responded, "Well, if I relieve you of classroom duties, I will have to account for your time in some way." I was not sure where she was going with this statement, although I had some inkling. I asked for clarification to be sure: "What do you mean, Marcia?" Her tone of voice changed. "Well, of course, the university cannot pay you to do nothing," she added. Finally the full truth was about to come out. "Marcia, are you thinking this is about trying to get two months' salary without working? Is that the dean's position?" She continued to reveal the university's true concerns: "He keeps asking me what you can actually do. He has asked me if I have actually seen you. He wants a clearer understanding of your limitations. The larger context that none of us shared with you is that the state is concerned about sick leave abuse. We are not saying that you are lying, but . . ." I did not need to hear more. Once again, I was insulted. I could not take it. The university had documentation from my physician. Dr. Kate had even called the university while I was in the hospital. In addition, I had done all of this communicating with my employer with noticeably impaired speech, and some colleagues and students had seen my physical impairments. I lost it at that point: "Marcia, you know what? I do not need you or anyone else questioning my integrity after all that I have been through. Fuck this job! You figure out what to do your damn self." I hung up in her face. I broke down again and sobbed at my desk for another twenty minutes. I felt myself falling apart. I watched the phone as it rang. I knew it was her calling back. I did not answer.

I drove home and did not take anyone's calls. I had reached a very low point. I was sad, but most of all I was extremely angry and offended. This was all about a racist and sexist work culture that held me to a different standard. My word was automatically suspect, and even if they did grant me my truth, I could never be too sick to return to work, no matter my condition. If I were not paralyzed and comatose, then I was well enough to come to work. Images of a "welfare cheat" kept playing in my head. Ph.D. or no Ph.D., tenure or no tenure, I was just like the rest of those lazy black folks: I'd do anything for a cheap ride. I'd take advantage of any situation. I'd exaggerate and manipulate good, responsible white folks who played by the rules, all to avoid my responsibilities. I thought to myself, "I cannot win." I knew and observed all of the regulations that came with the territory. If there had been a professor who was more conscientious about carrying out her duties, especially teaching, then I had yet to meet that person. I worked for an employer shamelessly out of touch with the human experience of serious illness and the trauma associated with its onset. Moreover, I felt foolish for thinking that a women's studies director would be more reasonable and humane and be willing to acknowledge my personhood while addressing the minor logistical challenge posed by my absence. Before I went to sleep that night, my prayer was very simple: "Whatever be your will, God." Nothing mattered to me at that moment. I crawled into bed, balled up in the fetal position, and rocked myself to sleep.

Sometime after 7:30 A.M. the next morning, I rolled out of bed. The events of the previous day seemed like a distant, very bad nightmare. After several minutes of prayer and meditation, I checked the numerous voice mail messages left on my home, cell, and office phones. There were messages from loved ones and from Marcia. First I called my two best friends, who are also academics. I explained, cursed, and cried to them. Both calmly shared their overall reaction: Chana, you deserve so much better. I thanked them as I exhaled fully. I felt my balance restored. I was not crazy or unreasonable after all.

Eventually, I returned Marcia's call. I requested that we meet in person, no more e-mail or phone conversations. She agreed that it was time to sit down and come to some understanding from our respective positions. When I arrived at her office, she seemed stunned to see my condition and to witness how producing intelligible speech was such a chore for me. I sat down and began with an apology for speaking to her so harshly and for hanging up on her. (In addition to loving, honest friends, few things restore perspective like a mortgage and a stack of hospital bills.) She apologized as well. She offered me an arrangement that would allow me to receive my regular salary and continued medical coverage. I would not return to the classroom. She had arranged coverage for my class. I agreed to create a teaching module for the multicultural women's course as my "work" responsibility for the remainder of the semester.

The next morning, I went to a place on my property where I go to reclaim strength and stability. I sat down in front of "Nat Turner" and "Ella Fitzgerald," two of the most unusual azaleas in my beloved collection. Three years before, I had rescued them from certain death. I pinched, pruned, and fed them without fail each season. Maybe it was my imagination or impaired memory, but it seemed that they did the improbable but not impossible that season—they bloomed twice. I smiled at them. It was the most uncomplicated moment that I had lived in over three months. I had reached the end of an emotional marathon that had kicked my butt. I had a long conversation with myself, the kind that I usually reserve for my journaling. I spoke aloud a wish list. I wanted nothing more than a sense of well-being. I wanted to be healthy again. I wanted to be happy. I wanted peace. I wanted order. I wanted to thrive once more. I knew that a beginning place had to be redefining my relationship to my job. I could not afford any more stress that might cause my lupus to flare up again and nearly kill me.

The following Sunday, I decided to continue my healing alone among relative strangers. I attended an early church service at one of Atlanta's gay-friendly churches, one of those huge megachurches. After I mingled with others during the morning greeting, I walked back to my seat. A very tall, elegantly dressed elderly sister held out her hands. "Good morning, beautiful." I thought she was speaking to someone else, so I turned around. She stopped me, "No, you. You look far away, like something heavy is weighing you." I smiled and sort of laughed as I responded, "Yeah, I have been on quite a ride of late. Not looking forward to the next test." She added, "Say no more. I understand. Sometimes being able to show up is all that matters. But remember that you are still here." She was right.

I am still here. Through it all, I am still here.[2]

NOTES

1. All names mentioned are aliases for actual persons.

2. Since this difficult experience of 2002–3, a number of colleagues in history and women's studies have stepped forward and offered a tremendous amount of support, from prepared meals and class coverage to donated sick leave. I am deeply grateful to them for their generosity in 2005 and 2006.

# Elsa Barkley Brown

## BODIES OF HISTORY

It is a vivid memory—one simultaneously amusing and painful. June 1988: The first Southern Conference on Women's History, sponsored by the Southern Association of Women Historians (SAWH), is meeting at Converse College in Spartanburg, South Carolina. I had been on the program committee and worked alongside a group of black and white women historians committed to making sure this conference is an inclusive gathering—fully incorporating graduate students, emphasizing a wide range of women's histories, ensuring that not only SAWH members but also a wide range of historians of women are recognized and participate as presenters and commentators. Yet by the time I arrive in Spartanburg on the evening of the first day of the conference, tensions between black and white women are evident—a situation that only increases throughout the next several days. As it is reported to me (multiple times by tellers both black and white), the precipitating incident had occurred in one of the first sessions, a session in which the papers were all on black women's history, the presenters were all white women, and the commentator was a black woman with a recently published biography of a prominent black southern woman activist. Whatever actually took place in that session, the legend of it grows over the next several days as black and white women struggle to engage each other as equals on the scholarly playing field. From the standpoint of most of the black women present, the problem is clear: white women, even many whose own work is deeply engaged with the history of black women, are for the first time having to accept black women themselves as historical authorities—not only on black women's history but also, and perhaps more difficult to accept, on women's history in general.

The details of that conference are clear to me nearly twenty years later, but even more impressed upon my memory is the response of black women, myself included, to an environment that seemed to have hoped for inclusion yet still resisted new histories and new people. Every time we returned to the dorm between sessions, I watched the black women around me re-emerge more "together" than before—lipstick freshly applied, now a touch of powder too, casual clothes giving way to more formal professional attire despite the summer heat. (I, on the other hand, got in my car and drove to K-Mart; purchased several spools of ribbon in various colors, needle, and thread; and, returning to the dorm, sewed bows on the socks that I always wore with my spike heels.) Throughout the conference, as other black women's makeup got more pronounced, the bows on my socks became larger and more numerous.

I tell this story not as a critique of the sawh or any of its members but as a comment on the setting in which we found ourselves—one that was managing to be more inclusive than most other sites within the history wing of the academy and at the same time struggling with what it would really mean to include new histories and recognize new people as historians.[1] I tell this story at the beginning of my essay because I understand the ways in which the members of the sawh have nurtured me, because it points to the ways in which questions of visibility and authority within the profession even among other women historians have been central issues for black women historians, and because it highlights the degree to which bodies as well as intellects are at stake in the discussion.

"We need to remember that when we really begin to include diverse experiences we have to think carefully about the other bodies we are bringing into the classroom." I am listening to a colleague talk about incorporating work on people of color into the curriculum. The talk is really quite good, but my mind is wandering. It is Maryland, June, hot, and the end of a long day. "Bringing bodies into the classroom" is a phrase I have heard often in reference to curriculum change. I'm imagining those bodies, wondering why they are almost always colored, considering what difference it makes that my colored body is already in the classroom, irritated that we are not going to discuss the meanings of bringing white bodies into the classroom—but, of course, they always belong there already.

### Learning and Learned Bodies

My earliest memories of something called "history" are in conjunction with my forced exile from the all-black (read: idyllic) setting of the Paul Dunbar School where I received my K–2 schooling to the formerly all-white Prentice Elementary School, thanks to Louisville, Kentucky's, experiment with voluntary and peaceful desegregation. Although the teachers and staff remained all-white, I was not the only colored body that had been transferred: a class photo from my fourth grade shows me along with three other black girls and three black boys in a class of twenty-nine students. While I longed to return to

Dunbar with my friends, school days at Prentice were not unpleasant. From a child's perspective, I viewed the teachers as treating us all as pupils who were there to learn. Nevertheless, I understood the idea of different bodies, unwanted bodies. In the spring of 1958, the unwanted body was mine when I took top academic honors for fourth grade, only to discover that there was no honor for me to have. The intended prize was a trip to a local historical landmark, but since the trip's sponsor, a local white women's organization, would allow no sponsorship of a little colored child, there was no prize for me.

If it weren't for my Aunt Augusta, this might have been a more devastating experience or might have made it more difficult for me to imagine the body of a little black girl moving through and invigorated by these kinds of designated "historical" spaces. Certainly the knowledge of being denied that honor would remain, but the next year, I had the satisfaction of having closer entry to historic spaces than even my teachers when Farmington, the main house of a nineteenth-century Kentucky hemp plantation, opened to visitors and my Aunt Augusta, employed there as housekeeper, became my entrée to the historical past. With Aunt Augusta as tour guide, I went through every inch of that house from inside the ropes that keep visitors at bay, and I touched, even helped dust, all the small ornamental displays that others would only get to peer at from afar. Years before changes in the presentation of historic sites would enable visitors to this place to be greeted with sights of the black slaves who had built and populated Farmington in the nineteenth century, Aunt Augusta made sure I knew about all the former occupants. And as would happen often in my childhood, a member of my family made it clear to me that important bodies were not always in the textbooks and learned bodies bore no necessary relation to occupational status and certainly no relation to color.

Bodies—movable bodies, unwanted bodies, surprising bodies, hardworking bodies, fun-loving bodies, light bodies, dark bodies, endangered bodies, dignified bodies, unscrupulous bodies—peopled my historical imagination as a child because bodies, named and anonymous, funny and grotesque, peopled the photographs and political cartoons my father produced, images that gave me a view of a wide landscape of African American life and politics and taught me that what we see is not always exactly what is. And bodies, specific, funny, contradictory, and amazing, peopled my mother's rich stories of generations of black Louisvillians, tales that seeded my sense of history with an appreciation for the experiences of ordinary people.[2]

Years later, it would be black working-class women's and men's bodies moving back and forth across another southern city that would help me catch a vision of history that could fuel a lifetime of work. As a professor at Emory

University in the mid-1980s, I regularly rode the subway and two buses from my home to work. Once those who worked in the central business districts departed, my fellow passengers on the final legs of the journey were principally black—men and women going to work at the hospital and women who would spend the remainder of their day cleaning house or caring for children in the elegant homes that surround the Emory campus. As the passengers thinned out, the conversations picked up. A central topic was the Reagan economy and presidency, but local political issues always got equal time. Individual conversations might involve sports, film, church, or other interests, but the political issues would often be the subject of buswide discussions. I noticed the way participants interrogated presidential statements or economic analyses, critiqued newscasts, disputed each other's claims, developed and exchanged knowledge. I began to see different forms of debate, different forms of political engagement, and, eventually, to understand the importance of this bus—of public transportation in general—in the circulation of ideas and in the construction of a late-twentieth-century black urban public sphere. Would it have been thus in the late nineteenth and early twentieth centuries? As I listened to these conversations happening outside the better-studied formal political spaces, I began to appreciate everyday talk as central to locating specific bodies within political cultures, to wonder about the ways that differently situated black men's and women's bodies traversed the city, to consider why those bodies were dressed as they were, to map out which bodies came into contact with which other bodies during the course of a day. It was on these bus rides, traveling through the city of Atlanta with these black working men and women, that I renewed my appreciation for the meaning of a learned body. When I gave my first paper at a major professional historical association meeting where I began to try to unravel ways to analyze gender, class, and African American political culture, my primary acknowledgment was to my companions on those early-morning bus rides.

### Professionalizing Bodies

It is a bit ironic, then, that it was the nonprofessionalized bodies that constitute the majority of most universities' employees with whom my first history department chair advised me against spending too much time. The year was 1979; I had just completed the first year of my first full-time academic job—teaching in history and African American studies—and I was receiving a performance review. My chair was affirming my work in the classroom and noting that my initial research was also promising. He did, however, have one serious criticism: I was too friendly with the office staff. Now what that really meant was disapproval of my friendship with the young black woman approximately the same age as me who was one of the two-person history office staff. It was important, he admonished, that I recognize myself and, especially, that the other history faculty recognize me as their colleague, and he emphasized the degree to which my friendship with this young woman would make that difficult. I didn't then and I don't now understand his position. I do, of course, recognize that one common admonition to the beginning woman professional is to be careful to distinguish oneself from the staff and to be open to socializing with one's peers (as professionally defined). And certainly I know that students and many others in the academy seem prone to assume that any black woman they see must be present in a capacity to serve them. I did, however, assume that my colleagues would not have trouble distinguishing my role since I looked nothing like this other young black woman. But, of course, this conversation with the chair wasn't really about recognizing my body in the literal sense; it was about recognizing it in the professional sense. It followed the same logic that to this day baffles me that requires professors' names to always be preceded by some title when being spoken to by the office staff and assumes without discussion that members of the staff have only first names, which not only professors but also students should freely use. This practice is one more way to stack the bodies, making verbally manifest what is already institutionally obvious—which bodies are on top.

This dilemma of too friendly relations between a young professor and the staff is no doubt something many new scholars face, and I would not advise anyone to overlook the importance of relations with one's professional colleagues. But in the case of a young, single mother of two in a new city, I would have been foolish to take too seriously my chair's admonition. After all, it was not my white male or female history professor colleagues who had helped me get settled in the city, volunteered to check out schools, introduced my children to their first playmates, or even invited me to dinner. And in the end, it wouldn't be they who worried most about helping this young historian enter the important professional bodies that would be central to my career.

At this stage of my career, in this particular setting, it was, in fact, another important office staff person, Barbara Hobson, the administrative assistant in African American studies, who foresaw the assistance I might need in order to begin to connect with other colleagues around the country in the field of African American history. She volunteered to babysit my seven- and eight-year-old daughters so I could go to my first Association for the Study of African American Life and History (ASALH) meeting in New York in the fall of 1979.

And the next year when the ASALH met in New Orleans, it was Hobson who made possible my attendance—and my beginning incorporation into institutional networks (the ASALH and the Association of Black Women Historians) that would be central throughout my career. Not only did she again volunteer to care for my daughters at no charge (as she did for other young single black mothers who came after me in the program), but recognizing that the combined expense of attending the conference—airfare, registration, hotel, meals—would be prohibitive for me (as she knew since she oversaw travel budgets), she hooked me up with a local black woman's group that was chartering a bus to New Orleans for some other purpose and agreed to let me ride along as a favor to her. From my vantage point as a young black female academic, the idea that I should distinguish my personal relations within the workplace along lines of professional versus nonprofessional status seemed not only inappropriate but also professionally shortsighted. But making manifest who should be where in academic spaces and how differently educated bodies should interact is a significant part of academia.

## Mothering Bodies

The notion of who should be where or what bodies should even be engaging in academic processes was, for me, especially relevant since, from the first day of graduate school, I would inhabit a mothering body. After all, it was my pregnant body—or rather an ill-conceived response to it—that thwarted my initial entry into graduate school. March 1971, my last semester of undergraduate study: I am delighted to receive a letter announcing that I have been accepted into a joint history/MAT graduate program, even more so because it indicates that I am being considered for a fellowship. An interview is required; I can travel to the campus or, with reason, request to be interviewed by a regional representative, and there is one in Indianapolis, only an hour's drive from my campus in Greencastle, Indiana. I request an interview, explaining that I am seven months pregnant and advised by my doctor not to fly. The reply is swift and unexpected: a woman with a small child does not belong in graduate school; not only am I no longer being considered for the fellowship, but my admission to the program has been rescinded! I understood the message: for these historians/educators, I had overstepped the line marking where the mothering body most appropriately belonged. But this was not the only time that I would learn that mothering bodies had to prove that they could/would withstand the pressures of the academy.

Three years later, when I arrived at Kent State University in the fall of 1974 to pursue a Ph.D., I had been forewarned by the history faculty at Ball State University (where I had done graduate work in the interim) that my new adviser, August Meier, would not have accepted me as a student had he known I had children. After reading my application, he had called to interrogate the Kent faculty about my preparation and abilities but also about whether there was anything in my life that would distract me from fully focusing on history. He had not asked specifically about children, and they had not volunteered the information, though they did inform me (perhaps with some slight hope that it might become true) that they had assured him I had "gotten over" my political phase and could be counted on to be single-focusedly moving ahead with my career. I took their advice (on the matter of concealing my children): this I could easily accomplish since I lived in Akron, Ohio, and commuted to Kent. It helped that other students' conversations soon made me suspect that Meier's concern had little to do with gender; within days of the opening of the semester, I met a white male student who had apparently lost favor with Meier because the previous summer he had married. Thereafter, he endured the reproach, "And I thought you were a serious student." Keeping mum about my children for a semester was one thing, but I had no intention of spending my entire graduate career doing so. On the day I turned in my final paper for the semester, I therefore brought my daughters, Ashaki (three years old) and Nataki (two years old), along to introduce them to my adviser. It is important to note that, after a significant period of flustered speech, Meier recovered quite nicely and accepted that this mothering body could meet his expectations.

I am certain that the professors at my first hoped-for graduate school as well as August Meier and many others had learned to think of mothering bodies as somehow incapable bodies in the world of academia. I am also certain that to the degree that my mothering body represented the changes that were taking place in society as a whole as well as in academia, my mothering body was to them a dangerous body.

### Dangerous Bodies

Certainly the prejudices against mothering bodies are hardly unique to black women. But the idea of the dangerous body in academe does have special salience for black women in general and me in particular.

This idea is quite often expressed in stereotypical renditions of black women's bodies. Those renditions might be most pronounced when disagreements arise. 1995: Arriving in a hotel lobby one morning for a breakfast meeting with a white woman historian whom I had never met but with whom I had engaged in a somewhat extended and less than pleasant (for both of us) disagreement several years before, I am greeted, "Are you Elsa?"

"Yes, are you——?"

"You don't look at all like I had expected."

"Oh, what had you imagined?"

"I thought you'd be bigger." (Here it is important to add a small bit of information about the body that I inhabited at the time of this exchange: it was about an 8/10 dress size.) The stereotype of the big angry black woman is an enduring one, though its expression generally comes in subtler forms.

But sometimes the black woman's body in the academy is not the danger but in danger. And when it is, who is going to notice?

When I moved to upstate New York in 1988 to teach at the State University of New York at Binghamton, a number of my white female colleagues kept pointing out to me that one of the virtues of the place was how safe it was. Finally, one day a young colleague was talking about how safe she felt in Binghamton when it hit her that I and most other black women with whom she had contact did not share her feeling of safety. Importantly, she acknowledged that she needed to be conscious that she, as a white woman, had a different experience than other black women and I had. What she did not recognize, however, was that she lived in an environment that she perceived as safe in large part precisely because I lived in an environment that I perceived as unsafe—that is, it was, in part, the small number of people of color in the area that made white women think of the place as safe and precisely the same circumstance that made me feel unsafe.

That point was vividly illustrated in the spring of 1989 when the Ku Klux Klan appeared on the Binghamton campus, invited by a professor into a government and politics class with no forewarning to the students. The black students in the class objected to the Klan's presence, arguing that they were unprepared to be—as they experienced it—in a threatened and assaulted position. Most white female professors with whom I talked who recognized it as a problem (most people either saw it as a free speech issue and supported the Klan's right to participate in classes or kept silent) saw it as a symbolic problem. All the black people—faculty and students—with whom I talked understood it as a potential threat to their lives. It was precisely their sense of the Binghamton area as a safe place that made it difficult or impossible for white women to see the Klan's presence on campus as a physical rather than symbolic threat, and it was precisely their reason for considering it a safe environment—lack of nonwhite population—that made the Klan more physically threatening to us. Not only were we up there all alone, as we often reminded each other, but we were up there all alone in a place where no one took our sense of danger seriously—and thus we were even less safe.

Recognizing that the academy and the classroom can be seriously dangerous places for some bodies can be difficult to come to terms with. In 1984 at Dartmouth College, it was the body of a black woman that students rejected as the appropriate authority to stand in front of a U.S. history survey class. Having the previous year taught a series of courses in African American history, I was assigned the second half of the U.S. survey course in the fall. On the first day of class in September, I walked into the room, set down the stack of syllabi I was carrying, and turned to face the students. Several, seeing no need to contain themselves, blurted out various forms of the question "Are you the professor?" though the answer was obviously clear to them. At the same time, the students rose, walked up one flight of stairs to the main office of the history department, and demanded another professor, using (I was told) some variant of the argument that "if we had wanted a black professor, we'd have taken a black history class." Clearly, at this moment, it was my body that was on the line. Yet my colleagues in the history department did all they could to obscure and then close their eyes to that fact. First the chair of the department, later that day the dean (who was also a historian), and eventually my other colleagues in the history department all asked me the same question: "What did you do to them?" My answer was always the same: "I am sure that had they given me the opportunity, I would have done something challenging that they did not like, but as I had not yet even opened my mouth in the class nor passed out the syllabus, I had done nothing to them other than appear in their classroom as their professor." Always I was met with a refusal to believe and explanations all around about how these were good students: "I have had — and — in my class, and they are just a joy to teach." There was no room in that place, at that time, for my colleagues in the history department to imagine that the nature of the student body might depend on the nature of the body that stood before them in a position of authority. Nevertheless, the department had no other faculty to offer the students, and since it was a required course for many, we were all eventually expected to return to that classroom. My sense of safety very much a question—both because of the students and because of the disbelief of my colleagues—I made a pact with another black woman in the university: she always would be by her phone during my class time; if within five minutes of the ending time of my class I had not called to say I was safely back in my office, she would set out to investigate. That plan never needed to be activated, but midway through the semester, I informed the chair that I would leave the university at the end of the term. No body needs to live with that kind of stress.

### Enabling Bodies

I have not meant this recounting to be a horror story. Despite the oft-repeated idea that academia is a solitary world, no body in academia ever survives or achieves anything without having been the beneficiary of a whole lot of enabling bodies. Mine have been numerous. Among them have been important institutional bodies, especially the Association for the Study of African American Life and History and the Association of Black Women Historians (ABWH). These organizations have made possible the fields of African American history and black women's history, creating the infrastructures to support them; providing the initial spaces in which numerous bodies could come together to share and debate their findings; offering an especially high standard of support to young, new, and unknown scholars; and building the networks that are necessary for professional development. It was in the fall of 1979 at the ASALH meeting in which the ABWH was founded that I first laid eyes on another black woman historian. I had met black male historians when August Meier invited prominent scholars such as Benjamin Quarles and John Hope Franklin to campus. Meier had a policy of arranging a dinner at his home attended by only his graduate students and the visiting scholar (not even Meier himself) so that faculty conversations would not overshadow student conversations with the scholar. And I knew of Darlene Clark Hine, who had been a Meier student at Kent State prior to my arrival there, but it would be several years later before we would meet.

Importantly, also through the ASALH and ABWH I met scholars who studied the history of black women and who welcomed and encouraged me to do the same at a time when I was engaged in a serious battle with Meier over the feasibility of such study. (He acknowledged the importance of Maggie Lena Walker but assured me that she was not only one of a kind but also the only woman I would find worth paying attention to as I developed the history of black Richmond.) Tom Shick, for example, listened to my research ideas during numerous extended lunches and imaginatively suggested avenues to investigate for sources. Some went the next step and kept me in mind as they did their own work; Jacqueline Rouse, for example, wrote to me when her research on Lugenia Burns Hope turned up items on Walker or other black women in Richmond. Over the years, the institutional sites of the ASALH and ABWH have remained central to the work I do, providing me a space to discuss new ideas; at least a partial sense of what Langston Hughes meant when he penned, "Oh sweet relief from faces that are white"; and an enormous amount of critique—of both my work and my painfully slow progress in developing a body of work.

Sometimes they have provided a critique of my physical body as well: It is the late 1970s, and I am excited to be at a meeting devoted exclusively to research in black women's history, part of a series of sessions being held around the country. The one I am attending is at the Mary McLeod Bethune House in Washington, D.C. I have driven up from Richmond to attend. It is the afternoon, and the session has broken into workshops where we can each discuss some of our own sources and findings. I am talking about a group of church people in Goochland, Virginia, whose trust I am slowly cultivating in hopes that I will be able to do a series of interviews with them, especially with one woman who is a graduate of Hartshorn Memorial College in Richmond, the first college founded exclusively for black women. Almost everyone is affirming that a necessary part of work on black women's history is often first developing the relations that will allow access to homes, churches, and other places where documents are stored as well as access to people whose stories will be important to preserve. I am feeling excited and supported when a very prominent African American woman historian whom I recognize but have never met, having surveyed my body from head to toe, interrupts me. "She sounds like an important source," the prominent historian says. "But you need to give her name to someone else because you are never going to get a look at her papers if you go there with your head looking like that." My hair is done in one of my favorite styles—numerous tiny, thin braids that have taken my oldest daughter many hours to put in. Even in the most supportive environments, bodies do matter. Especially among black women scholars, bodies do matter. (I should add that the critic of my hairstyle has over the years become a supporter of my work and not merely because my thinning hair now makes anything but a prim, pulled-back bun impossible.)

### Bodies Matter

Mid-1990s: She sits outside my door several times a week. I know she's there because I hear a page turn or a body shift; it will be for just a short time and then she'll be gone, to class or back to the library to study for her Ph.D. exams or off to home at the end of a long day. But in a few days, she'll be back, settle herself for a brief time outside my door, open her book, and read a little by the light through the hall window. And then she'll be off again. Sometimes I say nothing. Sometimes I call out, "——, is that you? Did you want to see me?" "No, I'm fine," she responds. "I just wanted to see that you're here."

I think I have always understood the difference it makes to young black women just starting out on the road to a career in history to have my body present in the department in which they will study and to have the many bodies of black women historians present at conferences, in associations, working in the fields in which they will work. But for myself, after twenty-eight years of teaching, how important could the mere presence of another black female body be?

Fall 2006: Walking down the hall of the history department at the University of Maryland, College Park, I pass one of the new faculty members. We are both in a hurry and only have time for a "hello" and a big smile. We both turn and look back at each other as we pass—it makes the greeting last longer. She has been in town a few weeks now, and we have had occasion to get together socially. But this is the first time I have seen her, now a colleague in my department, walking these halls. I rush on to my destination without delay partly because I am surprised at my visceral reaction. I had been very conscious that her arrival would mean I would no longer be the only black woman on faculty in the University of Maryland history department. It does not hit me until this moment, passing in the hall, that in twenty-eight years of teaching in numerous history departments, this is the first time that there has been another black woman faculty member in my department, sitting in meetings, passing in the halls. Mine is no longer the only black female body.[3] Is it possible that the first time I walk up to her office and knock on her door, whatever the ostensible reason I give for being there, my real purpose will be to say, "I just wanted to see that you're here"?

NOTES

1. It helps here to remember a point that is easy to forget—that often it is within those spaces that are most supportive and inclusive that one is most able to offer a critique, or at least a public one. It remains amazing to me that the civil rights organization that has received the greatest sustained critique of its sexism is the Student Nonviolent Coordinating Committee (SNCC), which arguably included the greatest numbers of women. Also, many female civil rights activists—black and white—credit SNCC with providing them the space to begin to assess the sexism in our society, both inside and outside SNCC.

2. Some of these intellectual debts are acknowledged in Elsa Barkley Brown, "Mothers of Mind," *Sage: A Scholarly Journal on Black Women* 6, no. 1 (Summer 1989): 4–11, and "Imaging Lynching: African American Women, Communities of Struggle, and Collective

Memory," in *African American Women Speak Out on Anita Hill–Clarence Thomas*, edited by Geneva Smitherman (Detroit: Wayne State University Press, 1995), 100–124.

3. Since I have always held joint appointments—usually with African American studies and now with women's studies—in the various institutions where I have taught, I have worked with other black faculty women in those departments. In the early 1990s at the University of Michigan, I first had black male colleagues in the history department: Earl Lewis and Robin D. G. Kelley. Nevertheless, the importance of this change is in how I experience being in a history department.

# Jennifer L. Morgan

## EXPERIENCING BLACK FEMINISM

It was 1984 and I was seventeen when I took Professor Adrienne Lash Jones's class "Black Women in America" at Oberlin College. Though I had taken courses in the Department of Black Studies before, I had avoided the Department of History, thanks to a youthful arrogance that I could craft a truer, more authentic narrative of the past through the literary and critical theoretical essays I'd encountered in other classes. Those essays, written mostly by women of color, shook me to the core. The work of black feminist writers and essayists pointed the way for me to become an academic. It did so in ways both predictable and surprising and positioned me in my current iteration as a feminist and a historian.

My freshman year at Oberlin coincided with a nearly volcanic outpouring of written work by black feminists. Like many of my generation, I felt as though something elusive and profound had slipped through my fingers by virtue of having been born just a little too late. I clung to the story of my parents finding each other in the crowds during the March on Washington in the summer before they married and worried that my attendance at the "No Nukes" and "U.S. out of Central America" rallies was little more than an anemic echo of something far more real. Taking history classes seemed to me similarly anemic. I wanted something in the here and now—the desire to be caught up in something important was, after all, precisely what had propelled me to Oberlin College in the first place. Oberlin's history as the first college to admit African Americans spoke to that teenage yearning for justice. So I immersed myself in classes on Third World revolutions and groups like the Student Organization against Racism (SOAR), where I connected with other students similarly engaged in figuring out the particulars of being black and female in such a rarified, if firmly righteous, place. When you get right down to it, I took Professor Jones's course because everyone else did—all of the black girls I knew and almost all of the political white girls as well. It wasn't entirely clear to me that I wanted to take the course, only that as a budding "race woman" I had to.

So what did it mean to aspire to such a status at the tender age of seventeen in the middle of the Reagan years? My family's move to Manhattan in 1976 deposited me on the Upper West Side, where my social life was entirely defined by a secular, predominantly Jewish, educated, middle-class cohort of friends and neighbors. At Oberlin, I was a temporary urban transplant, the child of an interracial upper-middle-class professional couple, the product of public schools, who tended toward the artsy outdated-hippie look while trying to re-create in Central Park the core scenes from *Hair* in the late 1970s. Oh, and, not incidentally, I was also the girl with her nose always stuck in a book, sheltering myself from the challenges of social interactions through a nerdiness borne of the self-conscious outsiderism that was the constant by-product of my interracial background. Grand Master Flash may be on my iPod, but anyone who knows me is aware that I own every Joni Mitchell album ever released—a complicated jumble of racial modifiers indeed.

I believe that the reason I was so strongly drawn to the feminists of color in the 1980s was because I hadn't yet learned to navigate the tangled demands of authenticity. In some of the most fundamental ways, I failed the test of racial legitimacy. My mother's early efforts to teach me to jump double-Dutch were disastrous, and my cultural references were far from those of the mainstream. My folk-festival ways set me outside a black peer group, and my unruly hair and family set me outside a white one. And thus, until college, in many ways my racial education came only at the hands of grown women—my mother, grandmother, great-grandmother, and great-aunts. While many may associate the early eighties with the burgeoning employment of a kind of essentialist racial roll call, the feminists anthologized by Toni Cade Bambara and Cherríe Moraga offered me a more complicated rendering of my own past, and thus of my present.[1] In a language of race and sexuality that my grandmother would never have sanctioned, they offered me a radical and accessible version of the explicit acceptance offered by my female kin.

My parents' marriage was the most fundamental illustration to me of the complicated intersections of race and subjectivity. My African American family comprised my immediate community; a descendant of Spauldings and Burghardts, I claimed membership (albeit distant) in the black political and economic elite. My grandmother had a degree in and later taught social work, and my uncle and aunt both worked (as accountant and administrative assistant, respectively) for the Rockefellers. Education and the expectation of a profession were a birthright and, indeed, a mark of racial identity. It was my father's kin for whom education was a surprise. The descendant of Kentucky farmers, my father's father worked on the B & O Railroad. My father retains a profoundly working-class worldview, despite the medical degree that separated him from his myriad cousins. Once he married my mother, his access to those cousins and his twenty-odd aunts and uncles was gone. I met my paternal grandparents at the age of six, and while my relationship with them became warm and important, they did not shape me. It was my mother's family who taught me, and they taught me that I was black, simply and, for them, without complication. Despite the fact that we were the only members of our family to have a white father, my brother and I were by no means the lightest-skinned people at my aunt's Thanksgiving table. Phenotype cast a wide and inclusive net over our gatherings, even as the two of us repeatedly encountered confusion and occasional hostilities from classmates and teachers. "What are you? Black or white?" In the context of our black family, it was a ridiculous question. And yet. . . .

By the end of the 1970s, the women who exemplified the activism of the civil rights era began to turn their energies toward teaching and writing, and those of us who came of age in the early 1980s were, profoundly, beneficiaries of this shift.[2] The work that characterizes this moment was about as important an outpouring of critical analyses of power as any work we have seen since the nineteenth century. It spoke with an urgency that continues to inspire even in the face of the upheavals and violence of the Bush years. At the time, these missives connected on at least two registers, one of which was political. In addition, I found a key to a much more personal alchemy of race, sex, and class. And so when Audre Lorde wrote that to merely tolerate difference between women is "the total denial of the creative function of difference in our lives," she offered me a way to resituate the signal of my differently raced body.[3] And when Donna Kate Rushin wrote, "I am myself struggling toward myself," I heard something like clarity there.[4]

Once I'd traversed the threshold of "Black Women in America," of course, I began to see the connection between the literary and political writings of contemporary theorists and the study of black women's history. In retrospect, there really is no more important writer in my development as a historian of the African American past than Audre Lorde. She set me on a path of discovery—one that changed markedly over time from an emotional quest to a quest that defined my professional life—and sparked a consistent resolve that I engage the past. Her insistence that we must do the difficult work to understand the complexities of our own locations was imperative to my burgeoning sense of self, both personally and professionally. At the forefront of what we have come to call intersectionality, Lorde paved the way for a critical black feminist politics in which interracial complications were not alarming but were, rather, fodder for a politics of location. During a visit to Oberlin in 1985, Lorde invited women of color to converse over breakfast about the associations between our distrust of one another and our desire for connection. I learned from her, and from my peers, that my racial identity—rooted in home, complicated by home—could be a source of engagement, not of embarrassment. Thus I entered Adrienne Jones's classroom looking for more than she could possibly have provided. I needed to put critical weight behind my own location. In the most straightforward sense, I needed to understand my lineage. I came of age at an opportune moment. The late 1970s and early 1980s were a crucial time for the kinds of political essayists who had already grabbed my attention, but they were equally important in the writing of African American and African American women's history.

I have written elsewhere about the pleasures I experience reading and writing, and those poised me for a life in academia rather than on other front lines.[5] In that first African American women's history classroom, I began to develop a sense of how ideologies of race and racial difference have shaped historical narrative in ways that have rendered my own embodied experience of race both visible and opaque. I understood that through the archives I might both craft a career and heed the call issued by Lorde and others that we use our gifts and our longings to enact social change in and around ourselves. I was taken with the African American women in the club movement in part because in them I listened for an echo from my female kin. But I also knew that demanding a place for Mary McLeod Bethune in the story of American history writ large changed more than just our canonical understanding of the American past. Doing history was itself a political act. It had serious consequences both for histories of activism and for our ability to conceptualize processes of crafting social justice. My questions about the proscriptive qualities of racial belonging remained and led me to begin to think carefully about how race, heredity, hierarchy, violence, and power had come to be linked in the first place. From there, the path to African American history—first an interest in the clubwomen and ultimately an engagement with the early modern histories of slavery and the slave trade—seems logical, if not inevitable.

An array of interdisciplinary anthologies on African American women's history that ranged chronologically from slavery through the twentieth century were published in the 1970s. Angela Davis's 1971 article-length work on women in slave communities inaugurated a wide range of scholarship on African American women that was organized around the nexus of family, sexuality, and resistance.[6] This meant that by the time I entered Professor Jones's classroom, anthologies like Sharon Harley and Rosalyn Terborg-Penn's *The Afro-American Woman* and Dorothy Sterling's *We Are Your Sisters* were there to greet us.[7] I accepted these books with a sanguine dismay that most were not even in paperback, not recognizing at the time that they represented a significant shift in the fields of African American and women's history. And while my attention was more diverted by the nineteenth and early twentieth centuries (this was also the year that Paula Giddings published *When and Where I Enter*, the hardback copy joining the others on my reading list), the histories of black women in slavery became increasingly interesting to me.[8] As part of a second course I took with Professor Jones on writing women's history, she brought us to the 1985 meeting of the Association for the Study of African American Life and History in Cleveland, Ohio. At a session on the history of slavery, I watched from a distance as Deborah Gray White introduced *Ar'n't I a Woman?* and urged members of the audience to take black women's history seriously.[9] This was for me, in retrospect, clearly no chance encounter.

By the 1980s, then, historical work on black women's lives both during and after slavery moved from margin to center. White's work on the American South initiated a number of studies, including Hilary Beckles's work on enslaved women in Barbados, Barbara Bush's study of gender in the British West Indies, and Marietta Morrissey's sociological work on the same topic.[10] There was also a surge of work from scholars in other disciplines such as Hazel Carby, Henry Louis Gates Jr., Deborah McDowell, and Hortense Spillars. Studies on women in slavery seemed destined to move, as the field does, in the direction of the particular—toward increasingly specific and less literary monographs in which the lives of these women moved irrevocably out of obscurity and stereotype. This was an extremely exciting time to be thinking about the political potential of doing academic work. The very entry of these texts into my canon was itself a portent of the powerful transformation wrought by those women of color feminists of the late 1970s and early 1980s.

It was in this context that I made the decision to begin graduate studies in American history, with a focus on African American women's lives. From 1988 until the mid-1990s, I attended Duke University, arriving at a moment of incredible intellectual and political convergence. I never needed to fight battles over the legitimacy of studying African American women's history; indeed, I don't believe there were many students there during my tenure who did not work on the intersections of race, gender, and class in the American past. But this did not entirely mitigate the intense sense of isolation I experienced as a black graduate student. Early in the fall semester, I was chatting at a party with Julius Scott, then a junior faculty member at Duke. "You realize," he said to me, "that all the black graduate students who've enrolled in Duke's history department in the past fifteen years are here in this room." I looked around in a fog of naïveté, searching for the crowd of alumni before realizing that he meant only me, himself, and Herman Bennett, a third-year student at that point and, incidentally, my future husband. A profound sense of hypervisibility compelled us, and those black students who would join the department in the coming year felt it as well. I was repeatedly reminded that, in 1988, there were only approximately 250 African American students enrolled in all of the history departments in the nation.

Together with Matthew Countryman and Lisa Waller, I helped to organize the first black graduate-student association at Duke, the Hurston-James Society. Ostensibly a place of cross-disciplinary intellectual exchange, Hurston-James was fundamentally a haven of privacy where we might temper the isolation we experienced in our respective departments. In this context, for me, the political imperative of African American social history intensified. Particularly since Duke University's Program in Literature reflected the ascendancy of postmodernism during those same years, I felt a visceral sense of the conflicting imperatives to both problematize and center on race as a historical and intellectual phenomenon. The challenge was, and is, to understand race as a lived experience while being attentive to the postmodernist and feminist critique of natural and embodied difference. These were academic questions that I felt intimately and that echoed the complicated terrain of my college years. Just as an earlier, more facile conflict on the grounds of popular culture had beleaguered me as a teenager, it was the convergence of my intellectual and political sensibilities as a feminist, a person of color, and a scholar of racial formation that made my footing unsure.

My journey from the twentieth century to the colonial period was influenced by that uncertainty. While the intellectual draw to early African American history was significant, I don't think I should discount the personal factors that pulled me back in time. My move to Duke had also been a kind of homecoming —Durham is where my mother's family has lived for generations, and the scarcities of graduate school were eased by my access to home-cooked meals and central air-conditioning at the homes of myriad "aunts" and cousins. My grandmother had sent me off to Duke with a request that I be certain to attend a football game on campus since she and her siblings had been barred from the university's segregated facilities. From my apartment near Duke's East Campus, I could see the logo at the top of the North Carolina Mutual Insurance Company headquarters, the heart of Durham's black middle class and the company owned and established by my extended—and, up until this point, distant— family. More than a few of my classmates at Duke were, indeed, studying the history of North Carolina Mutual and the black women in my family who'd been active in the struggles of the 1950s and 1960s.[11]

This overlap of my familial identity with the subject of history was ultimately an uncomfortable one. In effect, my proximity to the black community in Durham was yet another instantiation of racial (in)authenticity. I was, after all, not *of* this community even as I craved connection to it. I seemed, in some ways, to be impersonating the "goodlittlesmalltownColoredGirl" that Donna Kate Rushin evoked in 1983.[12] And so I needed to distance myself from these embodiments of the history that I imperfectly made flesh. The era of colonial contact was the primal scene for the racial ideologies and hierarchies I encountered at the end of the twentieth century. The study of gender and slavery became a means for a more intellectually critical and less emotionally fraught consideration of the complexities of race, sex, and power. Moreover, in the burgeoning field of slavery studies, the colonial period was an era in which questions were still in formation. Given the academic context in which my interest in black women's history was forged, I felt (erroneously, I now understand) that the antebellum period was "full," that studies of gender and slavery after the turn of the nineteenth century already saturated the field. But certainly there was historiographical support for further exploration of the lives of enslaved women in the earlier periods. And yet. . . .

By the end of the 1980s, Evelyn Brooks Higginbotham could still lament that "black women's voice[s] go largely unheard" in African American history, a lament that continues to resonate, particularly in studies of slavery, into the new millennium.[13] I am constantly surprised when I sit down to assess the scholarship on gender and slavery, as I have a number of times over the past few years. Among historical monographs concerned with enslaved women, there are only a few full-length studies: Deborah Gray White's *Ar'n't I a Woman?: Female Slaves in the Plantation South*, Marietta Morrissey's *Slave Women in the New World: Gender Stratification in the Caribbean*, Barbara Bush's *Slave Women in Caribbean Society, 1650–1838*, and Bernard Moitt's *Women and Slavery in the French Antilles, 1635–1848*. Stephanie Camp's *Closer to Freedom: Enslaved Women and Everyday Resistance in the Plantation South* and my own *Laboring Women: Reproduction and Gender in New World Slavery*, both published in 2004, brought the total to six, only three of which are geographically based in the continental United States.[14] Much powerful historical work has been generated on African American women in the nineteenth and twentieth centuries, work that also owes its genesis to the nexus of political activism and the forced integration of universities and curricula by black feminist activists. And, of course, there is also an entire field of studies on the slave family, for example, or community studies like those of Brenda Stevenson and Lorena Walsh in which women's lives are carefully centered. Or, indeed, studies like Sharla Fett's, in which enslaved and free women's interactions with one another and with the men of their communities receive rich and nuanced attention. My calculations also miss the work of scholars like Leslie Schwalm and Jane Landers, who, by examining transitions between slavery and freedom or interactions between free and enslaved women of African descent, have profoundly added to our understanding of the interplay between race and gender both during and in the aftermath of slavery.[15]

Studies that treat gender, race, and slavery in the context of emerging American colonies are more widespread and are deeply indebted (as is my own work) to historians of early American women. While initially constricted by a framework that focused primarily on the lives of white women, the fields of early American history, African American history, and women's history now inform one another as they always should have and intersect in studies such as Kathleen Brown's *Good Wives, Nasty Wenches, and Anxious Patriarchs: Gender, Race, and Power in Colonial Virginia*, a work that set the stage for early American histories that followed, such as Kirsten Fischer's *Suspect Relations: Sex, Race, and Resistance in Colonial North Carolina* and Sharon Block's *Rape and Sexual Power in Early America*.[16] Finally, I am well aware of a number of studies of women in slavery that are in the pipeline. Indeed, I have benefited tremendously from the ongoing work of Jessica Millward, Daina Berry, Erica Armstrong Dunbar, Barbara Krauthamer, Celia Naylor, Amrita Meyers, and others. But we continue to work in relative isolation in a bleak academic landscape that is highlighted by our insistent efforts to locate one another across the boundaries.

Having nurtured fantasies of progressive institutional changes myself, I perhaps should no longer be struck by the rarely explicit presumption on the part of my colleagues and peers that a veritable horde of women of color in the humanities are churning out studies on the intersections of race, class, and gender. While any number of factors may explain the significant gap that exists in historical studies on gender and slavery, racism in the academy is no doubt one of them. There are so few of us whose work has been nurtured by advisers, peers, presses, hiring committees, and tenure committees. There is a perception among many white academics that the work of integrating the academy has largely been completed. This is a misapprehension rooted in many factors, including a conflation between the insistence on attending to categories of race and gender in the disciplines and a presumption that, as a result, women and people of color are flooding the barricades.

In my final years as a graduate student and my first years as an assistant professor, I attended the 1994 "Black Women in the Academy: Defending Our Name, 1894–1994" conference at MIT and was on the planning committee for "Black Women in the Academy II: Service and Leadership" five years later in Washington, D.C. These were powerful events in my academic and personal life. They created an expectation that there were massive numbers of women of color in the academy and that the isolation of graduate study would soon be alleviated when we all joined the ranks of the professoriat. But gatherings like these aside, the fundamental isolation was not mitigated. Moreover, the expectation that there was a critical mass of black women in the humanities nurtured similar expectations about the growth of the field, and while I do not want to downplay the significant and groundbreaking scholarship that has emerged in this generation, I do not experience it as a groundswell—rather I see it as an uphill battle.

My decision to work on gender and slavery in early American history was a good one. My work continues both to engage me and to make the kind of political intervention that I most wanted from the beginning. I have centered the lives of the enslaved and argued that the exploitation of African women's bodies in the seventeenth century laid the groundwork for hundreds of years of slavery in North America and the Caribbean. My work has been well received, but a single monograph cannot, of course, account for the demands of the field—much less the lives lost to the violence of the institution of slavery. I am struck by how solitary this work on women in slavery continues to be. Having entered the field at a moment of such energy, I am still surprised at the small numbers of historians at work in this area in general, much less the numbers of black women historians.

The piece that I haven't talked about here—precisely because I haven't experienced it in ways that translate transparently—is the relentless violence of racisms both inside and outside the academy. I have come of age as a historian at a time in which the gains wrought by the post–civil rights generation—as moderate as they have been—have been strenuously under attack. Indeed, at precisely the moment when the claim that barriers to hiring women and people of color have fallen is made most emphatically, the actual numbers of faculty of color in universities across the country are declining. I can't fail to grasp the ways in which I present as a racial chimera to some, and there is no doubt that my career in the academy is firmly entwined in legacies of racial ambiguity. I have certainly benefited from those ambiguities, even as they have contributed to highly specific and personal loads to bear. I have gained some access to the significantly segregated fields of early American history and the history of the early Atlantic, access that is conditioned by the racial legacy that propelled me in this direction at the start. I come into the academy as both an insider and an outsider, and even in the communities of black scholars, both men and women, with whom I have grown as an intellectual and a historian and from whom I continue to learn, my presence isn't entirely without complications. I am, I imagine, a source of some confusion for those who can't quite locate me racially or, indeed, disciplinarily.

And yet in the context of such isolation, I continue to find and create spaces of community and exchange among women of color—whether it's at conference panels, through formal and informal seminars and working groups, or simply through the extensive networks of colleagues and friends that I believe we all are careful to generate and nurture. I have been enabled to do the work I do by the community of politicized women in whose company I continue to find myself.

This semester, I taught a course called "Black Feminist Theory and Practice in the Twentieth Century." Teaching the course put me in that most rare and uncomfortable position of trying to convey intelligent and articulate meaning about texts that are lodged deep inside one's own psyche. As I first pulled the dog-eared copies of *This Bridge Called My Back*, *When and Where I Enter*, *In Search of Our Mothers' Gardens*, and *Home Girls* down from my shelves, I realized that the usual tribulations of teaching would be significantly amplified by the challenge to not appear as some kind of sentimental old fool—clutching Audre Lorde's *Sister Outsider* to my bosom weepily, imploring my students to simply *see* its prescient radicality. I think I avoided such spectacle, but to be honest, I can't be certain. And yet I will endure this uncertainty again, as I fully intend to continue to teach this course. Teaching "Black Feminist Theory and Practice" gave me the opportunity to revisit texts and theoretical interventions that not only shaped my entry into the field of African American women's history but also continue to shape my work on gender and the slave trade in the early modern Atlantic. Revisiting that work is more than an exercise in nostalgia. I owe a considerable debt to those black women writers and activists of the late 1970s—all of us who work at the intersections of race and gender do— because their work continues to frame the crucial interventions that I intend to make in my field. If I am even moderately successful in moving the history of enslaved women from margin to center, it is because I came to the project with a presumption that to undertake it was an absolute necessity. I have never experienced a modicum of doubt about the importance of my scholarship. Doubts abound about my ability to shape my work in ways that are accessible and to use arguments that are persuasive. But about the work itself? About the time spent in the archive searching for a word or a gesture that allows me to sketch in the outlines of a woman's life? A life formerly lost to the violence and erasure wrought by her enslavement and wrought again by the archive constructed on her carcass? *That* time is always uncomplicated by doubts about the legitimacy of the work or by the demands of a profession that routinely sucks the energies and physical well-being out of the women of color who shoulder so much in the way of advising and teaching and rectifying the academy's deficiencies in department discussions, on committees, and at emergency meetings with administrators. Doing history has been, for me, a vocation that connects me to my past and to the possibilities of structural transformations in ways that continue to feed my spirit and my intellect. In other words, it seems that I have found what I went looking for in 1984 in Professor Jones's "Black Women in America" class.

NOTES

1. Toni Cade Bambara, ed., *The Black Woman: An Anthology* (New York: New American Library, 1970); Cherríe Moraga and Gloria Anzaldúa, eds., *This Bridge Called My Back: Writings by Radical Women of Color* (New York: Kitchen Table Press, 1983).

2. Kimberly Springer, *Living for the Revolution: Black Feminist Organizations, 1968–1980* (Durham: Duke University Press, 2005).

3. Audre Lorde, "The Master's Tools Will Never Dismantle the Master's House," in Moraga and Anzaldúa, *This Bridge Called My Back*, 98.

4. Donna Kate Rushin, "The Black Goddess," in *Home Girls: A Black Feminist Anthology*, edited by Barbara Smith (New York: Kitchen Table Press, 1983), 328.

5. Jennifer L. Morgan, "Why I Write," in *Why We Write: The Politics and Practice of Writing for Social Change*, edited by Jim Downs (New York: Routledge, 2006), 39–45.

6. I take as a starting point Sharon Harley and Rosalyn Terborg-Penn, eds., *The Afro-American Woman: Struggles and Images* (Port Washington, N.Y.: Kennikat, 1978), but one could look back to Bambara, *Black Woman*; Joyce Ladner, *Tomorrow's Tomorrow: The Black Woman* (New York: Doubleday, 1971); Gerda Lerner, *Black Women in White America: A Documentary History* (New York: Pantheon, 1972); Angela Y. Davis, "Reflections on the Black Woman's Role in the Community of Slaves," *Black Scholar* 3 (December 1971): 2–15; bell hooks, *Ain't I a Woman: Black Women and Feminism* (Boston: South End Press, 1981); and Angela Y. Davis, *Women, Race, and Class* (New York: Random House, 1981).

7. Dorothy Sterling, ed., *We Are Your Sisters: Black Women in the Nineteenth Century* (New York: W. W. Norton, 1984).

8. Paula Giddings, *When and Where I Enter: The Impact of Black Women on Race and Sex in America* (New York: W. Morrow, 1984).

9. Deborah Gray White, *Ar'n't I a Woman?: Female Slaves in the Plantation South* (New York: W. W. Norton, 1985).

10. Hilary McD. Beckles, *Natural Rebels: A Social History of Enslaved Black Women in Barbados* (New Brunswick, N.J.: Rutgers University Press, 1989); Barbara Bush, *Slave Women in Caribbean Society, 1650–1838* (Bloomington: Indiana University Press, 1990); Marietta Morrissey, *Slave Women in the New World: Gender Stratification in the Caribbean* (Lawrence: University Press of Kansas, 1989); Elizabeth Fox-Genovese, *Within the Plantation Household: Black and White Women of the Old South* (Chapel Hill: University of North Carolina Press, 1988).

11. Christina Greene, *Our Separate Ways: Women and the Black Freedom Movement in Durham, North Carolina* (Chapel Hill: University of North Carolina Press, 2005); Leslie Brown, *Upbuilding Black Durham: Gender, Class, and Black Community Development in the Jim Crow South* (Chapel Hill: University of North Carolina Press, 2008).

12. Rushin, "Black Goddess," 329.

13. Evelyn Brooks Higginbotham, "Beyond the Sound of Silence: Afro-American Women in History," *Gender & History* 1 (1989): 50. See also Elsa Barkley Brown, "Polyrhythms and Improvisations: Lessons for Women's History," *History Workshop Journal* 31 (Spring 1991): 85–90, and " 'What Has Happened Here': The Politics of Difference in Women's History and Feminist Politics," *Feminist Studies* 18 (Summer 1992): 295–311.

14. For studies of women in slavery, see White, *Ar'n't I a Woman?*; Morrissey, *Slave Women in the New World*; Bush, *Slave Women in Caribbean Society*; Bernard Moitt, *Women and Slavery in the French Antilles, 1635–1848* (Bloomington: Indiana University Press, 2001); Beckles, *Natural Rebels*; Fox-Genovese, *Within the Plantation Household*; Stephanie Camp, *Closer to Freedom: Enslaved Women and Everyday Resistance in the Plantation South* (Chapel Hill: University of North Carolina Press, 2004); and Jennifer L. Morgan, *Laboring Women: Reproduction and Gender in New World Slavery* (Philadelphia: University of Pennsylvania Press, 2004).

15. Brenda Stevenson, *Life in Black and White: Family and Community in the Slave South* (New York: Oxford University Press, 1997); Lorena Walsh, *From Calabar to Carter's Grove: The History of a Virginia Slave Community* (Charlottesville: University of Virginia Press, 2001); Sharla M. Fett, *Working Cures: Healing, Health, and Power on Southern Slave Plantations* (Chapel Hill: University of North Carolina Press, 2002); Leslie A. Schwalm, *A Hard Fight for We: Women's Transition from Slavery to Freedom in South Carolina* (Urbana: University of Illinois Press, 1997); Jane Landers, *Black Society in Spanish Florida* (Urbana: University of Illinois Press, 1999).

16. Kathleen Brown, *Good Wives, Nasty Wenches, and Anxious Patriarchs: Gender, Race, and Power in Colonial Virginia* (Chapel Hill: University of North Carolina Press, 1996); Kirsten Fischer, *Suspect Relations: Sex, Race, and Resistance in Colonial North Carolina* (Ithaca: Cornell University Press, 2001); Sharon Block, *Rape and Sexual Power in Early America* (Chapel Hill: University of North Carolina Press, 2006).

# Barbara Ransby

## DANCING ON THE EDGES OF HISTORY,

## BUT NEVER DANCING ALONE

What does it mean to be a black female historian in 2006? Some argue that it should simply mean being a good scholar and that's it. They contend that notions of race and gender are twentieth-century anachronisms that obscure more than they illuminate. I only wish it were true. My experience, and that of hundreds of other female historians of African descent working and struggling in the academy, tells a very different story. It is a story that reflects slow, erratic progress but also persistent, intractable prejudice augmented by the precedent of generations of institutional racism. It is a story about the sluggish, painful reconfiguration of a profession and its practitioners. African American women currently teaching in history departments at four-year colleges, community colleges, and high schools; working in museums, foundations, publishing houses, and nonprofit organizations; and working independently reflect a myriad of personal and career choices mapped out on the rugged and ever-shifting landscape of what we refer to inclusively as the historical profession. The terrain that we trek is similar, but the routes we have navigated and the challenges we have encountered are distinct, stretched across generational and geographic time zones. For me, political activism and parenting have presented added obstacles and added rewards. On the positive side, however, I have never felt alone in this journey. I was not a pioneer. I was not the Autherine Lucy, Charlayne Hunter-Gault, or Helen Edmonds of previous generations. I was not the first black woman to walk into an institution or one of the first to walk into the profession. Others had already walked that difficult path before me. So even though the work, culture, and at times scant sense of community have been frustrating, I have always had a handful of allies, mentors, and fellow travelers on the road.

I entered the university in the early 1980s as an undergraduate at a critical moment. The ranks of black and Latino students and faculty were larger than they had ever been. But in the wake of the civil rights and black power movements, when American universities opened their doors ever so slightly to scholars and students of color, that inclusion came with strings attached. Recently minted Ph.D.'s, valedictorians from predominately black urban high schools, and crossover professors from historically black colleges and universities (HBCUs) entered mostly white campuses in record numbers in the 1970s. But the message they received was mixed. "Come in and join us" meant "Come in and *be* us." And in many respects, that was the best-case scenario. At the other end of the spectrum was a begrudging tolerance. At the same time, universities extended their conditional acceptance letters to academics of color with the caveat that we be prepared to blend in and be quiet. Black communities and organizations, which were in no small part responsible for the desegregation of the academy, had their own expectations. Their message to the cadre of young black intellectuals who walked through those campus gates once they were pried ajar was "Don't forget where you came from. Remember who you are, where you are, and who helped you to get there." These are the clashing demands that black women academics, historians included, have faced for the past several decades. Most of us have navigated the minefield of academic life and community expectations with trepidation and varying degrees of grace and good humor.

The editor of this collection has invited contributors to be personal and candid in reflecting back on our careers, so I will do just that. I hope I do not offend or embarrass anyone in the process. There are many things that stand out as I think back over my twenty-six years of university life, from my experiences as a working-class undergraduate from the Midwest enrolled at an Ivy League college in New York, through my graduate studies at the University of Michigan in the 1980s, through the evolution of my career as a tenured professor at a public university in Chicago. In this essay, I will share some of my more salient memories and observations of my career as a historian in the hope that they will resonate with some readers.

As I say to my graduate students who sometimes wonder, as I did, "Do I really belong here? Is this the place and the work I really want to do?," the university is a big and contradictory place. There is still not nearly enough racial or class diversity and women are underrepresented in most of the sciences, but there are diverse views and values. And while I have encountered more than my share of blustering bullies and bigots who have made me feel unwelcome, I have also encountered others with status and power who have used their privileged positions to alter the climate and revise the culture of the university.

There were three men whose gestures of kindness and supportive collegiality at the outset of my academic career made me believe that the university was a place, problematic though it was, that I could do meaningful work and find validation: Eric Foner, Hollis Lynch, and Thomas C. Holt. And they were not the only ones. Ironically, even though my research interests were in black women's history and I was eager to identify a black female role model, my dissertation committee turned out to be all male: Michael Dawson, Robin Kelley, Aldon Morris, Earl Lewis, and Tom Holt. They were all enormously supportive and respectful. It was only later that I fully appreciated how rare this was. They were and are an exemplary group of men who refused to play the "good old boy" game or to bid for membership in the gentleman-scholar's club. There was never a hint of impropriety or condescension. They paved different and principled career paths for themselves and made it possible for me to do the same. I make this point for two reasons. First, even in situations where there is a lone black woman historian in a college or department, she need not be abandoned because there is no one who looks like her to provide support. Essentialist politics are a dead end in the larger world, and they are equally bankrupt in academia. We choose what side we stand on whoever we are. Second, my graduate-school experience suggests it is possible to create democratic oases within our otherwise undemocratic institutions.

Now back to the beginning of my journey. After working for six years as a community organizer and noncredentialed social worker in Detroit, I moved to New York City in 1980 and enrolled in Columbia University's School of General Studies for returning students. My initial intention was not to go to graduate school but to do something much more practical from my vantage point at the time—go to law school. I wanted to exact a greater margin of justice for black people and poor people from what I perceived as an extremely unjust legal system. Somewhere along the way, I met Hollis Lynch and Eric Foner, and practical intentions gave way to bigger philosophical and pedagogical ambitions. Two very different historians, these men made Columbia's campus open to me. Lynch supervised my undergraduate thesis on the Trinidadian black power movement, helped me locate sources, introduced me to key players in the struggle, and nominated the paper I had labored so hard on for a departmental award, which it won, much to my surprise. He also took me under his wing. With wit and good humor, he demystified the university and all of its pretensions and made me feel as if I were as smart as anyone else there.

For his part, Foner allowed me to talk my way into his graduate seminar on Reconstruction. I really didn't know what to expect in a graduate seminar, but I wanted to read W. E. B. Du Bois's *Black Reconstruction* and Foner was writing a book on the subject of Reconstruction, so it seemed like a match. Like Lynch, he was kind and accessible, encouraging and generous. We talked about history, politics, and life. And when I left class early to staff the anti-apartheid picket line or take my turn in the shanty we had constructed in front of Low Library, he smiled, nodded, and wished me well. It was his letter of support, I am sure, that got me into the University of Michigan graduate school and helped me to land a lucrative Mellon Fellowship.

When I arrived in Ann Arbor to begin the history Ph.D. program at the University of Michigan in the fall of 1984, I had a husband with his own busy career and, more important in terms of time demands, a six-week-old baby. While I was still pregnant, I had nervously waddled into the Mellon interview with a well-rehearsed speech explaining to my interviewers that despite my swollen belly I had every intention of being a serious historian and putting their fellowship money to good use if they were to select me. In other words, I felt I had to justify, or at least explain, my plans to be both a mother and an academic. Fortunately, the Mellon committee was sympathetic. I did not know whether my professors and advisers at Michigan would be as understanding or sympathetic concerning my situation. I was ecstatic to find that my new adviser, Tom Holt, was understanding and demanding in perfect balance. I never felt Tom expected less of me because I was a new mother or a committed political activist. There were no corners cut, no exceptions made, but there was enormous patience and nurturing support. The first time we met, I brought my nursing infant with me, and Tom made me feel as if it was the most natural thing in the world. It was as if all his first-year graduate students rolled into his office with notebooks and diaper bags in hand.

And then there were the politics. I was heavily involved in the Free South Africa movement when I arrived in Ann Arbor. I felt I couldn't go on sabbatical from my activism while I was in graduate school. After all, I had returned to school with the hope of making a difference in the larger world, not in order to insulate myself in the world of books and ideas. However, when my name and photo appeared in coverage of the protests by local newspapers, some of my professors were disapproving. More than one senior professor told me that I had to make a choice between being an academic who would be taken seriously and being an activist who would pursue an altogether different agenda. Tom Holt, who himself had come of age as a civil rights activist in Danville, Virginia, in the 1960s, told me I did not have to choose. I just had to be good at both. I don't think I ever thanked him enough for that life-altering reassurance.

Tom became not only a mentor but also an ally. When university administrators refused to give then-jailed South African leader Nelson Mandela an honorary degree in absentia, he led a committee of faculty to petition them to rethink the decision. Nearly a decade later, when I worked with a group of black women academics to launch African American Women in Defense of Ourselves in critical response to the Clarence Thomas Supreme Court nomination, Tom once again was a supporter. Over the years, he wrote me dozens of letters and offered calm, steadfast assurance that whatever political distractions or motherly duties had taken me away from the dissertation, I could always find my way back and finish. He also gave me confidence that what I had to say in my scholarship and what I had to say on the political platform were equally important. Without my undergraduate mentors at Columbia, I would never have started my Ph.D. training, and without Tom, I would never have finished it.

During my graduate years at Michigan, I remember quite vividly the daunting task of juggling parental responsibilities and graduate-school demands. I finished Eugene Genovese's *Roll, Jordan, Roll* sitting on a playground bench at Geddes Lake Park while my son fed the ducks. They were well fed by the time he and I finished. During the height of the campus anti-apartheid struggle, that same small boy accompanied me to the shanty that our student organization had built in the center of campus to express solidarity with the impoverished families of South Africa. I remember him looking at me with the utmost sincerity and asking, "Mommy, why is this house so small at your school?" After a brief political discussion, we were off to the library and then to the copy center to print leaflets, and by naptime, I was settled in to type up notes for my evening colloquium on comparative emancipations, hoping desperately that he did not wake up before I was done. With my good-natured toddler in tow and between regular visits to my ailing mother in Detroit, I went to campus rallies during the day and tedious planning meetings at night, strategizing about how to get Michigan to enroll more students of color and to hire and retain more faculty of color. We protested racist comments by university administrators, demanded policy changes, and pushed and petitioned for symbolic gestures, like the cancellation of classes on the Martin Luther King Jr. holiday.

At the time, it seemed like a hectic, schizophrenic existence, but in retrospect, I was learning invaluable lessons about theory and practice and work and ideas. I brought the skepticism and curiosity of a historian to my activist work, and I applied my compassion and sense of purpose as an organizer and activist to my historical scholarship. When Aldon Morris nudged me in the direction of Ella Baker for my dissertation topic, I was poised to ask key questions from one activist to another across the chasm of time. I used the skills I was learning as a historian to answer those questions as honestly and thoroughly as possible. Still, the actual work was tedious and fraught with challenges. Some of them were very personal. I had negotiated my graduate courses and passed my preliminary exams while raising a small child with a supportive partner, but as I headed into the final stretch of dissertation writing, my husband and I were expecting another child. It was a wonderful, exciting, and untimely surprise.

So ten years into my Ph.D. program, I was feeling a little weary and wondering if, as a soon-to-be mother of two, I would ever find time to finish. By January 1994, I was very, very pregnant with a strong-willed, hard-kicking little girl who was already making her presence felt in utero. Despite my size, stress level, and growing familial obligations and the threat of one of the worst snowstorms of the season, I set off for Boston to attend a historic conference organized by Evelynn Hammonds and Robin Kilson entitled "Black Women in the Academy: Defending Our Name, 1894–1994." I borrowed a red coat from a friend because mine no longer fit me. I arrived at MIT, the site of the conference, looking a bit like a happy, slow-moving fire engine, hoping the conference would reinvigorate my passion for historical scholarship, provide me with a greater sense of community, and give me the confidence to finally complete my degree.

I had grand expectations, and I was not disappointed. The conference represented different things to different women, and in the end, it was not rigidly exclusive. White women were there, as were Asian women, Latinas, and a very few Native Americans—but the overwhelming majority were women of African descent, as evidenced by the dreadlocks, gelées, shaved heads, perms, and Afros big and small. Sitting in the back of a large auditorium looking at the backs of all the heads in front of me, I was in aesthetically familiar company, at least on the surface.

Overall, the university can be a very cold place despite its pretensions to the contrary. But in the short-lived little cocoon at MIT on that frigid January weekend, I got a glimpse of what intellectual life could be like—more affirming, more humane, and less combative. Strangers sat cross-legged in hallways probing issues that had been raised in previous sessions. Three women shared coffee in an empty classroom, a more-experienced elder going over presentation points with her younger colleagues, presumably to ensure that the panel went smoothly. Perhaps most memorable were the open displays of tears as distinguished women scholars talked about the frustration, isolation, marginalization, and sometimes outright hostility they felt in all-white academic departments across the country. It was driven home to me that this was a space in which I could be both an academic and a whole person. I especially felt this as a visibly pregnant woman. Women helped me with my bags and pulled me out of a snowbank after I had inadvertently beached there as I was trying to cross the street, and a group of close friends gathered in my room to watch the feisty little girl in my belly do her nightly dance. Lunchtime conversations alternated between tips about breast-feeding and debates about critical race theory.

It was an unusually affirming and exhilarating moment—not to be too idealized because it was not utopian, but a moment in which we were all able to enjoy a different way of interacting, thinking, and working together. I didn't have to apologize for being pregnant and a historian. I didn't have to feel self-conscious about asking for help. I didn't have people look at me with surprise and skepticism when I cited examples of racism in the university. I didn't have to deny some part of my humanity, history, or sensibilities to be welcomed into a community of scholars. The gathering rescued me from my doubt and cynicism and reminded me that I was not alone. For most of us, that weekend stood in stark contrast to the academic worlds we routinely inhabited. I offer this vignette as both a counterpoint to my normal life in the university and a fantasy of what an intellectual community could be like. As a caveat, this is not to suggest that we have to be in totally homogeneous groups to feel secure. My undergraduate and graduate mentors are evidence of that. Moreover, the group that convened at MIT consisted of an extremely diverse cross section of mostly black women, and we were in no way monolithic in our views, backgrounds, or areas of research. That said, there was common ground, an appreciation for the complexities of our lives, and a mutual respect that allowed for healthy intellectual debate and disagreement.

I finished my degree in 1996, accepted a tenure-track job at a large research university, and meandered my way down the potholed road toward tenure. Somewhat naively I suppose, I expected to find the kind of mentors I had encountered at Michigan, Columbia, and the conference at MIT, but my first few years as an assistant professor were both sobering and distressing. One experience stands out as my baptism by fire in a less than hospitable intellectual environment. It was my first semester teaching an upper-level history seminar. As is typical of new teachers, I had overprepared. I was excited to be about to engage graduate students and upper-level undergraduates in some of the big ideas of history. I was even armed with humorous historical anecdotes to keep the three-hour-long discussion moving. Somewhere in the back of my mind I knew, and some of the students would tell me later, that I would be the first African American female professor most of these students ever had. We were about to begin this journey of discovery together, curious and eager, when in stormed harsh reality in the body of one of my older and notoriously grumpy senior colleagues. "I reserved this room. You'll have to clear out of here," he blurted out with a level of rudeness that left me uncharacteristically speechless. I regained my composure enough to muster: "There must be some mix-up." "There's no mix-up," he interrupted. "I have an important meeting scheduled in this room." Partly embarrassed and partly outraged, I suggested we "step out into the hallway, and discuss this privately." Professor X refused and stormed off to clarify things with the department secretary. A half hour later, class resumed—in the original classroom. The confusion had been his, not mine, and my students were appalled. "Doc," as one of them had already taken to calling me, "that dude showed some serious disrespect." "Yes, he did. Now let's talk about Fannie Lou Hamer and the black freedom movement," I continued, trying to retain my composure.

The offending colleague later offered a halfhearted apology via e-mail. I then dispatched a lengthy and detailed letter of complaint to my college dean and department chair expressing my outrage about what passed for acceptable collegial behavior. The dean never replied. The chair took me to lunch. And that was it. Fortunately, I had a joint appointment in another department, African American studies, where my colleagues were indeed aware of the challenges faced by young black women in the academy. There I found the encouragement to persevere.

In retrospect, what I would say about the classroom incident is that it had less to do with malevolent intentions or any deep-seated feelings of racial animus on the part of my colleague than with a much larger set of systemic problems. One problem is the gross underrepresentation of black women among senior faculty at my institution and most others. If the professor who sought to chase me out of *his* classroom saw more black female colleagues in the hallways, perhaps he would not have dismissed me as what he seemingly perceived as someone with less authority. Perhaps my new colleague assumed I was a teaching assistant or adjunct faculty whom he would not have to face later in departmental meetings. Given that the university hierarchy is gendered and color-coded, with women of color disproportionately at the bottom of the heap, all black women in the institution are more likely to be treated like subordinates. A principled response to this should be twofold: increase the number of senior black women faculty on the one hand and treat coworkers at every level of the hierarchy with greater dignity and respect on the other.

Another problem is the self-serving illusion, so popular of late, that racism is a thing of the past and that only hypersensitive "politically correct" zealots are still focused on the politics of interracial exchanges. In other words, many who are liberal on most matters think we are all too obsessed with race and we ought to just roll through the world as if race does not exist. The problem is that racism still impacts our lives in concrete ways whether we "believe" in it or not. The social construction of race has a material reality in the form of housing discrimination, racist epithets by public figures and celebrities, racial profiling by police, the long-standing deficit in economic and educational opportunities —the list goes on. Therefore, individual encounters happen against the backdrop of a society in which racism is still very real and prevalent.

Still, if my experience with a rude and insensitive colleague had been an isolated event, I too could perhaps write this incident off as a fluke. But there is more. During my first few years of teaching, I was one of only two black women in an otherwise all-white department of some thirty or so faculty. The other black woman colleague looked nothing like me and had an entirely distinct manner and carriage. She was tall, slender, brown-skinned, soft-spoken, reserved, and ten years my junior. Still, almost as if to offer comic relief during our stressful pretenure years, we were routinely confused with one another by several of our senior colleagues. It happened in elevators, in hallways, and even in meetings. No one intended to do this. And each time, there was awkward embarrassment and a polite fumble of an apology. Still, like something out of a Chris Rock or Dave Chappelle comedy skit, they just couldn't tell us apart. Well, one might think, if there were only two of you, how could they have been so confused? The point is we were in the same category. We were viewed as either the two black women who did African American history (a broad field) or the two affirmative action hires, which was not the case, but perceptions and misperceptions can be quite powerful. So despite our physical differences and distinct intellectual interests, we were easily reducible to a simple demographic designation, a rare one in that context. The colleagues I refer to were never the majority, but they were a conspicuous minority.

The university in many ways has always been a foreign country to me, one in which I am constantly being asked to show my passport and constantly being reminded that I am not a local. It is exciting, exotic, and far away from the home of my childhood. In the context of a work environment that makes one feel like an outsider, community is important. In other words, where is it that black female faculty feel at home on university campuses? Not surprisingly, it is often not in their home departments. And the largest community of black women on most campuses, big and small, with the exception of HBCUs, are not professors or administrators but clerical workers, janitors, and cafeteria workers—that is, women who take care of and take orders from someone else, women whose work is seen as low on the hierarchy of value. "Auxiliary services" is the euphemism for their work, but, of course, in reality what they do is quite essential. Black and brown women workers come in at night to empty the trash and clean the carpet. They make thousands of meals a day for generally unappreciative diners. They are the women who never seem to type, copy, file, or process information fast enough for the people who need those tasks performed. These women not only look like me in some superficial ways but also walk, talk, dress, and greet me as my grandmother (a onetime domestic worker and former sharecropper) or my aunt (a hardworking woman with a fifth-grade education and a strong belief in God) would have. In other words, their manner is familiar to me because of culture, community, and family. It is then not at all surprising that, at the end of a long and grueling day when I am leaving and she is coming in for the night shift, it is a custodial worker who has a kind word or a friendly smile for me, even knowing as she does the enormous and unfair disparities between my life and hers. For these reasons, and also because of my own political and moral sensibilities, I am offended when colleagues want to bond over how *bad* the help is. It is one more thing that alienates me from my presumed peers.

Not long ago, a friend of mine who is a black female professor at a large public university recounted a particularly egregious example of the harsh attitudes toward predominately black campus workers by supposedly liberal-minded white colleagues. In a discussion among faculty members, a senior white male administrator exploded in a torrent of complaints about the ineffectual office staff in his department (all of whom were black). They were "incompetent" and simply "not that smart," he insisted. They were "useless," he went on. The racial dynamic seemed totally lost on him, not to mention the sheer class arrogance. There was an apparent expectation of a high level of investment in a job that pays a fraction of what senior professors get. And there was the implied assumption that the staff should be happy about the blatant inequality and give a cheerful "Yessir boss" in reply to demands for service. To add insult to injury, the ranting professor expected his black female colleague to be sympathetic to his disparaging comments about the black workers. He was put off when she was not.

So then back to my initial question—what does it mean to be a black female historian in the early twenty-first century? For me, it is not about cosmetic diversity or phenotype but about remembering who I am in terms of the amalgam of experiences, people, and cultures that define my life. It means bringing that kind of diversity with me into the academy and into my historical research. It is this diversity of thoughts and lenses, curiosities and priorities, sensibilities and experiences that will make our collective intellectual lives more vibrant.

So what are the experiences I bring with me to my work, and why do they matter? I was born in 1957, three years after the U.S. Supreme Court declared racial segregation in schools unconstitutional but long before the impact of that decision would be felt on the ground. I went to all-black schools until ninth grade. My parents were working-class people who had migrated from the red clay towns of Georgia and the cotton fields of Mississippi in search of a better life in the crowded, dirty factories of Detroit and its environs. No one in my family had gone to college, and no one they knew had gone to college, let alone graduate school. I was adopted, and the only reason this personal tidbit is relevant here is that one related fact about my adoptive mother has always stayed with me. It is that by all indications she could not have a biological child of her own because she had had a hysterectomy, without informed consent, when she was in her twenties and still living in Sunflower County, Mississippi. In other words, she was a victim of forced sterilization in the Jim Crow South of the 1930s. This much seems clear even as the details of how and why remain fuzzy. This is only one of the many narratives that I carry with me quietly and invisibly into conferences and archives and classrooms as I go about researching, writing, and teaching the lives of black women in America. I remember that violence and vulnerability were dual pillars of reality for women like my mother. To be sensitive to that kind of experience and the beliefs and behaviors that it informs means remembering that I am my mother's daughter. As Nell Irvin Painter wrote some years ago in an essay in the *Journal of American History*: "In no case is history cut off from the political economy or the personal interests and demographic characteristics of each historian. What goes on in our institutions, our polity, and our experience affects our thought. Who we are as people enters into what we see as important historically and who we prize historiographically."[1]

Who we are matters. It doesn't dictate, proscribe, or determine, but it matters. Being who we are and refusing on some level to homogenize and become unrecognizable and inaudible to the communities we come from will broaden rather than fragment the university and enrich rather than impoverish the constructs of history and the history that we construct. In the words of Brown University president Ruth Simmons, a woman who also began her life as a sharecropper's daughter and now serves as the first black woman to head an Ivy League university: "There is nothing worse than a person who rises to high achievement and who thinks they did it on their own. . . . You owe to the world that has nurtured you, to the family and friends who have supported you, to the generations to come who will falter or thrive, depending on how well you make good on your duty to the general good."[2] I take her admonition very seriously.

One of my fondest memories of graduate school in Ann Arbor in the 1980s was the student/faculty parties that Tom Holt used to throw at his apartment on the outskirts of campus. It was not a staid academic party with neat hors d'oeuvres and neat conversation. There was no chitchat about promotions and hires, publications and dissertations. It was an intergenerational dancing party. The music was loud, and the bodies, with varying degrees of finesse and agility, wiggled, gyrated, and stepped to the music until we were all sweaty and speechless. It was an oasis of familiarity in a foreign country, and there was comfort in the many fellow exiles dancing along with me.

NOTES

1. Nell Irvin Painter et al., "Interchange: The Practice of History," *Journal of American History* 90, no. 2 (September 2003), <www.historycooperative.org>.

2. Ruth Simmons, "Design for Living: Digital Truth and Technicolor Dreams," commencement address at Washington University, St. Louis, May 10, 2002, <http://commencement.wust.edu/2002items/speech.html>.

# Leslie Brown

## HOW A HUNDRED YEARS OF HISTORY

## TRACKED ME DOWN

It is the fall of 2007 as I write this essay. I just finished writing a book. But my father couldn't read or write. The distance between us spans the hundred years of black history that I study.

Writing that statement makes me catch my breath, pained by the sharpness of the contrasts between our lives. My parents, the elderly couple who raised me, were born in the era of *Plessy v. Ferguson*, the U.S. Supreme Court decision that sanctioned Jim Crow. They farmed in the rural South, moved to New York with the Great Migration, and worked in the service sector well past a reasonable retirement age. The living history of slavery, passed on to them by their elders, passed directly to me because of the lack of a generation between us, along with the inherited history of Jim Crow. My parents measured their lives by looking backward to judge how far from slavery they had come. I accepted their hope but claimed membership in the generation that looked forward.

I was born the year of *Brown v. Board of Education*, the landmark Supreme Court case that pried open educational doors that had been closed to them. Willing to take on the risks of being among "the first, the only, and the few," I benefited educationally from the Great Society and affirmative action. But as one of the desegregation generation, I confronted some of the same race and gender challenges that my parents had known and some new ones that they could not understand. Indeed, as I achieved the aspirations my parents had for me, the distance between us widened. Their strategies for survival, experienced under segregation, grated against the ones I crafted to survive desegregation.

My generation occupied the space between American optimism and American cynicism. I started school in the dawning age of Kennedy's presidency. We rode the zeitgeist of direct action and black power and then graduated from high school during the fall of Richard Nixon and from college during Jimmy Carter's Great Malaise. My generation knew greatness and great oratory through Malcolm X, Martin Luther King Jr., Bobby Seale, and Bobby Kennedy, as well as Shirley Chisholm, Eleanor Holmes Norton, Angela Davis, and Flo Kennedy, whose ideas we debated and on whose leadership we depended. We also knew death at too young an age, having lost so many brothers and friends to a war abroad and so many national figures to the war at home.

A half step behind the activists of the 1960s, we were not on the front lines of creating change, but we were its inheritors. We were the third upwelling of modern civil rights activism. In college, Gil Scott Heron and Stevie Wonder hurled our anthems through the windows of Afro-House like rocks thrown at fraternity row (whose former residents, by the way, are now my colleagues). The year I graduated from college, Alex Haley won the Pulitzer for *Roots* and Robert Chambliss was convicted for his role in the bombing of Sixteenth Street Baptist Church in Birmingham. Shirley Chisholm had made her run for president, and the Supreme Court had issued the *Bakke* decision. Compelled—actually chosen—to transport black freedom, black power, and black feminism to the other side of *Brown*, "the first, the only, and the few" learned to move in circles that always had excluded blacks and women. We could get there only by looking forward.

Only through my work—teaching and research in history—have I come to understand how race and gender shaped not only my family's dynamics but also the dynamics of my encounters in the alien world of whiteness. But many other lessons have come from engaging this link between academic history and a personal past.

## *My People*

My people are from the Piedmont region of the Carolinas. My mother, actually my foster mother, was born Louana Alberta Woods in 1892 and was raised by her grandmother, who had been a slave. She was one of the many young women from Camden, Kershaw County, South Carolina, who moved to the North and found employment as household laborers. Her mother, Minnie, worked for a prominent white family and traveled north with them as their housekeeper every summer. In the early 1910s, Grandma Minnie brought along one of her daughters, my Aunt Grace, to work as a child nurse, and one year they decided to stay. My mother moved north to New York City not long after, and her best friend, Grace Alexander McGirt, came along. They later sent for Grace's sister, Molly, and her nieces, Emma and Hattie. My mother's sister, Aunt Maude (called Doc), also had moved north by 1920. Independent and fierce, all of these women saved their money, bought property, and drove big cars. My mother drove a cavernous two-tone blue Chrysler with an automatic transmission; Grace drove a two-tone yellow Buick.

It was into this circle of extended kin that I was born. My birth mother,

Charlotte, also from Camden, was Emma's best friend. Charlotte's job for the railroad kept her away all week. One weekend when the Camden women gathered at Grace's house, Charlotte brought me along. After a long discussion, the women decided to send me to Albany to be raised by Louana, who had moved from New York City to Albany during the 1940s. She had found work at the munitions plant and the army depot, where she had met my father, James Brown (called Brownie). Dad was originally from Salisbury, North Carolina; I don't know much more than that. He did time in a federal prison, although only my mother knew why, a secret she kept until his death in 1970. My mother continued to work, even after I arrived, but now she worked at night as a hotel maid. Dad worked in the evenings as a janitor and during the day as a trashman. He hauled refuse from the downtown restaurants, department stores, and banks and from the homes of their owners. He brought home whatever he thought might be useful, and in the building across the street from our house, my mother opened up a secondhand store, where she offered clothes, coats, dishes, and advice to neighbors down on their luck.

Our neighborhood was questionable and always in transition but interesting enough for a curious child to find a lot of entertainment. We lived on Market Street, on the shady side of the downtown business district. In the back room of my mother's store, men in dark suits and unbuttoned collars ran a horse-betting parlor. The local cops hung out in the Irish bar next door to the store. There was a nightclub around the corner and a gay bar up the street, and the "ladies" walked the corner at the end of our block. A fruit and vegetable warehouse took up the whole corner on the other end of the street, and I joined other neighborhood kids in stealing watermelons from there. Shops, restaurants, churches, and schools dotted the area, and we knew all of the merchants. Sal owned the corner store; Abrams, the liquor store; and Ainspan, the drugstore. We bought my father's work clothes from Rosen's, the uniform store around the corner. African Americans and ethnics usually greeted each other on the street and at the farmers' market, and they often stopped to talk. But they rarely visited each others' homes. Ours was a working-class district, multicultural and ecumenical in terms of its residents but not its institutions. The Italians went to St. Anthony's church and school, the Irish attended St. Patrick's, and the black Catholics went to St. John's. The other whites went to the Methodist church up the street. We belonged to Walls Temple AME Zion Church, and I went to the public school five blocks away.

My parents had little education—my mother attended South Carolina schools as far as sixth grade, and my father went to school hardly at all—so it was my responsibility to achieve, excel, and accomplish, especially when the racial barriers started to fall. Education was first and foremost in my mother's plans for me, including a political education. On Saturdays and Sundays, she sat on the stoop with my father and read the paper out loud, not just to him and me but also to gathering neighbors, some of whom could not read either. She stayed on top of the news, with the *Today Show* blaring in the morning and the *Huntley-Brinkley Report* in the evening. I always knew about national events, about Cuba and Castro and the Bay of Pigs, the civil rights demonstrations in the South, Sputnik and NASA. There was always talk in the kitchen about the possibility of war and whether the racial climate would really change.

My mother also had an entrepreneurial spirit. The local Democratic machine paid her five dollars for every voter she got to the polls. She ran a rooming house, so she could recruit a number of voters and earn extra cash in November. Renting to single men who needed a place but not much space, she played mother to two generations of men who lived on the third and fourth floors of our house. Uncle Larry moved in every time his wife threw him out. Manny lived there from the time he came to the United States from Puerto Rico until he got married. George Washington—to whom I sang Happy Birthday every year on February 22 before he chased me down the stairs—lived on the fourth floor until he died of tuberculosis. Doc came to stay with us while she was dying of cancer. I was around old people so much that I came to accept death as inevitable.

I was like most old people's children, wise and staid, a cautious listener, and a careful observer. Womanish is the perfect description for me at age seven, possessing too much knowledge, too much attitude, and too much mouth. Black people from down South, from the country, just out of the military, or just passing by the house, whether staying or going, provided a steady stream of visitors for me to interrogate, and I was nosy. With so many teasing adults around, though, I had to hone sharp defenses against being teased or tickled, developing the quick one-liner and quick reflexes. We owned a large dining room table with big lions' feet as legs around which an assortment of black folk sat on weekends and holidays. I would sit under the table on the feet and listen to the adults talk and laugh. Uncle Larry always told the story about me driving the car: one Sunday morning, I got into my mother's Chrysler with the keys (and the dog), turned on the engine, and put the car in reverse. I was four and lucky to live to see five.

The other stories were about the South, about a teacher who looked like Maggie from the comic strip "Maggie and Jiggs"; about pilot snakes, catfish, and a weed the old folks smoked called Life Everlasting (marijuana); about jackleg preachers and trifling ministers; about friendship, mutuality, and mean white folks. They also told stories about coming north: meeting someone from home at a club in Harlem, the last time they heard Billie Holiday sing, and fooling the employment agency into thinking they were Indians in order to get jobs. My aunt told a story about Adam Clayton Powell getting blacks in New York City to go to the utility company office and pay their bills in pennies to force the company to hire black clerks. Once someone told a story about the time Uncle Bruce asked a white shoe salesman in Camden why he didn't call his aunt Mrs. Woods. His friends spirited him out of town that night on the southbound train, figuring the mob would think he'd head north. After these kinds of stories, the bitter ones, they would laugh one last laugh and follow it with deep sighs and shaking heads full of memories they could not tell out loud.

As a kid, I wore these stories like armor. From them, I learned how to find humor in almost anything, to hold my own in an argument, and to get along with anyone, skills that developed beyond my conscious mind. Even more un- consciously, I learned history, culture, literature, anthropology, and antiquing. The not-so-subtle lessons were about manners and morals, about behaving like those in the respectable class. There were other lessons about "don't," the most important of which were "Don't make me have to tell you twice," "Don't make me come in there," and "Don't forget who you're talking to."

## Transition

The world of black ways gave way when urban renewal ripped through the streets and houses of the neighborhood. All the businesses closed. All my friends moved away, and eventually all the visitors stopped coming around. The area became hazardous, covered with empty lots strewn with bricks, glass, and pipes and empty buildings occupied by rats and rabid dogs. My mother, a stubborn soul, refused to let go of her house, so we stayed on Market Street until the city tore down every building in the neighborhood except ours and the two that were attached to ours on either side. Those were scary months of waiting and hearing my parents fight about something they could do little about. Eventually my father moved out. Unwilling to move to the projects, my mother used the last of their money to buy a house on Hudson Avenue in a white working-class neighborhood that did not welcome us. Our lawyer, who was white, bought the house and then turned it over to my mother. So the new neighbors were very surprised when we appeared. This was a new racial zone. One by one, the houses transformed from white homes to black until the only whites left were the ones who could not afford to move, though they were the majority. Eventually, the white kids stopped breaking our windows and throwing trash on our porch, and although black and white kids played (and fought) together on the street, we did not enter each others' houses.

The new neighborhood meant a new school, bright and clean and well ordered. The elders expected that I would step up to opportunity when it appeared, step in assertively, and pull everyone else in behind me. Of course, however rough it would be for me as the only black student in the class, my road of racial progress would be less treacherous than theirs had been. I wasn't so sure of that, however, the first day of fourth grade when I walked into my new school and an all-white classroom without a parent, the only black person in the room, knowing even then that the white parents there perceived my parents as less caring, less involved, and less committed to education. Not surprisingly, that first year was a struggle. After much debate and testing, I earned my place among students in the gifted class, but only one other black kid had been in their classrooms, and they were not too pleased about this one either. The first week, Miss Long warned me that she knew all about "you people" and that she would not tolerate the kind of deportment "you people" exhibited at "those schools" "you people" came from. Each year, I was pulled out of the alphabetized order of the class to sit at the left hand of the teacher, under excessive control, not because I behaved badly (I knew better) but because the teachers assumed I would if I was let loose on the other kids.

Suspicious of my academic abilities whenever my grades were good, teachers always challenged me. One set of homework problems done well was followed by another harder set and then another until Miss Long could say, "See, I knew you couldn't do it." Obstacles had been removed, but this did not mean race no longer mattered. Academic performance became a way for me to prove my equality, my belligerence, and my refusal to be intimidated. A steady performance made me safe in school. Outside school, I learned to bear racial insult, harassment, and assaults. I had to figure out when it was worth the punishment to fight back (and sometimes it was). Not trusting how my parents would react, I kept those altercations secret unless they left me with a bald patch on my head or a bruise on the side of my face.

Staying in the advanced class meant bearing the weight of race—not just the demand to prove my own capabilities but also the inability to look to my parents for academic support. I had to struggle through math, science, and English without very much help at home. Worse, as far as I was concerned, was bearing the cost of school. My mother did the best she could to keep a growing girl in clothes, but projects, trips, and supplies also cost money, and I grew tired of hearing that one pencil and one piece of chalk had to last all year. My parents had worked as children, and my mother, the more demanding of the two, had no concept of labor laws. I was willing to mow lawns, shovel snow, and babysit, but she got me jobs cleaning white people's houses on Saturdays. This I really resented, not just because I didn't want to give up my Saturdays but also because it was work I did not want to do. How could I tell someone who had spent her life doing that work that I was too good for it? So I didn't, and instead I perfected the silent seethe.

I was benefiting from newly opened doors, but that entryway became a divider. And over time, the fissure grew. Through Great Society programs, I participated in a wide range of activities that disadvantaged students rarely had access to. I attended the ballet, the symphony, and the theater, and I took classes in writing and elocution. Too immature to figure out how to switch languages between home and school, I sensed my family's growing resentment. I was becoming something they didn't know, understand, or tolerate, and they had become something I didn't want to be.

As the educational divide played out at home, I occupied a space between black and white at school. Even when the class divided between boys and girls, I remained an outsider to my female cohort. Most black students conveyed hostility toward me by tagging my academic achievement as "acting white." The white boys mostly were mean, especially junior high adolescents seeking easy targets. All but a few curious white students avoided me. For the most part, neither my classmates nor their parents were acquainted with any African Americans other than the ones who worked in their homes. I did not know how to react when I arrived at a classmate's house to find one of my mother's friends working as the housekeeper for the family. Other family friends staffed the school cafeteria and tended the locker rooms. This meant, of course, that there was little I could get away with since each of them reported my activities to my mother. I made new friends the week Martin Luther King Jr. was assassinated when the white kids seeking safety walked with me to the bus stop for the first time.

By 1969, ninth grade, the tide of love and brotherhood had turned enough for me to collect a range of acquaintances, black, Asian, Jewish, and international. The daily task of school was less difficult, yet I was all the more discontent. My father spent that year and most of the next in and out of the hospital, and I went to visit him every day. He died in the summer of 1970. I felt relieved, guiltily, because his passing freed me to get more involved in school activities. Clubs and sports kept me away from home and from my own sadness. They filled the gaping hole between where I came from and where I wanted to go.

When Dad died, I started thinking about my own life. Adolescent angst and self-possession were not privileges that my mother had known, and she did not understand. Nor was she one to soften the blow. It had been my hidden aspiration to go to Howard University. I failed to heed, or did not understand, her warning that I was not like those Howard people; I didn't have good hair or good clothes. I took these comments as criticisms until I got the chance to visit the D.C. campus. When someone asked what my people did, I answered honestly that my mother was a kitchen worker and my father had passed away, only to watch faces fall and backs turn as the Howard students met my enthusiasm with contempt. Their response conveyed that no black college would welcome me, a message reinforced when the admissions person warned me that Howard did not have a lot of money to give out in scholarships. Financial aid was a necessity for me, as it was for most black students, but my mother, like most black parents, was reluctant to reveal the personal information required for the application. When I finally got her to cooperate, I was shocked at how little we lived on and promised myself that I'd never ask her to pay for anything again. As soon as I turned sixteen, I got a job at McDonald's. One of the first women and one of the first blacks hired, in order to keep the job, I had to learn to put up with a lot (and to give it back) and to do the work better than everyone else.

The gifted program led to advanced classes in high school, so I stayed with the cohort I'd known in elementary school. I knew very few people who had attended college, only my cousin who was a teacher, one of my high school teachers, and the daughter of one of my mother's friends. And I knew little about applying to college, except for the names of the schools that my classmates talked about. Once the SATS, rankings, and National Merit scores came out, the college-recruitment process began, and my classmates' tolerance turned into hostility. Through minority-student recruitment programs, I received a lot of personal attention from admissions people at the schools my classmates were applying to. Tufts University was the backup for those who aimed for the Ivies and the reach school for those applying to liberal arts colleges, so it was on everyone's list. In the end, I was one of only two students from my high school who got accepted at Tufts that year. Most of my teachers were pleased and encouraging; they had written my letters of recommendation. One of the few who were not supportive remarked, "You don't deserve it; you don't work hard enough, and you're not that smart. You only got in because you're black." So despite having applied to many other schools, I selected Tufts out of spite, increased my hours at McDonald's, and worked full-time through the spring of my senior year and overtime in the summer.

I was in love with the idea of college, but I found the reality disappointing. Tufts was unlike any place I had ever known, comprised of wealthy students from all over the country and all over the world, which made it all the more distant from my mother's dining room table. Many had attended New England prep schools I had never heard of, such as Choate, Northfield–Mt. Hermon, and Deerfield. Nor did I know that black people could have so much money. Light-skinned, fine-haired, and well-dressed, most of the black students drove nice cars and wore expensive clothes. A poor kid with bad skin and a wardrobe of jeans and T-shirts, I didn't fit in with the crowd, but I could compete in the classroom. Still, I could not relieve my restlessness until I found courses in black history, black literature, and black politics. These introduced me to issues and writers that I didn't know much about: Frederick Douglass, W. E. B. Du Bois, and John Hope Franklin in history, and Langston Hughes, Richard Wright, Ralph Ellison, and Gwendolyn Brooks, the only black woman writer I read, in literature. These courses were taught by black faculty, but they were the only courses black faculty taught and the only black-focused courses offered. Once I took them, there was no place to go to quench my thirst for more.

These courses, along with a summer internship with the Massachusetts legislature's black caucus, heightened my racial consciousness and brought me out as a black person. I found words for my frustration and discontent and became active in local civil rights issues, which in Boston centered on busing and electing a black councilperson. Outside of the institutional setting of the college, I started to focus on who I was and what I cared about but kept those matters separate from my education. By my senior year, Tufts had recruited more black students like me, disadvantaged and eager, and I felt less isolated in some ways. Of the three black faculty members I had known, only one remained at the university until I graduated, and she seemed miserable.

### Passing On

While most students faced the tough decisions of senior year, mine came quite easily. I had thought briefly about graduate school and had hoped to stay in the Boston area, but my mother, very aged by then, had become frail. If I considered, however briefly, not coming home, my relatives were happy to remind me of my obligations. She had taken me in as family, and now it was my turn to care for her. The generational divide created more resentment on both sides. I had never known that my family thought I had done the wrong thing by going off to college instead of staying and helping at home. We all agreed that my place was at home now, but they would not tolerate my putting my mother into a nursing home. Black people didn't leave the care of their elders to someone else; parents were not supposed to be palmed off on other people.

Stepping up to my adult role, I took the best-paying job I could find—I returned to McDonald's, this time in management and field operations and again as one of the first women and one of the first African Americans to work at the corporate level. Well-paying but very hard work, it provided the income I needed to support myself and my mother, whom I lost to Alzheimer's over those years. After she died in 1982 at the age of ninety, I quit my job at Mickey D's. For a while, I bummed around, despondent and dejected, wasting years. I took a job as a retail manager, then as a driver for Ryder Truck Rentals. I became a bartender and a bouncer and a hard-partying lesbian, overwhelmed by hopelessness.

The fog began to lift when I found a position in college admissions recruiting minority students and then accepted a job as the director of a program that recruited and admitted disadvantaged students at a small upstate New York liberal arts college that resembled Tufts. With the program staff, I created mentoring, counseling, and academic-support programs, each of which improved the students' academic performance but did not enhance their sense of belonging. Enlivened by increasing the number of minority students enrolled, the program itself provided a strong community base, attracting a range of people, including blacks, Latinos, and townies but also gays and lesbians and the politically active. My students' experiences reflected the sense of anomie that had possessed me in college. They too were overwhelmed by the cultural change but felt isolated from home and increasingly unwilling to return to a place that signified limitations. It became my job to play mother, sister, aunt, cousin, and confessor to every student of color on campus (and every student who knew a student of color or who had never known a person of color but wanted to) and every gay student as well. Gay students' struggles with sexuality encouraged me to come out as a lesbian—to be visible and, to the surprise of many, functional, and, to my own surprise, relieved.

But administrators can do only so much to support students trying on new identities, particularly since so few administrators of color understand the transformation that occurs among the economically disadvantaged who enroll in college. They can offer support but not the kind of intellectual engagement students of color want or need. It is hard to feel a part of a community when you have no representatives at its core. These students were learning what I learned but could not articulate: that education pulled them further from their roots, even as they worked to fulfill family aspirations. And in the way it was populated, college provided more evidence of constraints than of opportunities.

The hierarchy of higher education reflects the hierarchy of race that the civil rights movement was supposed to have toppled. It was our collective observation that those of us who had desegregated colleges in the 1960s and 1970s had done little more than that. Three decades after *Brown*, African Americans worked mostly in service jobs at the institution, some in administration, but none (or very few) could be found among faculty. This troubled me on behalf of my students. What does it mean for students of color to not see themselves represented among the institution's primary intellectual achievers? And what does it say to white students? Without people of color—or many women— among the professoriat, I wondered, can students of color view academia and intellectual pursuits as viable realms of achievement? More important, if faculty hold—or believe they should hold—intellectual authority and control over the curriculum, doesn't the absence of black and Latino professors reiterate a racial hierarchy of power and influence and thus undermine the assumption of education as an equalizer? Or at least nullify the equal educational opportunity implied by admission to the college?

These questions transcended matters of culture or specific scholarly disciplines, for not all black and Latino faculty teach black and Latino subjects. Rather, the wide-angle lens on the landscape of higher education revealed the breadth of the problem. What my students and I saw and experienced was that the dynamics of educational achievement remained within the domain of mostly white males. Where can students of color get intellectual validation that does not require them to so fully assimilate that they lose the best of themselves, their families, and their cultures? It occurred to me that through grade school and high school we had learned to compete, to keep up, but not to surpass; to stand alongside but not in front; to fit in but not to reshape.

The answers kept coming back to the presence or absence of black faculty as fully participating members of the academic community. Through meetings, panels, and discussions ad nauseum centered on what became known as "the black faculty issue," the students and I raised challenging questions that the faculty had to grapple with, if for no other reason than the fact that we refused to back down. Arguing for diversity for diversity's sake failed to shake traditional hiring practices. When equality equates with sameness, it defeats innovation. We turned our attention to the relationship between intellectualism and race as it played out in our everyday college lives and beyond.

The circular problem of supply and demand threatened to defeat any initiatives: there were few black Ph.D.'s, and moving the same faculty members from place to place (or raiding the historically black institutions) did nothing to increase the quantity available. Without a professoriat of color, students rarely viewed such positions as viable careers. How, furthermore, could we encourage students who were pressured, like I was, with family obligations to continue in school for three more years?

I found a number of women on campus who supported the cause and who facilitated my connection with other faculty. But it was my students who finally asked me, "Why don't you go to grad school?" To be honest, the question caught me off guard. I knew one black person with a Ph.D. but no others who had even studied for a doctorate. When I asked her what one needed to get a Ph.D., she answered, "You need to be crazy." My students presented me the same challenges that I had presented them. Their pestering (and my time on campus) did rekindle a small part of my disappointing love affair with academia as an undergraduate. So with support from my campus allies, I gave graduate school serious thought.

Still, I had reservations about returning to school after a dozen years out. You just don't up and apply for grad school like it was this morning's great idea. The students wisely pointed out that I could take undergraduate courses as refreshers. Rolling toward forty, however, I thought a lot about my age, about having a tenure party and a retirement party at the same time. It was my 105-year-old Aunt Grace, who was always the hardest on me, who dismissed my reservations about returning to school. "So what if you don't finish until you're fifty," she said. "You'll be fifty years old with a Ph.D. or fifty years old without a Ph.D.; either way, you're going to be fifty." You can't argue with old people; it's like arguing with a drunk—they're always right. And you cannot talk to black people who grew up in the Jim Crow South about feeling inferior. Nor can you talk to them about having to climb the racial mountain because they have already climbed it. I certainly could not talk to Aunt Grace about my reluctance to bear the harshness of crossing one more race obstacle.

## Ironies

Lest I suffer the embarrassment of not getting in, I told only a few people that I had decided to go to grad school. I decided that if I got in, I would also be prepared to flunk out; in fact, I made flunking out the default position and assumed that my job would still be there when I came back. Then there was the question of which program would be worthy of making me give up my home and my community. This question was the easiest to answer because I got accepted at only one place.

Graduate school at Duke University in the early 1990s was just the opposite of what I had expected. Given the faculty picture at most institutions, I assumed that Duke would be the same or, as a southern school, worse and that the faculty would be hostile toward black students or the study of black history. Instead, Duke (as I call the experience, the program, and the place) was a place of renewal and sustenance. The graduate program in history was the hardest thing I ever did, but it was also the best thing I ever did. For the first time in my educational history, perhaps my adult life, I did not feel intellectually or socially isolated. Nine African American students enrolled in the graduate program's first-year class (more than I had ever known among any previous cohort), and we joined a group already enrolled in the two previous classes. Moreover, it was a place that had a history of graduating black scholars, thus a difficult path had been smoothed. There were more black professors in the department than I'd had as teachers in all my years of schooling. I discovered the life of the mind, which is where I lived most of the time anyway. Being a student felt like re-decorating my interior life. I felt a joy I had not known before in being among a legion of students of color, women, gays, and women my age. But there was more. Much as I had found at the college where I had worked, I met allies and supporters among the white faculty, men and women who believed in taking action toward change. And I met my partner, Annie, at Duke; we have lived together now for some fifteen years.

My graduate cohort worked together as graduate assistants and research coordinators on a project called "Behind the Veil: Documenting African American Life in the Jim Crow South." The project included an academic conference, a summer institute for faculty, a graduate class, an undergraduate curriculum, and a field research component that focused on collecting oral history interviews. As the conference organizer, I met, to my great delight, African American faculty. They gave me a sense of pride, confidence, and comfort. Even more important, it was inspiring for me to meet African American women scholars who gave papers, chaired sessions, and spoke up in breakout groups. I realized that I was in the presence of people who had written books, and I was in awe. This was an achievement I never thought I'd meet.


### Finding Home

For the "Behind the Veil" project, I crisscrossed the South in the company of other explorers, sharing a journey that began on an intellectual level but cut deep into a place that I had long forgotten. Everywhere the stories of elderly southerners echoed the ones I had heard sitting beneath my mother's dining room table, but I listened with the ear of a historian, not that of a child. They told stories about hard work, community, and mean white people; about teachers they recalled as inspiring, the churches they had attended, the jokes they had played. These were people whose voices were rarely heard, and since my college years, I had almost forgotten them. I engaged their cadences, so much slower than my New York pace, the softness of their southern accents contrasting with my upstate twang. Through these interviews, I found a place I had lost. The further I delved into the study of African American and women's history, however, the closer I came to reclaiming my personal history. And as much as I struggled with theory, it did give me a way to read a connection that I didn't immediately understand. The people I met through the project gave me a sense of pride as well as stories that countered the assumptions that white people held. The work made me feel capable in a way I'd never known. I developed the indefinable skills needed to record their histories, read their sources, and forge respectful analyses.

The topic of the Jim Crow South reconnected me to the past and made me feel like part of my family again. I understood what my parents had not been able to explain. And I have wondered ever since if they were angry or ashamed. And if it really was different on this side of the civil rights era. As I grasped the complexities of Jim Crow, I wondered how they stood the arbitrariness of the system. Where did they get such patience? Jim Crow caused and maintained their poverty and crushed any aspirations they had for themselves, but they found solace and support in their communities and families and avoided confrontations with whites. And although I had grown up in an integrated setting and had to be part of it to get a good education, my parents never trusted white folks, and they would have preferred that I had little to do with them.

I came to understand the intricacies of their network and the meaning of kith and kin. And I realized that black family is and always has been strong even if scattered, linked together by friends reconstructed as relatives. Moreover, I came to appreciate my family members as historical actors—their participation in the drudgery of farming, their excitement about moving north with the Great Migration, and their insistence on voting "even if they ran a dog for dogcatcher." The study of race, gender, and class gave me a new appreciation for my mother's role in the neighborhood as an adviser whom everyone consulted before taking action and as a bridge linking different groups of people together. I learned how it was possible that my father attended school but never learned to read or write and why my mother always kept me close by.

It was not my intent to turn my family into an intellectual exercise. That I could access my family's stories in academic ways made the "Behind the Veil" project all the richer and made it easier to comprehend the stories of interviewees. Through the interviews, I also came to appreciate the reasons for my parents' strictness and their stifling protectiveness. It was their way of trying to prevent me from having to endure things that had happened to them or to someone they knew personally. The research also helped me to understand their approach to politics and infrapolitics, the ways they manipulated difficult circumstances to find space for their dignity. Through the research, I became better able to think about my family's history in terms of who raised whom, how, and why. I felt like I was bringing my family into the academy they had never been able to approach. I heard their voices, reactions, and interpretations when I read documents. I heard them speak to me through oral history; they explained their world to me as I traveled throughout the South.

Finally, through graduate school, I found my own feminist sensibility, which I admit had always been subsumed by race until I discovered Alice Walker's 1983 book, *In Search of Our Mothers' Gardens*. Its themes resonated with me and refreshed memories of my mother's front window full of plants and her back-yard full of roses. I grow roses now to honor her. In my first week, Anne Firor Scott gave me a copy of Deborah Gray White's book *Ar'n't I a Woman?*, the first book I ever read in black women's history. It forced me to own the stories of slavery that I had always wished to cast off. Darlene Clark Hine's book *Black Women in White* reminded me of my godmother, who was a graduate nurse. At the "Behind the Veil" conference, I heard Elsa Barkley Brown and Evelyn Brooks Higginbotham talk about women and mutual aid. Sharon Harley talked about work; Roslyn Terborg-Penn, about voting. These women schol-ars, and many more, had already engaged in the intellectual warfare that I had anticipated, but I suspect that their graduate years were not as comfortable as mine.

I am well aware that my Duke experience was exceptional and that graduate cohorts like mine come around once in a generation. This became clear when I started going to conferences, where African Americans and especially black women still struggled for visibility. It was clear that much of the scholarship on women excluded women of color and much of the scholarship on African Americans excluded women. And it was still a battle to get African American women's history taken seriously as a field. Alienation and isolation were the overwhelming circumstances of most black women students and faculty. This I understood as I moved through my graduate-school years.

I'd like to be able to say that the glow has lasted throughout my scholarly career, but, of course, it has not. Some days, I feel like I'm back at McDonald's. Even as surprising changes unfold, gender and race politics play out every-where. I was elected the first graduate representative to the Executive Council of the American Historical Association. At a forum to discuss critical graduate issues, a young white man stood up in the back and said, "You're making it hard on the rest of us. You black women are getting all the jobs." Be that as it may (and it was certainly not true), if the few of us on the market got all 700 offers made to historians every year, we still could take only one each. That left the other 695 jobs for others. That was just a taste of what was to come.

My first job came easily enough. I was hired at the University of Missouri at St. Louis, but it was quite an adjustment. I was one of two black women in a department of five or six faculty members. Except for my research and my engagement with the profession outside of the university, my alienation recalled my college days. Although there were three black faculty in history, the hostilities from other faculty were almost as bad as those I had sometimes known in grade school. The chair hung a noose in his office. I heard a group of senior men telling "colored people" jokes in the hall. Several of them never even spoke to me when we passed in the hall. One demanded that I give up the seminar room where my class met so that he could hold his class there. They might have thought they were enforcing some junior/senior hierarchy, but I interpreted such actions as motivated by issues of race and gender. When I moved from UMSL to Washington University, in the same city, they did not wish me luck. Rather, they probably expected that I would never make it to tenure there.

And so here I am, wondering how tenure will play out. Inasmuch as Duke was my coming-out party, Washington University is my life in the open. I am out as a lesbian to my colleagues, my students, and the administration. Since I am an African American woman, my presence at the university takes on a political cast. The crusade for black faculty continues, but I do have colleagues of color who are also in the fray and a coterie of students coming through the pipeline. Undergrads have entered grad programs, and I mentor grad students of my own. The freedom of the university is something that my parents would have never expected. I teach what I want, and my research agenda focuses on African American women without challenges to its credibility. For that, I can thank the sister scholars who have come before me. The students lined up outside my door attest to the popularity of my courses and my dedication to those who enroll. My classes become a forum for race and gender issues in historical context and in the present, heated by invigorating discussions that continue even after class lets out.

Education and the academy have changed dramatically since the 1960s, but they have not been transformed. As an African American woman professor, I am called upon to do much more in the Washington University community than is demanded of my white colleagues, and in this way, the race and gender paradigm is little different than it was in the past. I am not entitled to be difficult, a tactic that keeps my white tenure cohort out of committee work, or I risk being labeled as detached, noncollegial, and obstinate. Nor can I teach with mediocrity lest I be accused of laziness. Each semester, at least one student evaluation complains that I must have been an affirmative action hire, short-hand for being incapable, unqualified, and incompetent. Others accuse me of racism because the white experience is marginalized, ironically in classes specif-ically designated as African American studies. In addition to the usual faculty load, I still play mother, sister, aunt, and cousin to too many students of color, as well as gays and lesbians. Diversity programs, women of color conferences, speaker series, and black history celebrations all take pieces of me.

And yet I love my job and can't think of anything I'd rather be doing. I was born a historian, practiced in the art of interrogation. I'm never happier than when I'm in the classroom. And I know from my own experiences that my visible presence on campus proffers special meaning to students who come to Washington University, even the Republican ones. I am here, for the most part, for students of color, who, like me, feel anxiety about an environment that is so unlike home, students who are searching for something about themselves in the academic arena and seeking a way to sustain the connection between their families and themselves. Just how much has the academy changed?

### Postscript

Not until recently did I realize how close black history cuts to my personal life. Through an alumni website, I got a message from Cecelia Jackson, which I promptly ignored since I did not remember the name. I opened the e-mail the third time it announced itself to find a message I did not expect. My sister Cecelia was searching for me. We shared the same birth mother and possibly the same father but had only seen each other once, at a meeting that included my birth mother, Charlotte, and Charlotte's three sons. Charlotte had passed away by the time I got the message, but Cece was living in Portland, brother Brian was in Washington, Martin was in Atlanta, and Raymond was still in Camden. Our conversations—Cece talking about family and me talking about my research—traced a direct line between us and the past. Apparently, my oldest living relative still holds down the family roots in Camden. Thomas "Daddy Mac" McLester, now ninety-four years old, was the son of Thomas and Elise McLester. Thomas "Daddy Tom" McLester was the son of Hugh McLester and a slave named Ellen, who had been given to Hugh as a gift from his father, Archie. Archie McLester originally had rented Ellen from the Boykin family, as in Mary Boykin Chesnutt, the Civil War diarist who wrote with disgust about her husband's mistress and his mixed-raced offspring.

Tracing the story forward revealed even more irony. Through Cece I met my uncle, Jerry Raymond, my birth mother's brother. I told him about my research, a study of the black community of Durham, North Carolina. When he finished laughing, he told me that he (we) had an aunt who had been a teacher in the segregated Durham public schools; that his uncle (and mine), Rev. Charles McLester, had been the minister at Mt. Vernon AME Zion Church; and that Uncle Charles's wife, Johnnie McLester (called Johnnie Mac), had been active in a statewide women's mission society and the YWCA. I had interviewed Johnnie McLester in Durham in 1993, not knowing then that she was my great-aunt. Hers was the first interview I did. Her keen insights into black Durham's backstage allowed me to see the complexities of the black community. By the time I learned she was my relative, she had passed away. I love this story, nonetheless, because it illuminates so well the importance of family stories in African American history. How do you talk about the rest?

There's a book in here somewhere.

# Crystal N. Feimster

## NOT SO IVORY

### AFRICAN AMERICAN WOMEN HISTORIANS
### CREATING ACADEMIC COMMUNITIES

*This kind of testimony makes a difference, I still think, and I hope you'll share*
*it with everyone you know—as a warning and as a statement of solidarity with*
*those who have encountered similar situations and concluded in their isolation*
*that the difficulties were somehow their fault. Your letter can help break down*
*the isolation that is poison to people like us.*
—*Nell Irvin Painter to Crystal N. Feimster, April 1997*

In the spring of 1997, after attending my first graduate-student conference at the University of Mississippi in Oxford, where, as the only African
American participant, I was virtually ignored and my work on the lynching of
black and white women viciously attacked, Nell Painter welcomed me "to the
long-suffering, much-abused community of black women academics." Painter
was responding to my article in the Coordinating Council of Women's Historians newsletter, "An Open Letter to My Advisor." In it, I recounted in detail
how I was treated at the conference. A third-year graduate student at Princeton
University, I should not have been surprised at how shabbily I was treated at Ole
Miss. It was not the first time that I had been mistreated because of my race and
sex; however, it was the first time that my work had been openly dismissed as
irrelevant and unworthy of study. The problem I faced, however, was not simply
my sex and race but also my ease with theory and my being from Princeton. Not
completely naive, I understood that not everyone in the profession was happy
to see more African Americans and women joining the ranks, but somehow I
had convinced myself that such prejudice would not affect the reception of my
work. I believed that my scholarship, if well researched, written, and argued,
could stand alone. So as you can imagine, this conference was a rude awaken-
ing. How, you might ask, could I have been so unprepared for the harshness of
this experience? The answer to that question has to do with not only the
generation of African American women historians who paved the way for me
but also the intellectual communities of support that both people of color and

women have been able to create within the ivory tower. As an undergraduate in the early 1990s, a graduate student in the late 1990s, and an assistant professor beginning in 2000, my experiences in the academy are quite different from those of the generation of scholars who came before me. My relative shock at how badly I was treated at Ole Miss is in many ways a testament to how much these scholars have done to change the academy. Indeed, my experiences are a reflection of the success of the women and faculty of color at my undergraduate and graduate institutions as well as scholars in the field of African American women's history at creating welcoming and supportive environments in which I could learn and develop as a historian.

## The Birth of a Historian:
## The University of North Carolina at Chapel Hill, 1990–1994

I did not always know that I wanted to be a historian. In fact, I had convinced myself that I wanted to practice law when I entered the University of North Carolina at Chapel Hill as a freshman in 1990. I had decided on a career in the legal profession not out of some compelling interest in law but because it gave me a valid excuse for turning down a four-year academic scholarship that required a commitment to teaching in the North Carolina public schools upon graduation. I had been awarded the North Carolina Teaching Fellows Scholarship, and if I had accepted the award, it would have meant not only having to commit to teaching but also having to give up my dream of attending the University of North Carolina at Chapel Hill because the fellowship committee required that I attend the university of its choice—Appalachian State University. Thus, I believed it was necessary to have a respectable alternative to teaching to justify my decision to turn down the scholarship. Having been born to teenage parents who did not graduate from high school and were for years forced to work in the North Carolina textile and furniture factories, I understood the importance of a college degree and a well-paying job. I wanted to go to the best school I could get into, and for me, that school was UNC–Chapel Hill.

I must confess it was not easy to look a gift horse in the mouth. Indeed, many of my white high school teachers were horrified that I would even consider not accepting the scholarship because, as they were so eager to point out, my mother was a single parent with two college-age daughters. My sister, who was a freshman at South Carolina State, was struggling to pay her out-of-state tuition, and my father, who was serving the second year of a seven-year prison sentence, was in no position to help. If I wanted to attend UNC, I would have to take out loans and work part-time. Against the wishes of my high school teachers but with my mother's support, I turned down the scholarship and headed to Chapel Hill in the fall of 1990.

When I arrived at UNC, a major in history was the furthest thing from my mind. During my senior year in high school, I had suffered through a college history course that I was convinced had forever turned me off of history. More important, credit in the course meant I was exempt from having to take the Western civilization course that was required of all UNC undergraduates. Thus, with my history course requirement behind me, I imagined with delight an undergraduate career free from memorizing dates, names, and the life stories of a bunch of dead white guys. The English department, I decided, would be my intellectual home. A major that would allow me to spend my days reading novels, plays, and short stories seemed perfect, and I enrolled in an English course entitled "William Shakespeare's Plays." What I had not imagined, however, was a professor with an eye patch and a cane who did not share my enthusiasm. Determined to teach her class without freshmen, she used every scare tactic in the book to convince those of us who did not have more than three semesters under our belt to drop the course. I, however, dropped not only the course but the major as well. With the drop/add period coming to a rapid close, I was desperate to find another course and more than willing to take the advice of a football player who suggested that I take "Introduction to Women's Studies," a lecture course with an enrollment of 250. He had earned a B in the course and was convinced that I could do even better. Clueless as to what women's studies was about but desperate for a course that would both fit into my schedule and fulfill a General College requirement, I added the course. I had no idea that enrolling in this course would put me on the path to becoming a professional historian.

While "Introduction to Women's Studies" was not a history course, a historian, Barbara Harris (chair of women's studies), taught it. The course was an interdisciplinary exploration of intersections between gender, race, class, and sexuality in American society and internationally. Topics included work; sexuality and sexual identity; gender relations and images of women and gender in literature, religion, art, and science; and the history of feminist movements. Course readings were drawn from the humanities and the social sciences, and to my surprise, I found the essays written by historians the most compelling. Feminist theory was a revelation when I heard Harris's lecture on the topic. I enjoyed the readings, lectures, and discussions so much that at the end of the semester, I asked Harris what she would be teaching in the spring semester; "European Women's History from 1750" was her reply. I not only signed up for the course but also convinced Harris to hire me as a work-study student in the women's studies program.

The history department at UNC was an exhilarating place in the early 1990s when I arrived. Scholars like Nell Painter, Colin Palmer, and Herman Bennett had moved on to other institutions by that time, but it was clear that they had changed the department for the better and made it easier for those who would come after them. Among the faculty were women and people of color interested in a diverse set of fields. Women and African American faculty were in a minority but still more numerous than in most history departments, and for the first time, I would be taught by women of color and scholars in the fields of women's history and African American history. In the spring of my sophomore year, I declared myself a history major and enrolled in four history courses. When I signed up for the twentieth-century American history survey, I knew nothing about the professor, except that his/her last name was Hunter. On the first day of class, I was thrilled to see a young African American woman standing at the front of the classroom. Tera Hunter, a Yale University Ph.D. who was writing a book on southern black women and labor in the postwar South, taught me that placing women and people of color at the center of American history was both possible and necessary. After learning from Barbara Harris that I might be interested in pursuing a graduate degree in history, Hunter wrote me a note encouraging me to apply for an internship at the Martin Luther King Papers Project at Stanford University. Not quite ready to give up the idea of law school, I decided not to apply to the program that year but promised her I would consider applying in my junior year.

During the same semester, Darlene Clark Hine visited UNC as the Hanes-Willis Visiting Professor and gave a series of talks on African American women's history. While I attended all three of her lectures, it was the first, "The Intersection of Race, Gender, and Class in the Lives of Black Women," that I found most compelling. "I had discovered that there is power in history," she explained; "one makes claims on society to the extent that one has made contributions." Black women, she argued, had made significant contributions to the survival of the black community, yet their histories had been overlooked. She noted: "A decade ago, it would have been impossible to find books dealing with black women." I was impressed by her argument that black women sought to protect themselves and their self-esteem from negative sexual stereotypes and degrading racial images by opting to become invisible as a defensive survival strategy. Invisibility, however, did not necessarily mean powerlessness, she argued. I had never thought about history in such terms. Hine's lecture challenged me to think about the ways that history can effect change in society and exposed me to the power of African American women's history.

On a mission to motivate me to think seriously about graduate study in history, Barbara Harris arranged for me to have lunch with Hine. Taking the opportunity to make the case for graduate study in history, Hine asked me why I wanted to go to law school. I babbled on about wanting to make a difference as a civil rights lawyer and not being sure that I could make a difference in the world as a historian. She was quick to challenge my assumptions about history and reiterate her argument about its empowerment. She contended that it was important that historians take black women's experience seriously and that black women historians lead the way. She explained that of those receiving Ph.D.'s in history since 1975 only 2.2 percent had been African American women. At the end of the meal, Hine made me promise to think seriously about pursuing graduate study in African American history.

During my junior year, I took a range of courses such as "Women in Latin America," "Women in Africa," "Women, Race, and Class," and "Performance of Women of Color." I began to think seriously about graduate school and the possibility of entering a joint J.D./Ph.D. program. I completed a research seminar in African American legal history with Genna Rae McNeil, an independent study with Jacquelyn Dowd Hall, and an American women's history course with Suzanne Lebsock. Following up on Hunter's suggestion about the King Papers Project at Stanford, I submitted an application. I was thrilled to be selected as one of four interns who would spend eight weeks working at the project. The work would involve a mix of tasks, some more enjoyable and satisfying than others: entering document records into the computerized inventory system; photocopying and filing documents; transcribing documents and tapes; researching volume chronologies; and doing directed research on annotations for the volume on the Montgomery bus boycott and other subjects.

Before heading off to Stanford in the summer of 1993, I attended the Ninth Annual Berkshire Conference of Women Historians at Vassar College. The three-day conference drew more than 2,300 historians from 220 colleges and universities in 31 countries. The conference made me more enthusiastic about the possibility of becoming a professor of U.S. history focusing on the experiences of African American women. It was incredible to see so many scholars in the field. I was fortunate to meet and talk with Nell Painter, Evelyn Higginbotham, and Paula Giddings and reconnect with Darlene Clark Hine. Panels entitled "Ida B. Wells and the Meaning of Black Women's Leadership," "Three Modern Biographies of Sojourner Truth," and "African American Women and Radical Grassroots Politics, 1960s and 1970s" fed my curiosity and passion to learn more about African American women leaders. I met Rhonda Williams and Stephanie Camp, African American graduate students studying women's history with Evelyn Higginbotham at the University of Pennsylvania. Most important, I was able to witness African American scholars at work, exchanging ideas, creating historical knowledge, interpreting sources, challenging and encouraging one another. Patricia Williams's keynote address reinforced my growing belief that the mastery of one's history is empowering. Indeed, for the first time, my young mind was able to see that the study of the past could both inform the present and allow the envisioning of a new future. I was inspired.

The Berks, combined with my experience as an intern at the King Papers Project in the summer of 1993, solidified my decision to pursue a Ph.D. in history. The King Papers Project provided me with a clear idea of how to undertake historical research and reinforced my growing commitment to understanding the diverse ways in which black women have shaped the American past. While working at the project, I was drawn to the role of black women in the civil rights movement. Although the project is organized around King and his contributions to the movement, I learned from reading the documents that black women's participation, organizing skills, and networks were crucial to the movement's success. I discovered that while black women were not spotlighted as leaders of the movement, they were in many ways the driving force at the local and grassroots levels. Ella Baker, Fannie Lou Hamer, Daisy Bates, Diane Nash, Rosa Parks, Pauli Murray, and Jo Ann Robinson stood out among the countless numbers of black women who had risked their lives in the fight for civil rights. These women and their stories, thanks to a handful of African American women scholars, were slowly becoming a part of the larger historical narrative, and my work at the project convinced me that I wanted to join these scholars in writing and teaching black women's history. Another intern who was also interested in African American women's history, Erica Armstrong (an undergraduate at the University of Pennsylvania), enhanced my experience at the project. We developed an enormously important relationship that continues to have far more significance than what I learned at the project. Our friendship and shared interest enabled us to talk about the professional possibilities and options facing women of color in an academic world that is still predominately white and male.

During our senior year, Armstrong and I were among over 2,000 black women who attended the "Black Women in the Academy: Defending Our Name, 1894–1994" conference at the Massachusetts Institute of Technology in Cambridge. Organized by two historians, Evelyn Hammonds and Robin Kilson, the conference was an attempt to "provide a public forum for black women academics in order to address issues of research, survival in the academy, and the repressive political climate of the 1980s and 1990s, in which black people had been constructed as the domestic enemy and black women, in particular, vilified as welfare queens, whores, breeders and quota queens."[1] One could not ignore the historical significance of the conference since it marked the hundredth anniversary of the formation of the National Federation of Negro Women in Boston, when 100 black clubwomen met to organize a national response to the vilification of Ida B. Wells in the press and to challenge the negative stereotypes of black womanhood. Lani Guinier, Johnnetta Cole, and Angela Davis gave keynote addresses, and fifty-four panels convened in the two and a half days of the conference. We heard a range of papers and discussions on issues such as black feminism, pedagogy, university politics, sexuality, working-class women's politics, black women's biographies, black women and welfare, and black women's history. Unlike the Berks conference, where I was inspired by black women's intellectual work and camaraderie, at MIT black women's narratives of alienation, oppressive loneliness, and marginalization within the academy overwhelmed me. As we listened to women recount war stories and feelings of isolation, Armstrong and I counted ourselves lucky and hoped that our experiences would be different.

In the fall of my senior year, I began investigating graduate programs and wrote letters to scholars across the country working in the fields of African American history and women's history. I sent letters to Nell Painter, Wilma King, Elsa Barkley Brown, Raymond Gavins, Earl Lewis, Carol Karlsen, Christine Stansell, Kevin Gaines, Thomas Holt, Robin Kelley, Sharon Harley, Mary Frances Berry, Deborah Gray White, Manning Marable, Barbara Fields, Elizabeth Blackmar, William Chafe, and Nancy Hewitt. I was overwhelmed by the positive and encouraging responses I received from Nell Painter, Wilma King, Kevin Gaines, and Ray Gavins (this was in the days before e-mail when folks still wrote letters). I recall vividly my excitement when Elsa Barkley Brown called and spent over an hour talking with me about the different graduate programs. When the graduate-school letters began arriving in the spring, I was overwhelmed by my choices. I had applied to eight graduate programs (I had planned to apply to more but could not afford the application fees) and was accepted by six: Princeton, UNC–Chapel Hill, Michigan State, the University of Michigan, Columbia, and the University of Pennsylvania. I was able to immediately eliminate two schools: Columbia because it had not offered me any funding and the University of Pennsylvania because Evelyn Higginbotham was planning to leave there for Harvard. Even though I was tempted to stay at UNC, I took the advice of my mentors, who told me I needed to spread my wings. So in the end, my choices came down to Princeton and the two Michigan programs. It was a tough decision. Darlene Clark Hine, who had in many ways played an important role in my decision to pursue a graduate degree, was at Michigan State; the University of Michigan not only had three scholars of African American history (Elsa Barkley Brown, Robin Kelley, and Earl Lewis) but also had a joint J.D./Ph.D. program; and Nell Painter and Kevin Gaines were at Princeton, which had at the time the top-ranked history program in the country. During my visit to the University of Michigan, Robin Kelley told me it was an easy decision—"You have to go work with Nell Painter at Princeton!" After meeting with faculty and graduate students at all three campuses, I decided to attend Princeton.

I graduated from UNC–Chapel Hill in the spring of 1994 with a double major in history and women's studies. From six different women professors, I had taken eight of the eleven courses needed for the history major. At the time, four of the professors were senior faculty members, one was chair of women's studies, and another was director of the Southern Oral History Program and held an endowed chair. Two of my history professors were African American women; of the three white male history professors, one considered himself a feminist and the other encouraged my interest in women's history. Even now it is hard for me to believe such an experience was possible. In an academic world that is predominately white and male, I found women (both black and white) who served as role models, provided me with the skills I would need to engage in the professional study of history, and encouraged my interest in African American women's history. Indeed, I embarked on my graduate career with a female cheering squad.

### The Making of a Historian: Princeton University, 1994–2000

In the fall of 1994, I arrived at Princeton to begin my graduate training. Princeton had admitted seven Americanists in the history graduate program, five of whom were African Americans (Kenneth Mack, Marie Taylor, Barbara Krauthamer, Dylan Penningroth, and myself). I entered my graduate program as one of four African Americans (Dylan Penningroth had decided to attend Johns Hopkins University), three of us women. Since three African American students, two of them women (Cheryl Hicks and Shalanda Dexter), had entered the program the previous year, African American women were the majority in many of our classes. Our presence changed the dynamics of the discourse; as a group, we had to be acknowledged. When we arrived in Princeton for minority-recruiting weekend, we first encountered the racism and hostility of students who either resented our presence or were absolutely unprepared for our arrival. I was sitting in the history lounge with the other recruits when a white female student who was apparently shocked by our numbers asked, "What are they doing, busing you guys in here?" We all looked at one another as if to say, "Did she really say that?" Having one another, as well as an adviser with whom we could talk about such issues without feeling as if we were being hypersensitive, provided the support and affirmation so many students of color lack at institutions of higher education.

I had come to Princeton to work with Nell Painter, and my graduate experience cannot be understood separate from our relationship. She created an environment that made my survival possible. Her efforts to recruit both students and faculty of color had a tremendous impact on my studies. Before arriving at Princeton, I had no idea what it meant to be a black woman at a predominately white Ivy League institution. That first semester, I felt marginalized, and outside of Painter's class, I could hardly find the courage to speak. While I have no doubt that my other professors were concerned about my silence in their classes, it was Painter who best understood my intimidation and discomfort, and it was she who made sure I was fully armed and prepared when I entered my second semester of course work. In my first year, she taught me that my success depended not on saying what I thought she or other professors wanted to hear but on asking questions and seeking answers. If I did not understand the material or my classmates' comments, it was okay to ask for clarification. In fact, I remember that after reading an essay by Homi Bhabha or Derrida—I can't remember which—Painter came to class with a handout and said, "I did the readings with the eyes of a first-year student and thought it might be helpful if we start by going over some of the key terms." At the same time that Painter taught me how to read theory, she taught me to question everything and take nothing for granted. "What do you mean when you say THE black community?" "Whose South are you talking about?"

I could easily argue that the ways that Painter was a wonderful adviser had nothing to do with her racial identity, but I do believe it was her experience as a black woman historian that made my experience at Princeton a less painful one. As a role model and inspiration, she helped prepare me for the often-harsh realities of being a black female academic. Indeed, she taught me how to take care of myself and how to build community and support beyond institutional affiliations. More important, she did the work of training me as a historian of African American women. In her classrooms, in her scholarship, and in the way she lives her life, Painter taught me to ask questions—in other words, "to transgress," to go beyond limits, to cross boundaries, to struggle against convention. She inspired me with her brilliance, awed me with her determination, and amazed me with her resistance. She shaped and defined the way I think and write about the American past. In her *Southern History across the Color Line*, Painter reflects on her career:

> Despite much success, I have experienced my work as a struggle against the conventions of American education and scholarship. I feel I have wrestled for half a century with what I have been taught. For this black woman, at least (and I do not pretend to speak for any but myself), Western knowledge is not to be trusted. Everything in it needs careful inspection for insults and blind spots, which turn up all too often, diminishing the authority of prominent authorities in my eyes. Such a critical process means that education proceeds slowly and patchily. But I have kept at the struggle. Therein lies the key to what kind readers see as my originality. I question (nearly) everything, and so many questions produce some good answers.[2]

Painter's struggle against convention and her persistent questioning have produced more than some good answers. Her scholarship and teaching have made possible the work of those of us who follow in her footsteps. While Painter concludes that Audre Lorde may have been right "that the master's tools cannot take down the master's house," she does not leave us empty-handed. Indeed, *Southern History across the Color Line* provides us with what I like to call "Painter's Tools" for navigating and reinterpreting the past. I am convinced that "Painter's Tools" will either serve to dismantle the master's house or allow us to construct a new one.

During my graduate studies, I never felt alone or isolated. Not only did I have a community at Princeton that sustained me, but I was able to tap into a larger community of scholars in the fields of African American history and women's history. At Princeton, I was also able to work with Christine Stansell, Elizabeth Lunbeck, and Kevin Gaines. Both Joan Scott and Jacquelyn Dowd Hall served as outside readers on my dissertation committee, and Glenda Gilmore read every chapter of the dissertation. I remained in constant contact with Erica Armstrong, who was in the history program at Columbia University, and I received continued support from Barbara Harris, Tera Hunter, and Darlene Clark Hine. Leslie Harris, who was a graduate student at Stanford when I was an intern at the King Papers Project, offered encouragement and guidance throughout my graduate career. Painter introduced me to Deborah Gray White and Linda Reed, and at conferences, I had the opportunity to meet and network with other African American women historians, such as Ula Taylor, Barbara Ransby, Barbara Savage, Leslie Brown, Mia Bay, and Jennifer Morgan. Through my work as the graduate-student representative on the Coordinating Council of Women's Historians, I met and worked with many women's historians, including Eileen Boris, Nuper Chaudhuri, and Peggy Pascoe.

## A Historian of African American Women's History, 2000–Present

Since completing my degree at Princeton, I have taught at Yale University, Boston College, and UNC–Chapel Hill. As a predoctoral fellow/postdoctoral fellow in the history department and African American studies department at Yale, I joined a community of scholars that included Glenda Gilmore, Hazel Carby, Nancy Cott, Heather Williams, Katherine Charron, and Adriane Smith. When I joined the history department at Boston College as an assistant professor, I was the only tenure-track woman of color in the department. There were two other African Americans in the department: Davarian Baldwin, a junior colleague in the field of African American history, and Karen Miller, a lecturer in the department who had been denied tenure. It was the first time I found myself without a senior African American woman colleague. Despite the small number of women and faculty of color in the department (of the forty faculty members, there were only eight women and two African Americans), I was able to create and build community, which proved especially important in a department that was not used to working with people of color. I suspect the challenges that I faced at Boston College were not unique, ranging from fighting battles over the department's commitment to affirmative action to enduring racist and sexist comments in faculty meetings. With the support of colleagues like Virginia Reinburg, Karen Miller, Deborah Levenson, and Davarian Baldwin, I never had to confront these issues alone. More important, because of the large number of universities in the Boston area, I was able to tap into a community of scholars in the area interested in race and gender. In the fall of 2006, I began teaching at UNC–Chapel Hill, where I am one of six African Americans (four women and two men) in the history department. While I have not been here long enough to reflect on my experience at UNC, I can say that numbers make a difference.

In both my research and my teaching, I have been able to draw on the rich literature of African American women's history that has been produced over the last three decades. It was this work, much of which was written by many of the historians in this collection, that led me to consider a project on women and lynching. Indeed, my dissertation, "Ladies and Lynching," was made possible because of these historians' insistence that black women's experiences are essential to understanding the American past. The scholarship on black women shaped the central themes of my project and defined the questions I would eventually set out to answer. Emphasizing the inseparability of race, class, and gender, scholars of African American women's history are redefining and enlarging traditional notions of historical significance. The writing of a new history that includes and accounts for black women's experience depends on the development of both race and gender as categories of analysis. It has not been enough for us to prove either that black women had a history or that they participated in the major political upheavals of the American past. The challenge, as Evelyn Higginbotham concluded in "African-American Women's History and the Metalanguage of Race," requires the creation of theoretical formulations that will question "many of the assumptions currently underlying Afro-American history and women's history . . . and that will problematize much of what we take for granted."[3] It has been with these specific instructions that I have approached my work.

Indeed, much of the scholarship on lynching and rape reflects the efforts of feminist historians to theorize about race and gender. In *Revolt against Chivalry* (1979), Jacquelyn Dowd Hall argued that sexual and racial violence are intricately entwined and posed questions regarding the various ways in which black and white women engaged the rape/lynching discourse that historians are just beginning to answer. In the 1980s, scholars such as Rosalyn Terborg-Penn, Darlene Clark Hine, Nell Painter, Deborah Gray White, Angela Davis, and Hazel Carby (to name only a few) grappled with theoretical questions regarding the impact of racial and sexual violence on African American women and the world in which they lived. The 1991 Anita Hill/Clarence Thomas hearings, however, underscored the urgency of doing this work and led to the proliferation of new theoretical scholarship in the field. Scholars of African American women's history were among the first to challenge Judge Thomas's representation of the hearings as a "high-tech lynching" and called into question a history of lynching that ignored sexual and racial violence against black women. In her essay, "Imagining Lynching," Elsa Barkley Brown asked: "I wonder why it is that people don't remember the lynching of Black women and the brutality of the experience. . . . Why is it that lynching (and the notion of it as a masculine experience) is not just remembered but is in fact central to how we understand the history of African-American men, and indeed the African-American experience in general. But violence against women—lynching, rape, and other forms of violence—is not."[4] Nell Painter, in "Who Was Lynched?" in *The Nation* and in an essay in *Race-ing Justice, En-Gendering Power: Essays on Anita Hill, Clarence*

*Thomas, and the Construction of Social Reality*, declared: "Black women, who have traditionally been discounted within the race and degraded in American Society, are becoming increasingly impatient with our devaluation. Breaking the silence and testifying about the abuse, black feminists are publishing our history and dissecting the stereotypes that have been used against us."[5]

In many ways, "Ladies and Lynching" was an attempt to rise to this challenge. When I started the project in the spring of 1996, I set out to write a paper about the black female victims of lynching we had heard so little about. I began by tracking down the names of women who were lynched. I searched for references to female victims in secondary sources, went through the Tuskegee Newspaper File and records of organizations that campaigned against lynching, and contacted all the folks I knew who might have come across sources that would be useful. Early in my research, I was fortunate to find a pamphlet entitled "Women Lynched in the United States since 1889" that was compiled by a black women's group called the Anti-lynching Crusaders. It contained the names of female victims and when and where they were lynched. To my surprise, there were white women on the list. By the time I completed my research, I had found 160 cases in which black and white women were executed by southern mobs—of those, 132 were black and 28 white—but I had also found hundreds of cases in which mobs raped, tarred and feathered, beat, and tortured women for transgressions as minor as refusing to step off the sidewalk for a white person. As my sources continued to reveal women who were not merely victims of rape and lynching but key actors in the rape/lynching drama, the scope of the project broadened. No longer a study about women's victimization, it examines the ways that black and white women responded to sexual and racial violence and manipulated the rape/lynching discourse for their own personal and political empowerment. It includes not only female victims of lynching but also women who participated in mob violence, sought to reform rape laws, campaigned against lynching, resisted racial and sexual violence, and challenged racist and sexist stereotypes that informed the rape/lynching myth. The manuscript maps out a dense cultural grid through which conflicting and overlapping representations of racial and sexual dangers circulated in the New South. In so doing, it brings together two bodies of historical literature—work on racial violence and civil rights and work on sexual violence and women's rights—and makes use of three decades of evolving race and gender theory.

Before I was able to take on Higginbotham's theoretical challenge to problematize the assumptions embedded in African American and women's history, I had to face the problem of locating sources. When I first proposed the project, the issue of sources was the furthest thought from my mind. It never occurred to me that the reason no one had written on the lynching of black women might be related to the lack of sources. I'm part of the generation that grew up on Deborah Gray White's *Ar'n't I a Woman?* If she could write a book on black women and slavery, why couldn't I write one on black women and lynching? Some of my advisers asked, "What sources will you use and where are they?" I was a Nell Painter student and had been trained in theory, taught to read the silences and against the grain, and instructed that the fact that my sources were not nicely collected in folders filed numerically in cardboard boxes neatly stacked on shelves in some university archive didn't mean that such a history couldn't be written. But I would need sources, and I had enough sense to know that I could not write a whole dissertation on silences. It will take years of research, I was told. Why not consider a dissertation on Mary McLeod Bethune— no one has written about her, and her papers are in Washington, D.C., at the Library of Congress, someone sensibly suggested. I refused to be dissuaded. Tera Hunter is writing a book in which black washerwomen take center stage, and their papers are not nicely tucked away in some archive, I told myself (her book has since been published—*To 'Joy My Freedom*). I must confess that I did experience a moment of panic. It didn't last long, however, because, as those of us who do African American women's history know, there are sources—plenty of them. It is just a matter of locating them. In my case, it was not a matter of finding completely new sources but retracing the steps of those who had researched and studied lynching before me. In some instances, I merely had to look where they pointed, and in others, I had to reexamine what they had ignored or discarded as unusual or irrelevant.

## Conclusion

Ten years ago, when Painter welcomed me to the "much-abused community of black women academics," she warned me that my experience in Oxford, Mississippi, would "occur again and again." She wrote:

Those people will try to make you feel unwelcomed, weird, not-good-enough, lucky, dumb, out-of-step, and insufficiently respectful to your historiographical elders for as long as you remain productive. Needless to say, this gets pretty old pretty fast, but once you start to recognize the patterns and learn to protect yourself somewhat, you won't be so vulnerable. But I don't know anyone who has completely overcome such vulnerability. The only way I know to deal with it is through sharing, as you have done. Then your buddies can tell you how lame your assailants were and how something similar (but worse) happened to them somewhere else. Every black woman academic I know has stories after stories to tell. We survive by supporting each other and getting together on a regular basis to celebrate our survival.

Painter was absolutely right. What happened in Oxford was the first of many such experiences, but more important, as she so eloquently states, with community, survival is possible. In this essay, I have tried to focus on what has gotten me through—the community of scholars who continue to guide me, support me, and make my work possible. Like Mary Church Terrell once said, "In myself I am nothing, but with the loyal support of conscientious, capable women, all things are possible." Thus, it is with gratitude and admiration that I dedicate this essay to scholars of African American women's history.

NOTES

1. Saidiya Hartman, "The Territory between Us: A Report on 'Black Women in the Academy: Defending Our Name, 1894–1994,'" *Callaloo* 17, no. 2 (Spring 1994): 439–49.

2. Nell Irvin Painter, *Southern History across the Color Line* (Chapel Hill: University of North Carolina Press, 2002).

3. Evelyn Brooks Higginbotham, "African-American Women's History and the Metalanguage of Race," *Signs* 17, no. 2 (Winter 1992): 251–74.

4. Elsa Barkley Brown, "Imagining Lynching: African American Women, Communities of Struggle, and Collective Memory," in *African American Women Speak Out on Anita Hill–Clarence Thomas*, edited by Geneva Smitherman (Detroit: Wayne State University Press, 1995), 101.

5. Nell I. Painter, "Hill, Thomas, and the Use of Racial Stereotype," in *Race-ing Justice, En-gendering Power: Essays on Anita Hill, Clarence Thomas, and the Construction of Social Reality*, edited by Toni Morrison (New York: Pantheon, 1992), 214.

# CONTRIBUTORS

ELSA BARKLEY BROWN is associate professor of history and women's studies at the University of Maryland and an affiliate faculty in African American studies and American studies. She received her Ph.D. from Kent State University in 1994. Her dissertation, "Uncle Ned's Children: Negotiating Community and Freedom in Postemancipation Richmond, Virginia," examines southern urban African American political culture in the late nineteenth and early twentieth centuries, with a focus on the meanings and processes of community. Barkley Brown is a co-editor of *Major Problems in African-American History* (2000) and *Black Women in America: An Historical Encyclopedia* (1993). Her articles have appeared in *Signs, Feminist Studies, History Workshop, Sage, Public Culture*, and the *Journal of Urban History*. She has twice been awarded the Letitia Woods Brown Memorial Publication Prize by the Association of Black Women Historians for best article in African American women's history. She has also won the A. Elizabeth Taylor Prize for best article in southern women's history, the Martin Luther King Jr. Prize for best article in African American history, and the Anna Julia Cooper Award for Distinguished Scholarship in Black Women's Studies.

MIA BAY, associate professor of history at Rutgers University and assistant director of the Rutgers Center for the Study of Race and Ethnicity, received her Ph.D. from Yale University in 1993. Her dissertation, the basis for her first book, *The White Image in the Black Mind: African American Ideas about White People, 1825–1930* (2000), examines African American ideas about white racial character and destiny in the nineteenth and twentieth centuries. She is also the author of " 'See Your Declaration Americans!!': Abolitionism, Americanism, and the Revolutionary Tradition in Free Black Politics," in *Americanism: New Perspectives on the History of an Ideal*, edited by Michel Kazin and Joseph McCartin (2006), and "In Search of Sally Hemings in the Post-DNA Era," *Reviews in American History* 34, no. 4 (December 2006). Currently, she is completing two new projects: a biography of antilynching activist Ida B. Wells and a study of African American views on Thomas Jefferson.

LESLIE BROWN is assistant professor of history and African and African American studies at Washington University, St. Louis, where she teaches a range of content and methodology courses in race, gender, and public history. She served as an administrator in admissions and student affairs at Skidmore

College in Saratoga Springs, New York, before attending graduate school at Duke University, where she earned her Ph.D. in 1997. From 1990 to 1995, she co-coordinated "Behind the Veil: Documenting African American Life in the Jim Crow South," a collaborative research and curriculum project at the Center for Documentary Studies at Duke. She is the author of *Upbuilding Black Durham: Gender, Class, and Black Community Development in the Jim Crow South* (2008). Based on her dissertation, "Common Spaces, Separate Lives: Gender and Racial Conflict in the 'Capital of the Black Middle Class,'" the book examines the gender and class dynamics of the black community at the high tide of the Jim Crow era in Durham, North Carolina.

CRYSTAL N. FEIMSTER is assistant professor of history at the University of North Carolina at Chapel Hill, where she teaches a range of courses in African American history, women's history, southern history, and oral history. She earned her Ph.D. from Princeton University in 2000. She has published "A New Generation of Women Historians," in *Voices of Women Historians: The Personal, the Political, and the Professional*, edited by Nuper Chaudhuri and Eileen Boris (1999), and "Muriel Snowden," in *Notable American Women* (2005). She is currently working on a manuscript titled *Southern Horrors: Women and the Politics of Rape and Lynching in the American South*, to be published by Harvard University Press. Based on her dissertation, "Ladies and Lynching: The Gender Discourse of Mob Violence in the New South, 1880–1949," the book examines the ways that both black and white female victims of racial and sexual violence manipulated the rape/lynching narrative, asserted their presence in a sexually charged public sphere, and influenced the racial and sexual politics of lynching in the New South.

SHARON HARLEY is associate professor and chair of the Department of African American Studies at the University of Maryland, College Park. She received her Ph.D. from Howard University in 1981. She is the editor of *Sister Circle: Black Women and Work* (2002) and *Women's Labor in the Global Economy: Speaking in Multiple Voices* (2007), publications based on research seminars funded by the Ford Foundation that she directed and codirected. She is currently working on a monograph titled *Dignity and Damnation*, a historical study of the intersection of gender, labor, and citizenship in the lives of African Americans in the United States. Her dissertation, "Black Women in the District of Columbia, 1890–1920: Their Social, Economic, and Institutional Activities," examines the images and expectations of black middle-class women and compares them to the experiences and desires of black women of the working class.

WANDA A. HENDRICKS, associate professor of history at the University of South Carolina, received her Ph.D. from Purdue University in 1990. Her dissertation, which became the basis of her first book, *Gender, Race, and Politics in the Midwest: Black Club Women in Illinois* (1998), examines the social and political activism of African American women during the height of the Jim Crow era. She has published several articles and essays on black clubwomen, including "Child Welfare and Black Female Agency in Springfield: Eva Monroe and the Lincoln Colored Home," *Journal of Illinois History* 3, no. 2 (Summer 2000), and " 'Vote for the Advantage of Ourselves and Our Race': The Election of the First Black Alderman in Chicago," *Illinois Historical Journal* 87, no. 3 (Autumn 1994). She is also a senior editor of the 2005 Oxford edition of *Black Women in America*. She is currently working on a biography of Fannie Barrier Williams, one of the most influential African American intellectuals and social-welfare reformers of the late nineteenth and early twentieth centuries.

DARLENE CLARK HINE, former John A. Hannah Professor of History at Michigan State University, is currently the Board of Trustees Professor of African American Studies and History at Northwestern University. She received her Ph.D. from Kent State University in 1975. Her dissertation, which became the basis for her first book, *Black Victory: The Rise and Fall of the White Primary in Texas* (1979), examines the black struggle to regain the ballot, a struggle that affected both jurisprudence and the shape of national and southern politics in the twentieth century. She is a past president of the Organization of American Historians and the Southern Historical Association and the winner of many honors and awards. Her numerous publications include *Black Women in White: Racial Conflict and Cooperation in the Nursing Profession, 1890–1950* (1989), *Hine Sight: Black Women and the Re-Construction of American History* (1994), *The African-American Odyssey* (1999), and *A Shining Thread of Hope: The History of Black Women in America* (1999). She is a member of the American Academy of Arts and Sciences.

CHANA KAI LEE is associate professor of history and African American studies at the University of Georgia, Athens. She received her doctorate from the University of California, Los Angeles, in 1993. Her dissertation became the basis for her prizewinning biography, *For Freedom's Sake: The Biography of Fannie Lou Hamer* (2000). She is a senior editor of *The Encyclopedia of Women in World History*, which is forthcoming from Oxford University Press, and her *Rosa Parks: A Movement Life* will appear in Pearson Longman's Library of American Biography Series.

JENNIFER L. MORGAN is associate professor in the Department of Social and Cultural Analysis and the Department of History at New York University. She received her Ph.D. from Duke University in 1995. Her dissertation became the basis for her first book, *Laboring Women: Reproduction and Gender in New World Slavery* (2004), which examines the complex circumstances under which early American enslaved women gave birth and African American women became the foundation of the fortunes of American slaveholders. She is currently working on a study titled *Accounting for the Women in Slavery*, a project that considers colonial numeracy, racism, and the rise of the transatlantic slave trade.

NELL IRVIN PAINTER, former Edwards Professor of History at Princeton University, studied at the University of California, Berkeley; the University of Bordeaux; the University of Ghana; and the University of California, Los Angeles, before receiving her Ph.D. from Harvard University in 1974. Her books include *The Narrative of Hosea Hudson: His Life as a Negro Communist in the South* (1979), *Standing at Armageddon: The United States, 1877–1919* (1987), *Sojourner Truth: A Life, a Symbol* (1996), and *Southern History across the Color Line* (2002). Her dissertation, a study of the migration of ordinary people from Louisiana, Kentucky, Texas, and Tennessee to (Free) Kansas in response to the white-supremacist terrorism that ended Reconstruction, became her first book: *Exodusters: Black Migration to Kansas after Reconstruction* (1976/77). Her sixth authored book, *Creating Black Americans: African-American History and Its Meanings, 1619 to the Present* (2006), won a Gustavus Myers Award. Winner of many honors and fellowships, Painter has served as president of the Southern Historical Association and the Organization of American Historians. She is a member of the American Academy of Arts and Sciences. See <www.nellpainter.com>.

MERLINE PITRE is professor of history and dean of the College of Liberal Arts and Behavioral Sciences at Texas Southern University. She received her Ph.D. from Temple University in 1976. Her dissertation, "Frederick Douglass: A Party Loyalist, 1870–1895," examines Douglass's relationship with the Republican Party. Her most notable works are *Through Many Dangers, Toils, and Snares: The Black Leadership of Texas, 1868–1898* (1985), which was reissued in 1997 for use in a traveling exhibit on black legislators by the Texas State Preservation Board, and *In Struggle against Jim Crow: Lulu B. White and the NAACP, 1900–1957* (1999). Pitre has received grants from the Fulbright Foundation, the Texas Council for the Humanities, and the National Endowment for the Humanities. She is also a former member of the Texas Council for the Humanities, a past president of the Southern Conference on

African American Studies, and a former member of the nominating board of the Organization of American Historians.

BARBARA RANSBY is associate professor in the Departments of African American Studies and History at the University of Illinois at Chicago. She received her Ph.D. from the University of Michigan in 1996. Her dissertation became the basis of her biography, *Ella Baker and the Black Freedom Movement: A Radical Democratic Vision* (2003). The book examines Baker's entire political career and its impact on African American and progressive politics. Ransby is the past recipient of a national Mellon Fellowship in the Humanities and a Ford Fellowship. Her book on Baker has won eight national awards of distinction, including the Joan Kelly Prize from the American Historical Association (AHA), the James Rawley Prize from the Organization of American Historians, and the Letitia Woods Brown Memorial Publication Prize from the Association of Black Women Historians. Ransby is also the author of numerous popular and scholarly articles. She serves on the boards of many publications and nonprofit organizations and is the chair of the Committee on Women Historians of the AHA. Ransby's two current activist projects are Public Square, a nonprofit group that organizes public forums and discussions on social issues, and Ella's Daughters, an international network of women working in Ella Baker's tradition. Her forthcoming book with Yale University Press is a biography of Eslanda Goode Robeson.

JULIE SAVILLE, associate professor of history at the University of Chicago, received her Ph.D. from Yale University in 1986. Her dissertation, which became the basis of her first book, *The Work of Reconstruction: From Slave to Wage Labor in South Carolina, 1860–1870* (1996), examines the social expectations that former slaves brought to emancipation and analyzes their patterns of behavior in the context of the repressive policies of former slaveholders. Her publications include "De l'esclave au citoyen: Les rituels politiques des ouvriers agricoles des plantations à l'époque de la guerre de Sécession américaine et de la Reconstruction," in *Esclavage et dépendances serviles: Histoire comparée*, edited by Myriam Cottias, Alessandro Stella, and Bernard Vincent l'Harmattan (2006), and "Rites and Power: Reflections on Slavery, Freedom, and Political Ritual," in *From Slavery to Emancipation in the Atlantic World*, edited by Sylvia R. Frey and Betty Wood, special issue of *Slavery and Abolition* 20, no. 1 (April 1999). She is currently working on a history of slave emancipation in the Windward Islands of the Caribbean in the aftermath of the French and Haitian Revolutions.

BRENDA ELAINE STEVENSON is professor of history and chair of the Program in Afro-American Studies at the University of California, Los Angeles. She received her Ph.D. from Yale University in 1990. Her dissertation, which became the basis of her first book, *Life in Black and White: Family and Community in the Slave South* (1996), examines family and community life among four groups of people who resided in the Upper Piedmont region of Virginia: planters, yeoman farmers, free blacks, and slaves. She is the editor and annotator of the *Journals of Charlotte Forten Grimké* (1988), co-author of *The Underground Railroad* (1998), and senior editor of the 2005 Oxford edition of *Black Women in America*, among other works.

ULA TAYLOR is associate professor in the Department of African American Studies at the University of California, Berkeley. She received her Ph.D. from the University of California, Santa Barbara, in 1992. Her dissertation, which examines the activist and personal life of Amy Jacques Garvey, became the basis of her first book, *The Veiled Garvey: The Life and Times of Amy Jacques Garvey* (2002). She is also the co-author of *Panther: A Pictorial History of the Black Panther Party and the Story behind the Film* (1995). Taylor's articles on black feminism and black nationalism have appeared in the *Journal of Women's History*, *Feminist Studies*, *Race & Society*, *Black Scholar*, and the *Journal of Black Studies*.

ROSALYN TERBORG-PENN is professor emeritus of history and former coordinator of graduate programs in history at Morgan State University, where she helped develop the university's history Ph.D. program. She earned her Ph.D. from Howard University in 1978. Widely published, Terborg-Penn has written over forty articles. She has authored or co-edited six books. Best known for her award-winning study, *African American Women in the Struggle for the Vote, 1850–1920* (1998), she was one of the co-editors of *Black Women in America: An Historical Encyclopedia* (1993) and a co-editor of *The Columbia Guide to African American History since 1939* (2005). She is the cofounder of the Association of Black Women Historians and a former chair of the American Historical Association's Committee on Women Historians. A 2003 recipient of the Distinguished Black Marylander Award conferred by Towson University, in 2005 Terborg-Penn was elected to a three-year term on the nominating board of the Organization of American Historians. Terborg-Penn's dissertation, "Afro-Americans in the Struggle for Woman Suffrage," identifies the African American men and women who were involved in the woman suffrage movement from 1830 to 1920. In an effort to dispel the myth of black apathy toward woman suffrage, it examines the activities, ideas, and arguments that grew out of black concerns for black and human rights.

DEBORAH GRAY WHITE is Board of Governors Professor of History and Women and Gender Studies at Rutgers University. She received her Ph.D.

from the University of Illinois at Chicago in 1979. Her dissertation became the basis for her first book, *Ar'n't I a Woman?: Female Slaves in the Plantation South* (1985), which presents a gendered analysis of the institution of slavery. She is the author of *Too Heavy a Load: Black Women in Defense of Themselves, 1894–1994* (1999), several K–12 textbooks on U.S. history, and *Let My People Go: African Americans, 1804–1860* (1999). She is also a senior editor of the 2005 Oxford edition of *Black Women in America*. A former chair of the Rutgers University Department of History, White is also a former co-director of "The Black Atlantic: Race, Nation, and Gender," a two-year seminar and conference project of the Rutgers Center for Historical Analysis. As a recent fellow at the Woodrow Wilson International Center for Scholars in Washington, D.C., she conducted research on her forthcoming monograph, *Can't We All Just Get Along?: American Identity at the Turn of the Millennium*.